The

GRANDE
ODALISQUE

*VIVÈS / RUPPERT
+ MULOT*

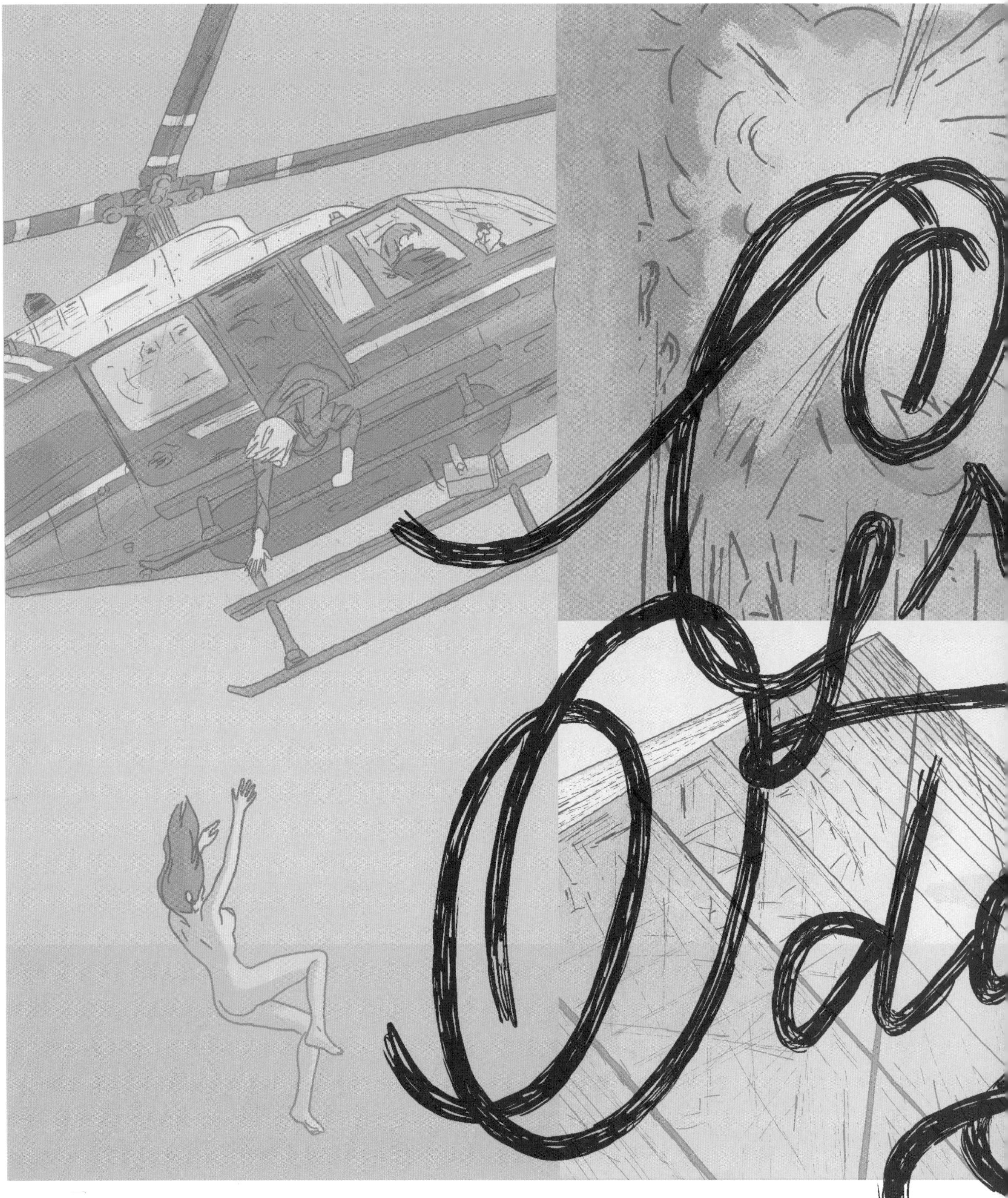

VIVÈS / RUPPERT + MULOT

Color by Isabelle Merlet

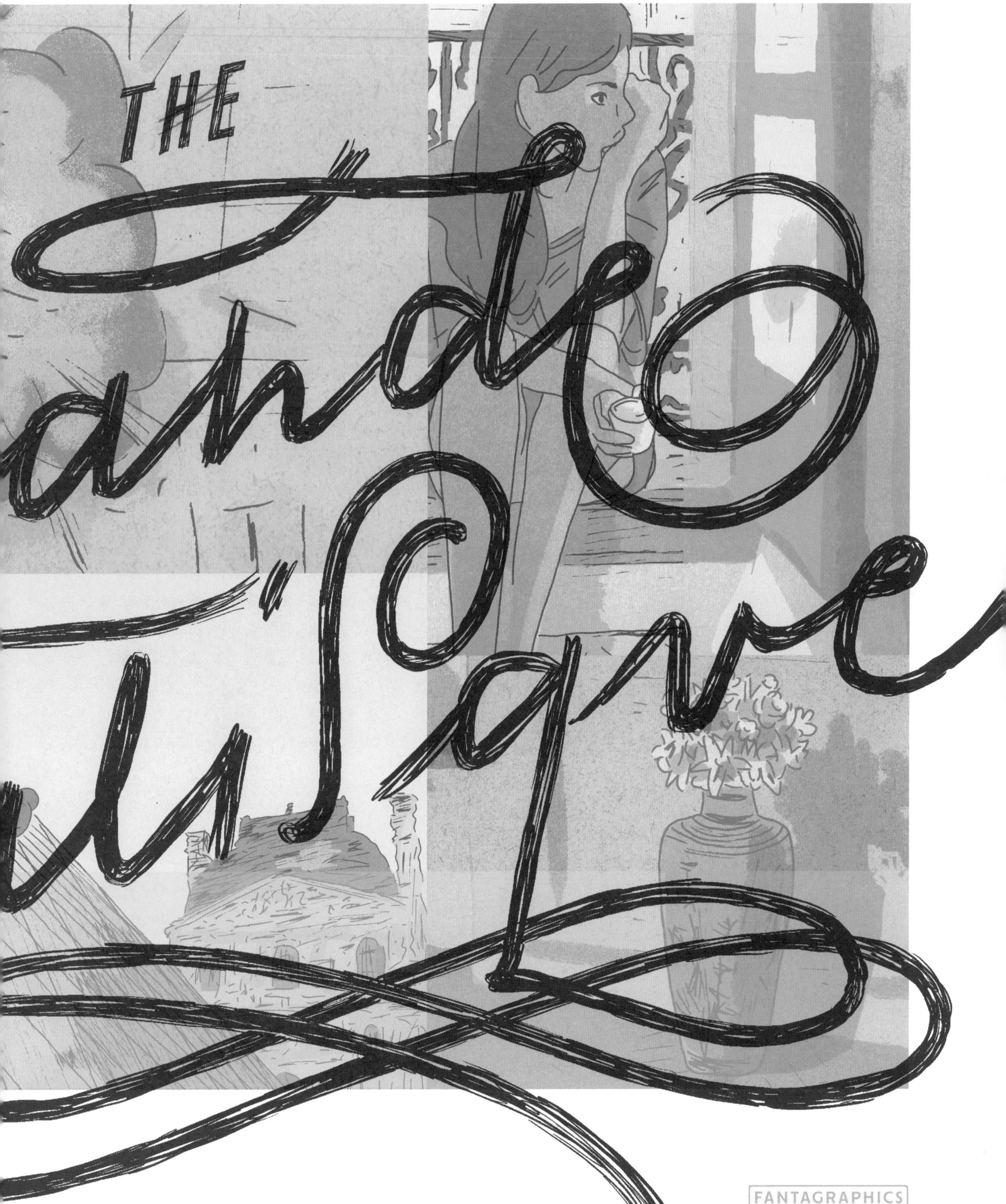
THE

FANTAGRAPHICS

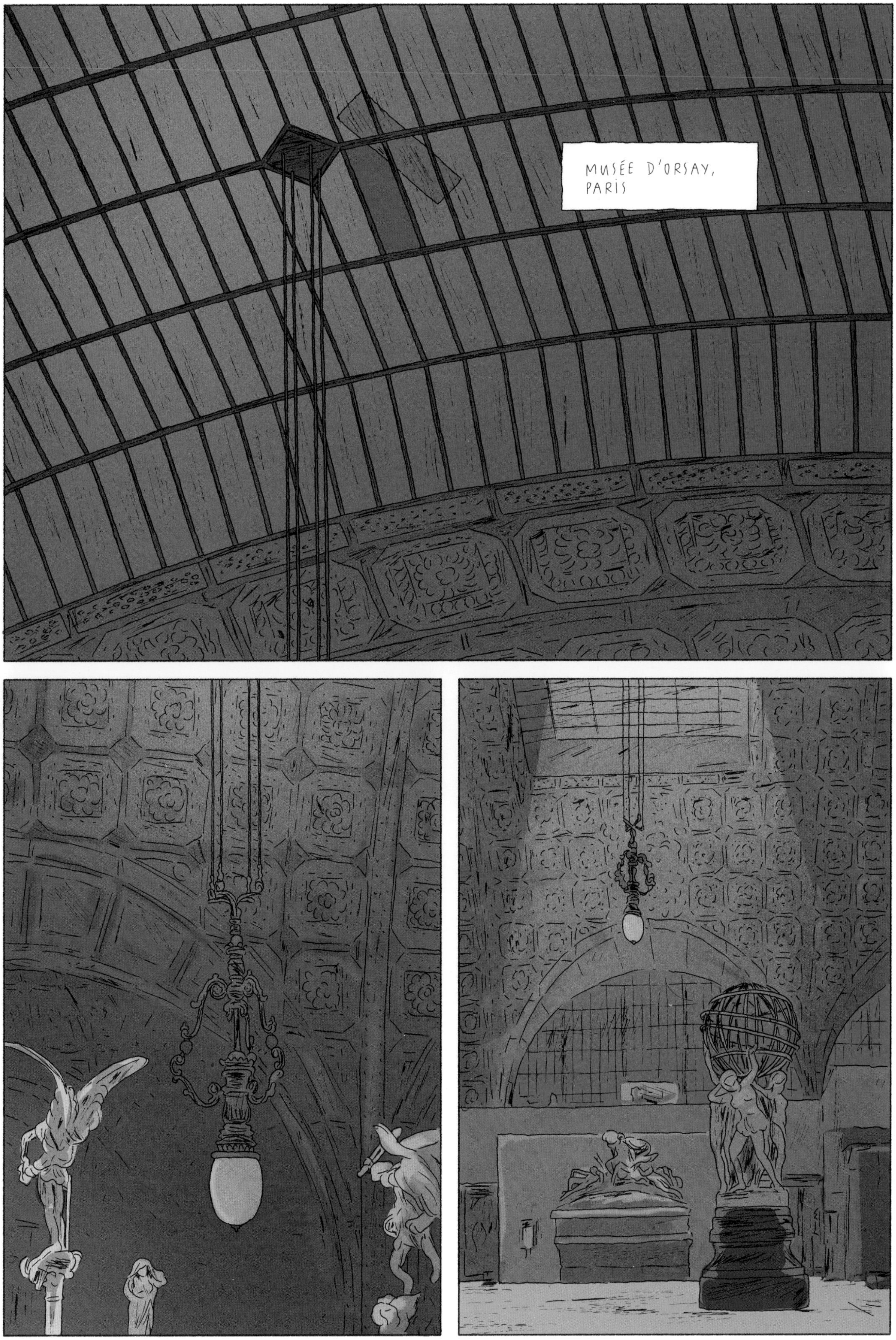
MUSÉE D'ORSAY,
PARIS

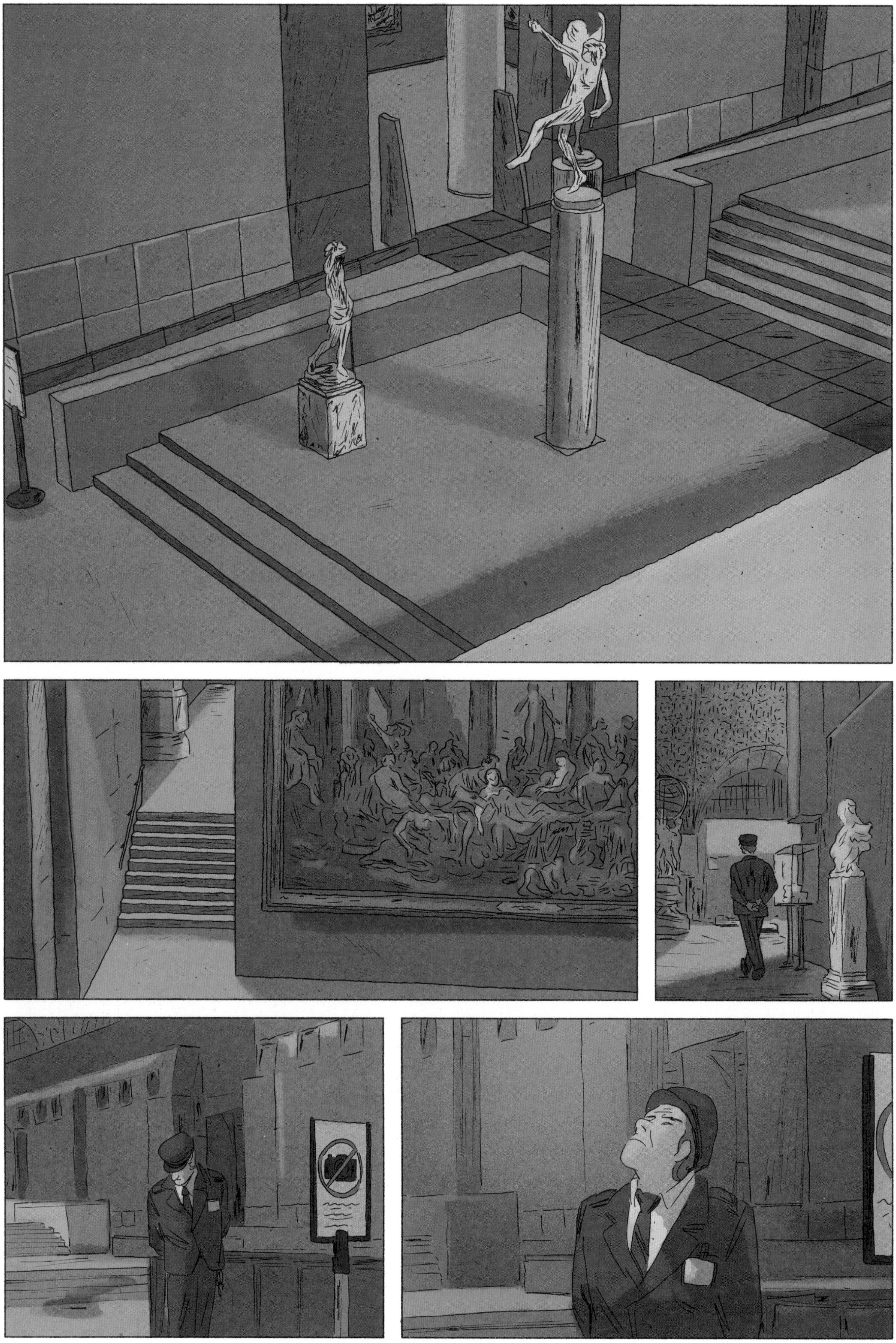

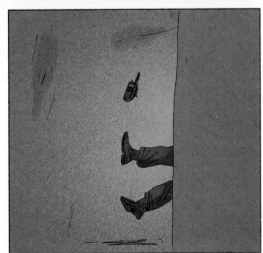

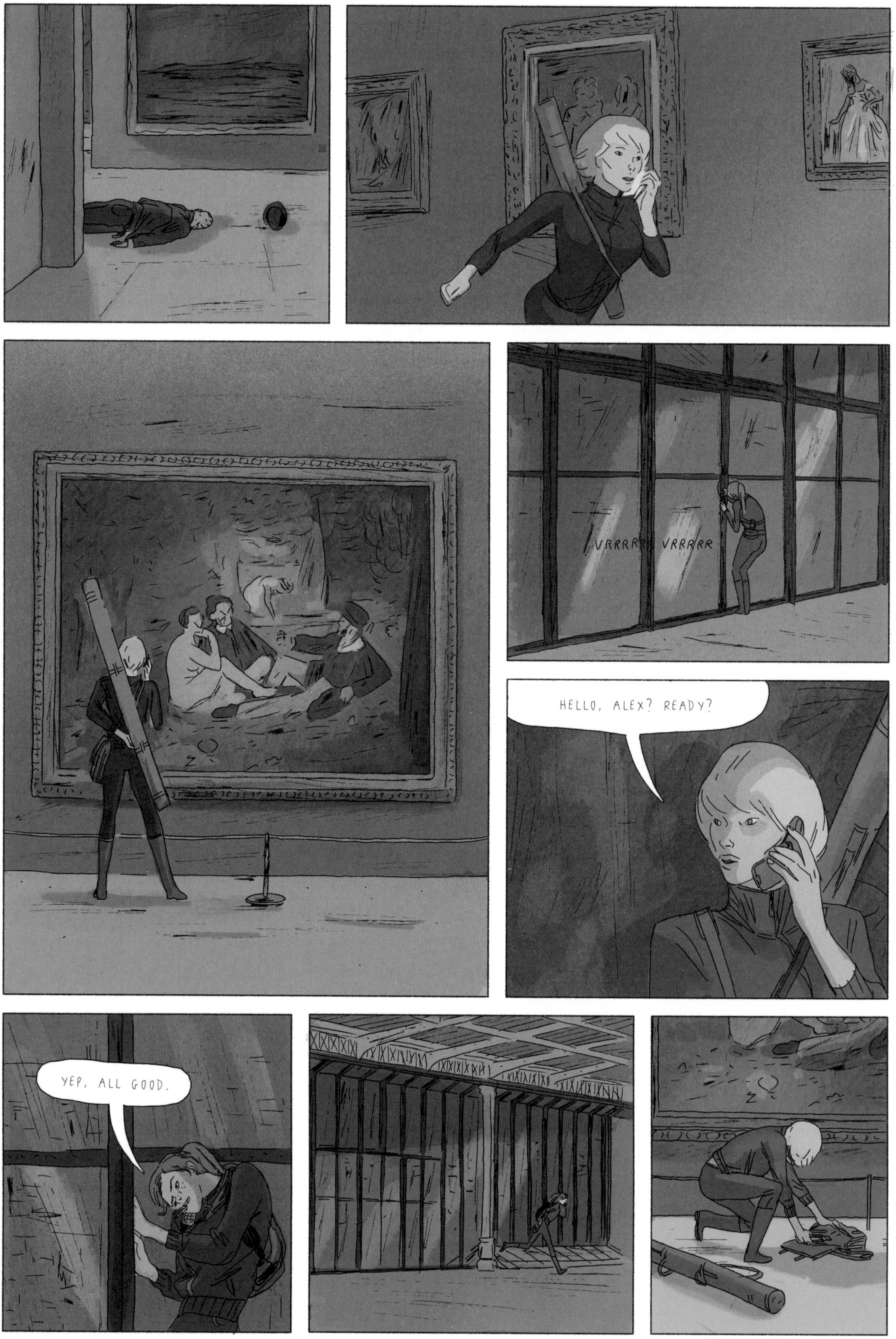
VRRRRRR VRRRRR
HELLO, ALEX? READY?
YEP, ALL GOOD.

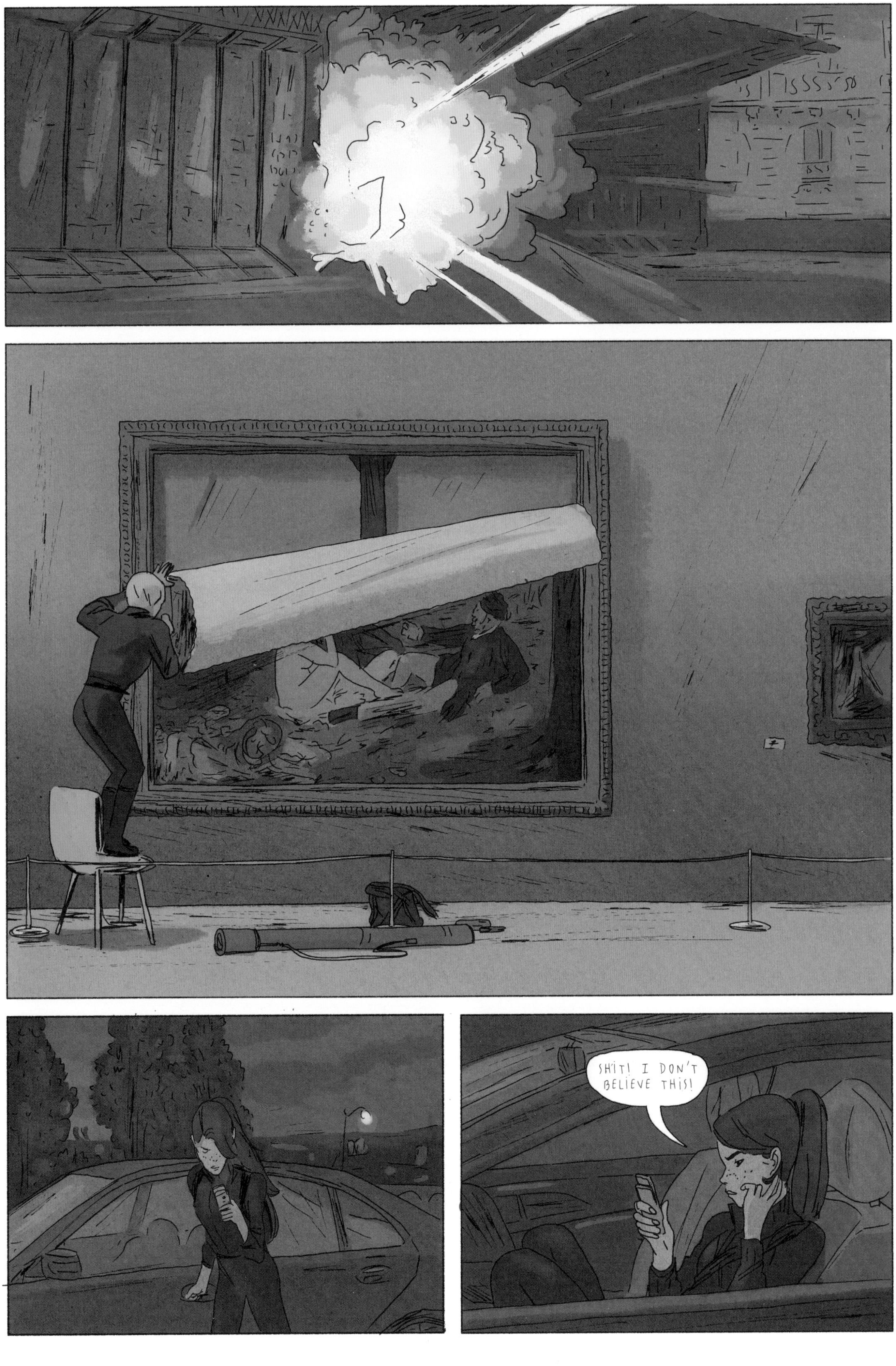
SH!T! I DON'T BELIEVE THIS!

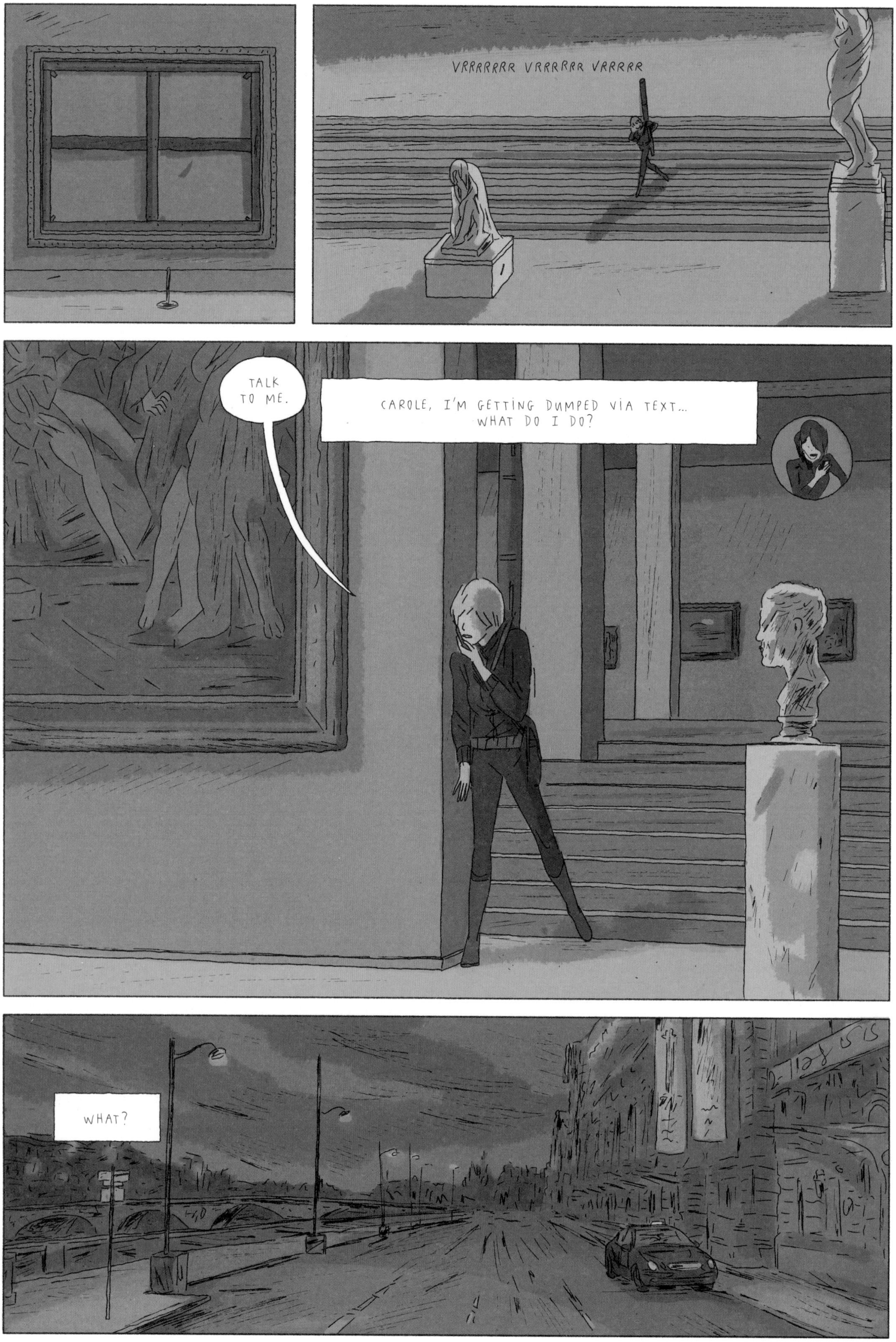
VRRRRRRR VRRRRRR VRRRRR
TALK TO ME.
CAROLE, I'M GETTING DUMPED VIA TEXT... WHAT DO I DO?
WHAT?

ARE YOU KIDDING? I NEED YOUR ATTENTION ON ME!
I'M AT THE ENTRANCE. THERE'S THREE GUARDS PLUS THE DOG.
ALEX, NOW IS WHEN YOU HONK TO GET THEIR ATTENTION--
ALEEEEX!
WOOF WOOF
COME OOOOON!

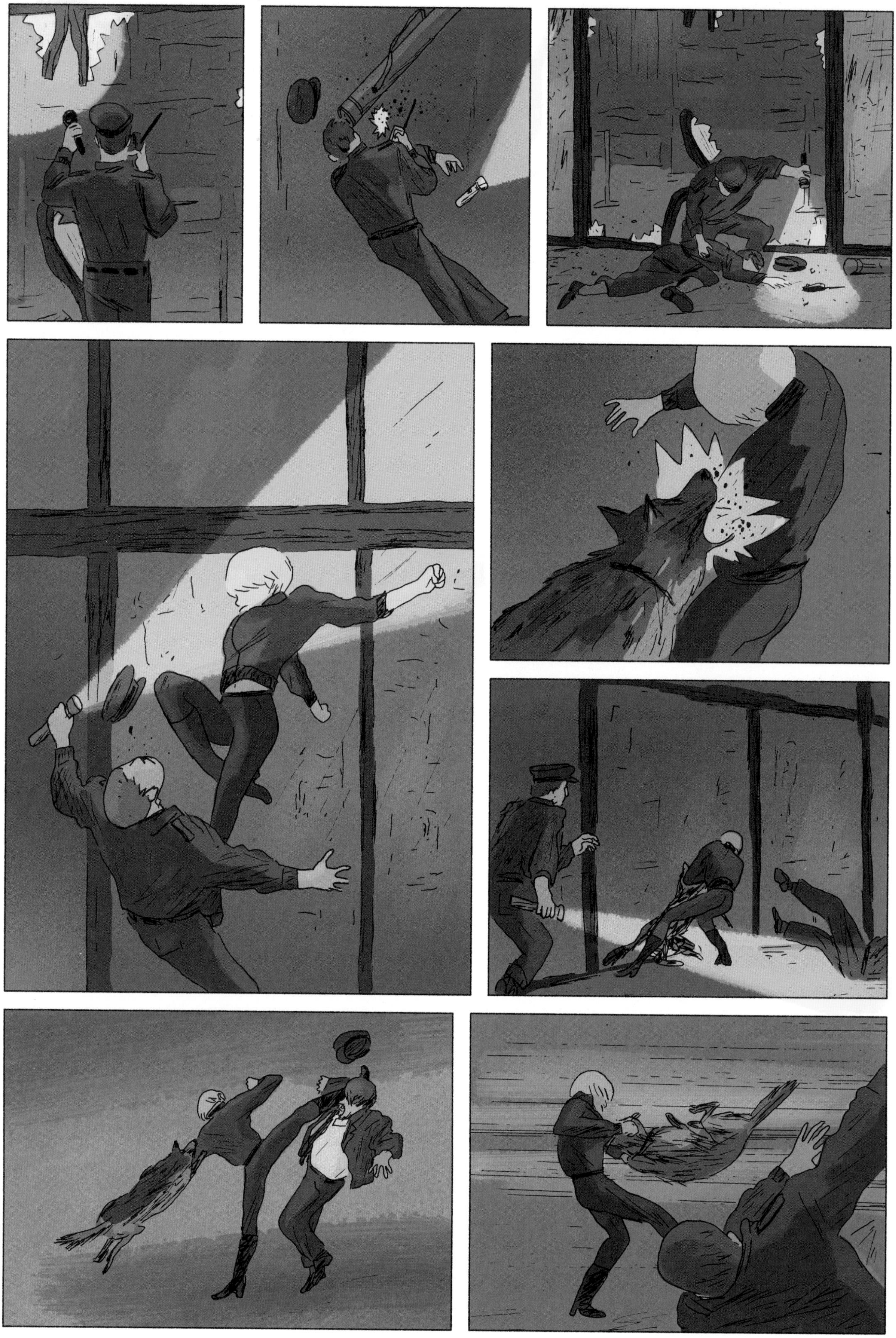

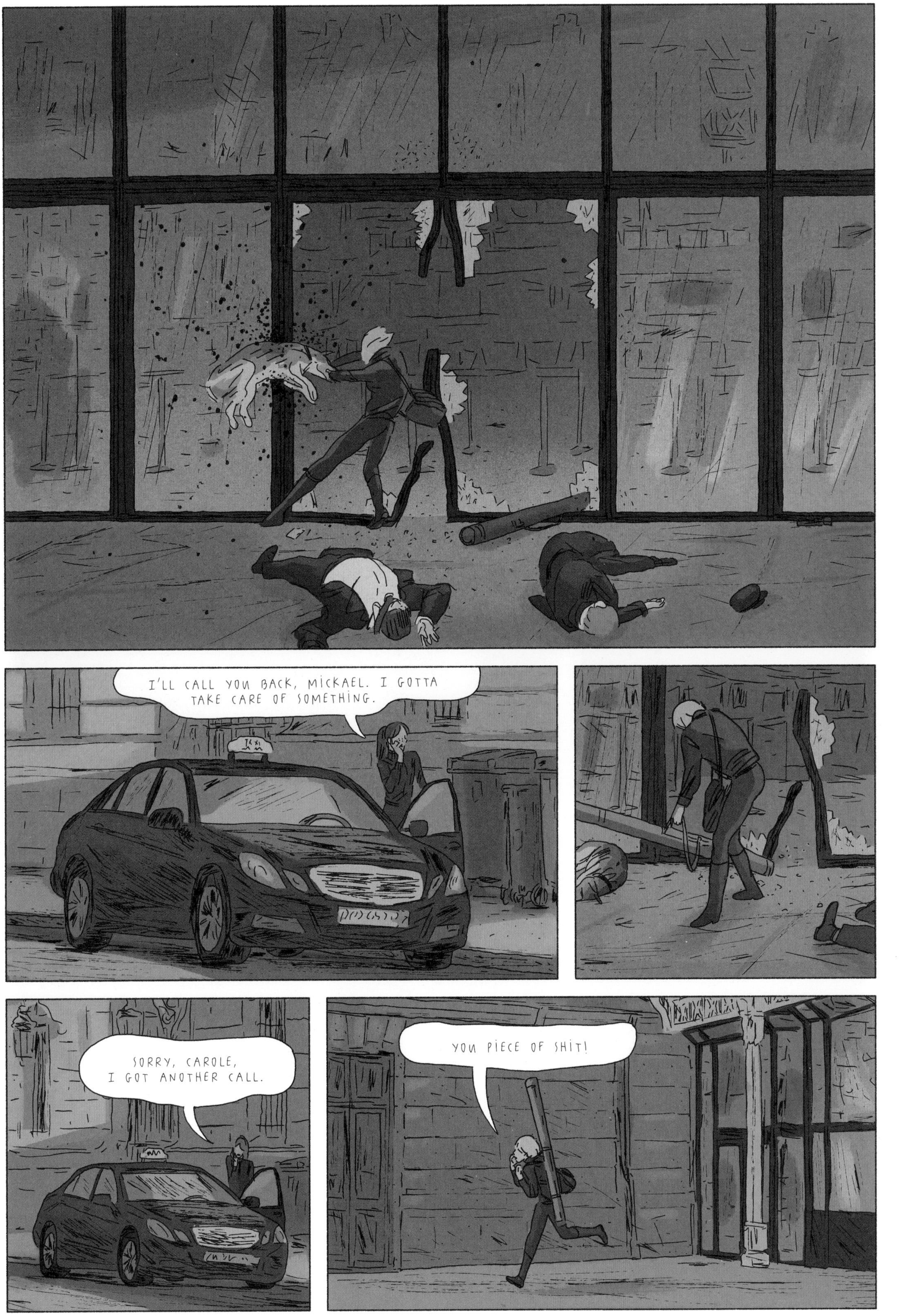
I'LL CALL YOU BACK, MICKAEL. I GOTTA TAKE CARE OF SOMETHING.
SORRY, CAROLE, I GOT ANOTHER CALL.
YOU PIECE OF SHIT!

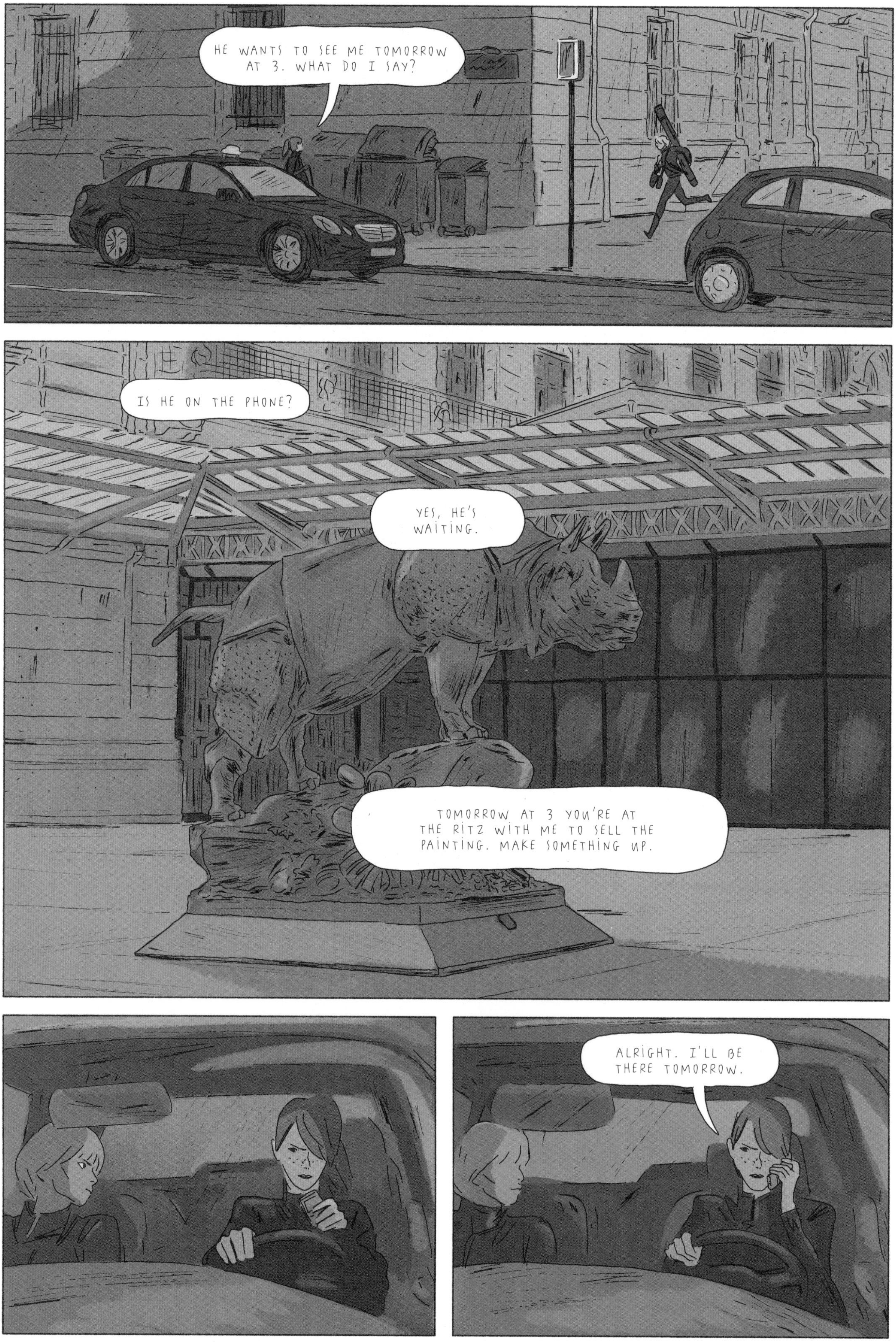
HE WANTS TO SEE ME TOMORROW AT 3. WHAT DO I SAY?
IS HE ON THE PHONE?
YES, HE'S WAITING.
TOMORROW AT 3 YOU'RE AT THE RITZ WITH ME TO SELL THE PAINTING. MAKE SOMETHING UP.
ALRIGHT. I'LL BE THERE TOMORROW.

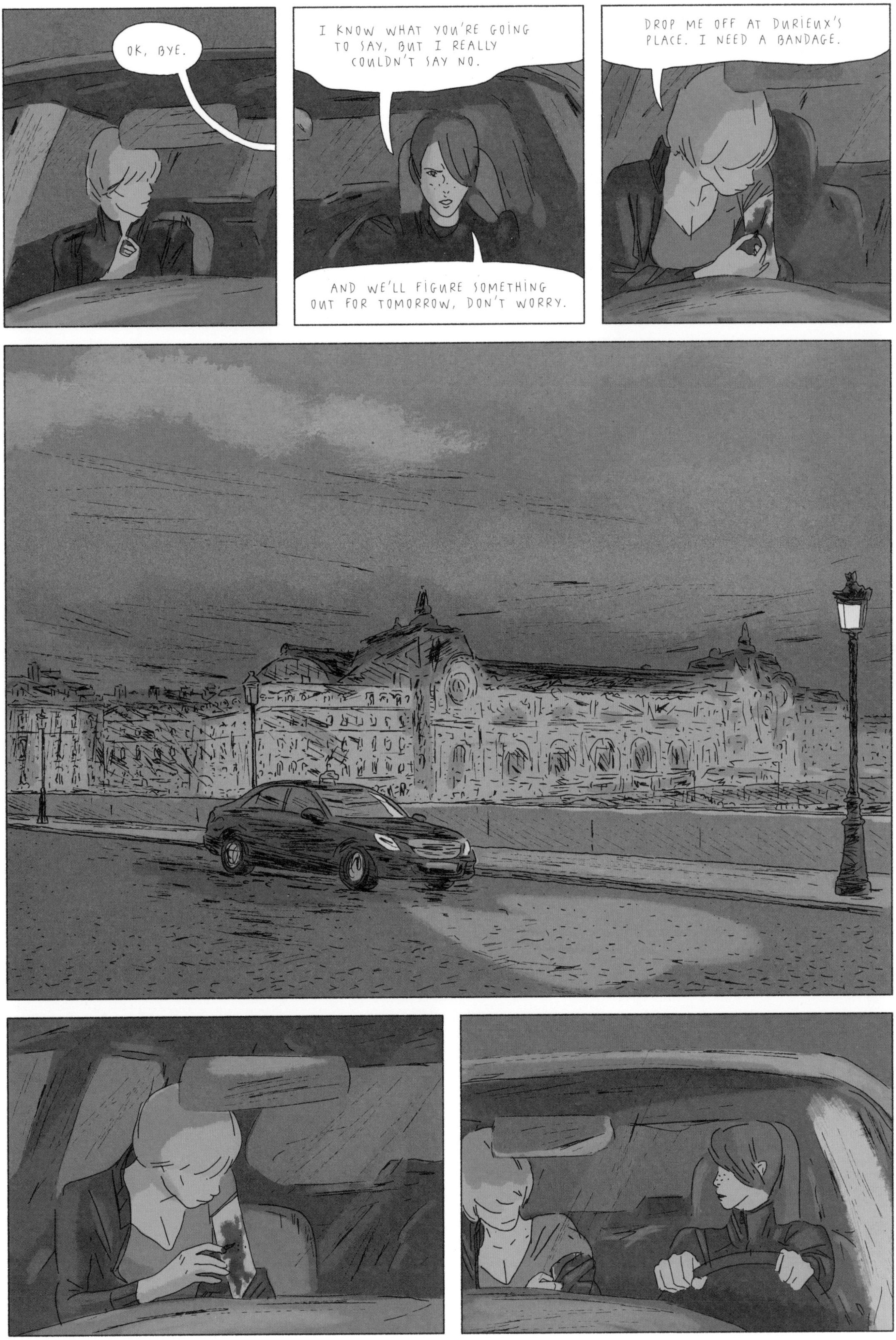
OK, BYE.
I KNOW WHAT YOU'RE GOING TO SAY, BUT I REALLY COULDN'T SAY NO.
AND WE'LL FIGURE SOMETHING OUT FOR TOMORROW, DON'T WORRY.
DROP ME OFF AT DURIEUX'S PLACE. I NEED A BANDAGE.

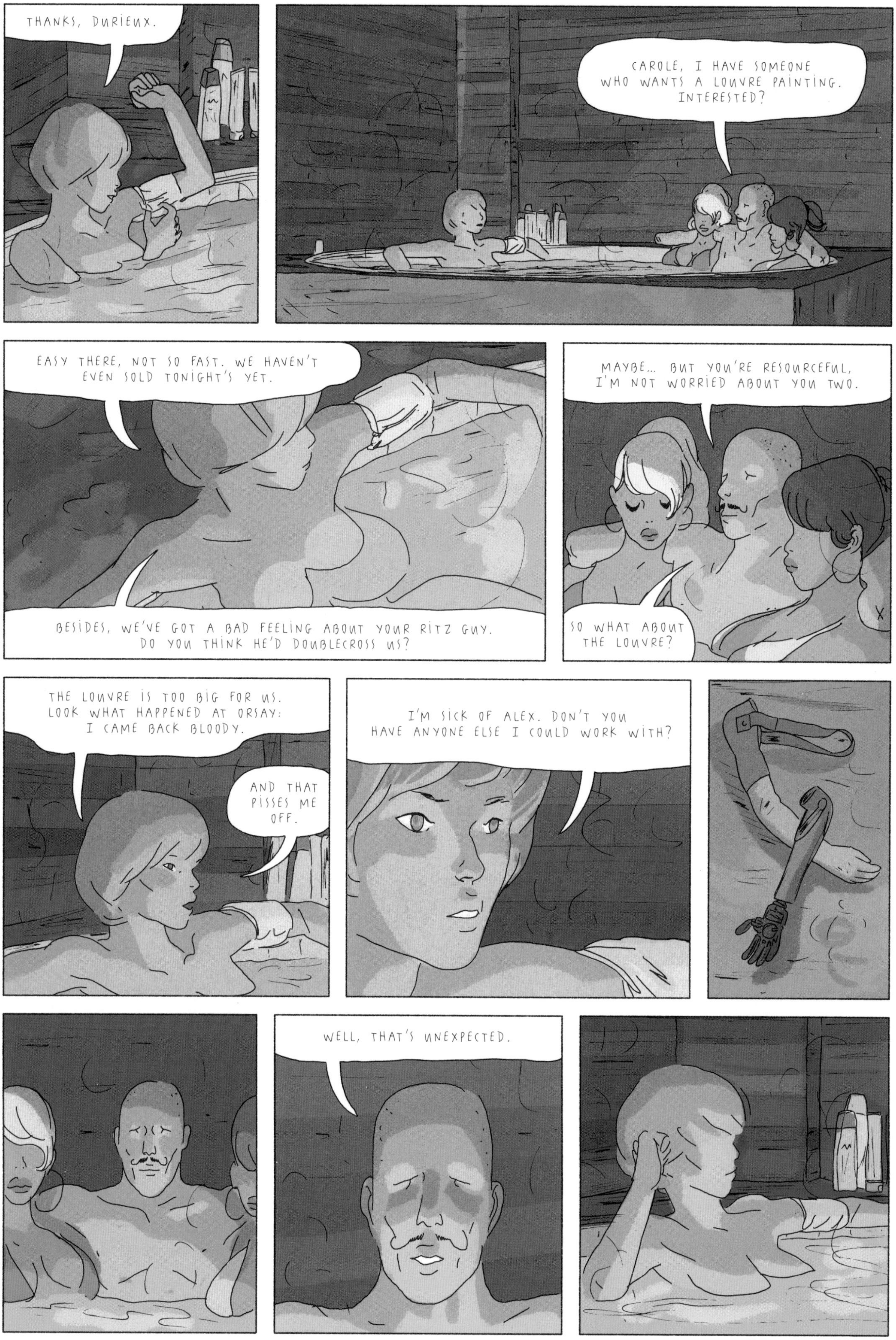
THANKS, DURIEUX.
CAROLE, I HAVE SOMEONE WHO WANTS A LOUVRE PAINTING. INTERESTED?
EASY THERE, NOT SO FAST. WE HAVEN'T EVEN SOLD TONIGHT'S YET.
BESIDES, WE'VE GOT A BAD FEELING ABOUT YOUR RITZ GUY. DO YOU THINK HE'D DOUBLECROSS US?
MAYBE... BUT YOU'RE RESOURCEFUL, I'M NOT WORRIED ABOUT YOU TWO.
SO WHAT ABOUT THE LOUVRE?
THE LOUVRE IS TOO BIG FOR US. LOOK WHAT HAPPENED AT ORSAY: I CAME BACK BLOODY.
AND THAT PISSES ME OFF.
I'M SICK OF ALEX. DON'T YOU HAVE ANYONE ELSE I COULD WORK WITH?
WELL, THAT'S UNEXPECTED.

YOU'VE BEEN WORKING TOGETHER FOR TEN YEARS, YOU'RE LIKE SISTERS.

NINE YEARS, ACTUALLY.

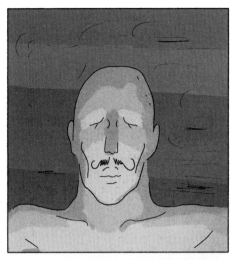

WELL, NOW, YOU'RE BEING HARSH. THAT'S NOT LIKE YOU.

RIGHT. I'M OFF TO THE SAUNA. SHOULD I SEND YOU SOME COMPANY?

NO THANKS.

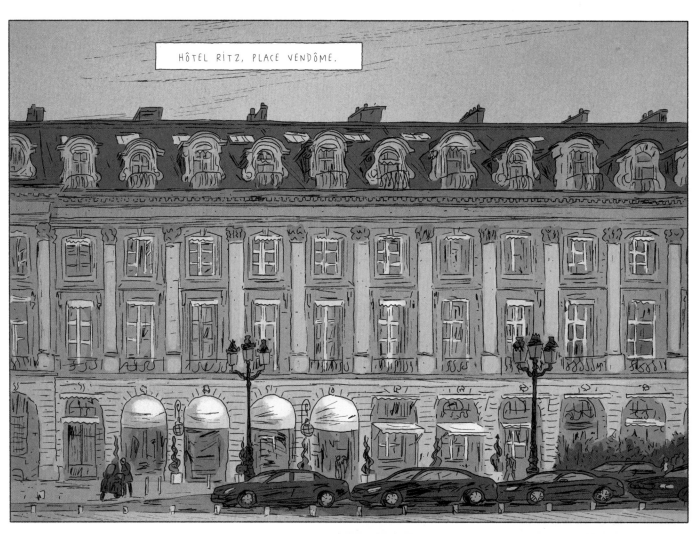

HÔTEL RITZ, PLACE VENDÔME.

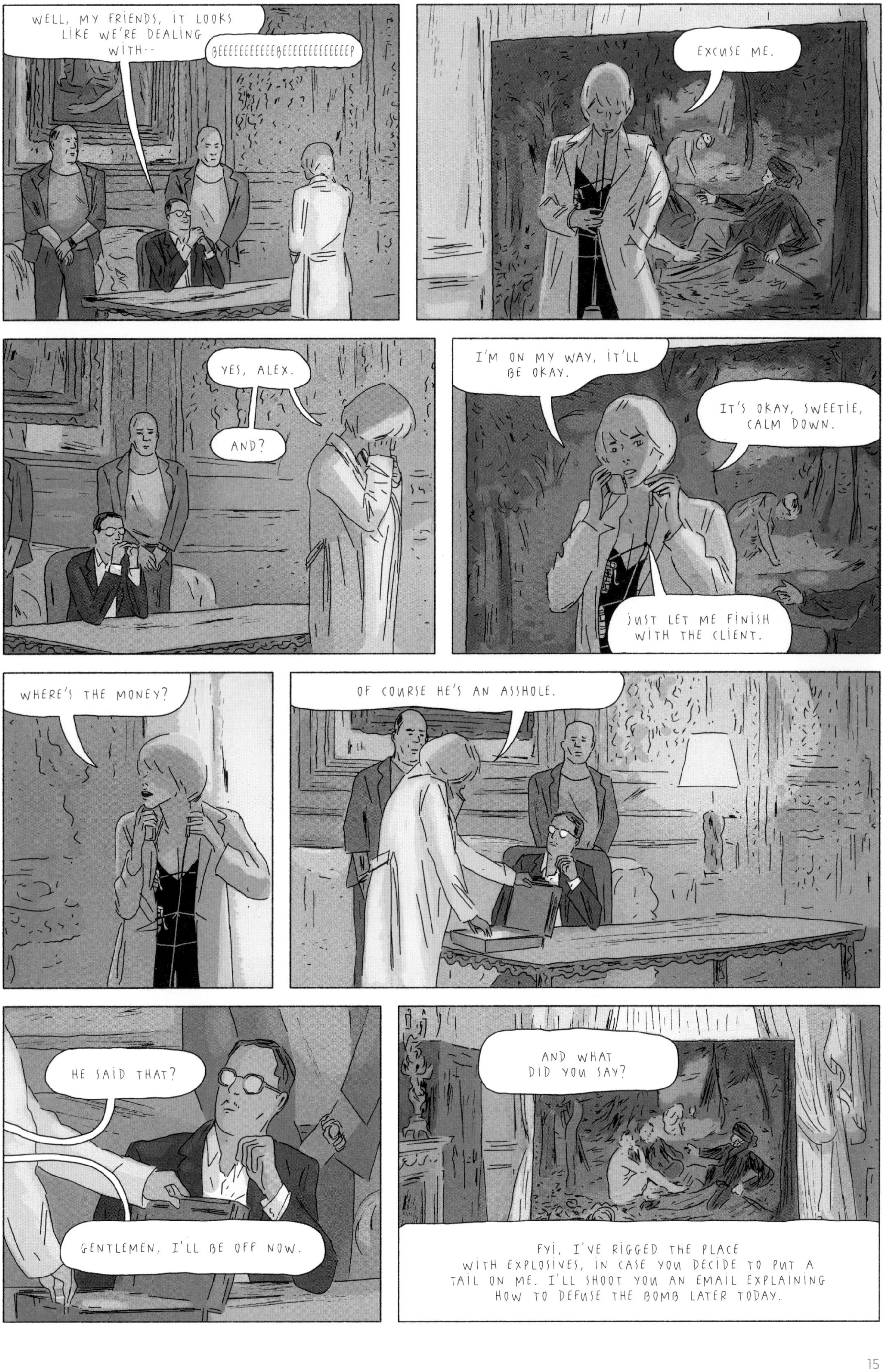
WELL, MY FRIENDS, IT LOOKS LIKE WE'RE DEALING WITH--
BEEEEEEEEEEEBEEEEEEEEEEEEEP
EXCUSE ME.
YES, ALEX.
AND?
I'M ON MY WAY, IT'LL BE OKAY.
IT'S OKAY, SWEETIE, CALM DOWN.
JUST LET ME FINISH WITH THE CLIENT.
WHERE'S THE MONEY?
OF COURSE HE'S AN ASSHOLE.
HE SAID THAT?
GENTLEMEN, I'LL BE OFF NOW.
AND WHAT DID YOU SAY?
FYI, I'VE RIGGED THE PLACE WITH EXPLOSIVES, IN CASE YOU DECIDE TO PUT A TAIL ON ME. I'LL SHOOT YOU AN EMAIL EXPLAINING HOW TO DEFUSE THE BOMB LATER TODAY.

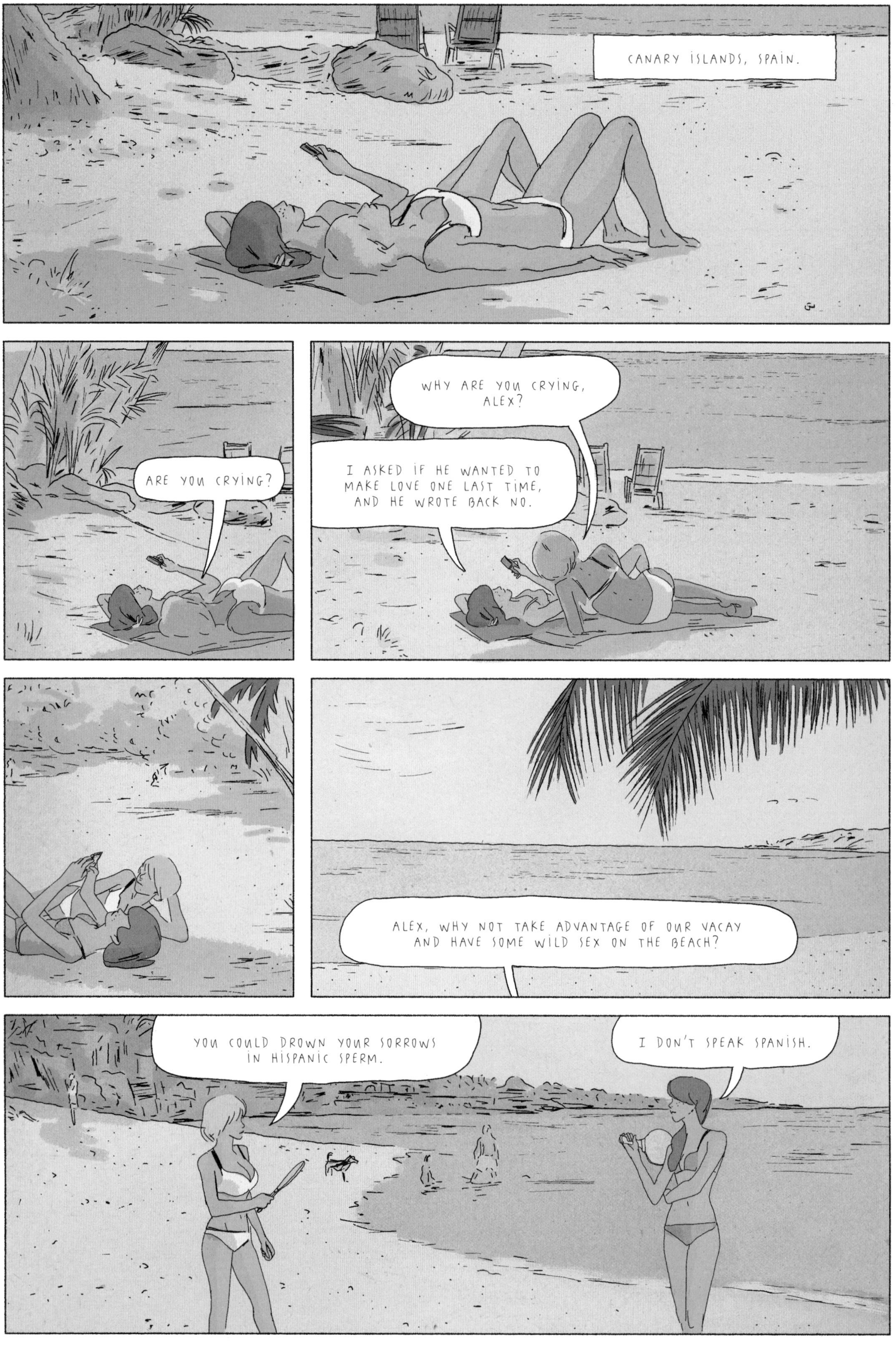
CANARY ISLANDS, SPAIN.
ARE YOU CRYING?
WHY ARE YOU CRYING, ALEX?
I ASKED IF HE WANTED TO MAKE LOVE ONE LAST TIME, AND HE WROTE BACK NO.
ALEX, WHY NOT TAKE ADVANTAGE OF OUR VACAY AND HAVE SOME WILD SEX ON THE BEACH?
YOU COULD DROWN YOUR SORROWS IN HISPANIC SPERM.
I DON'T SPEAK SPANISH.

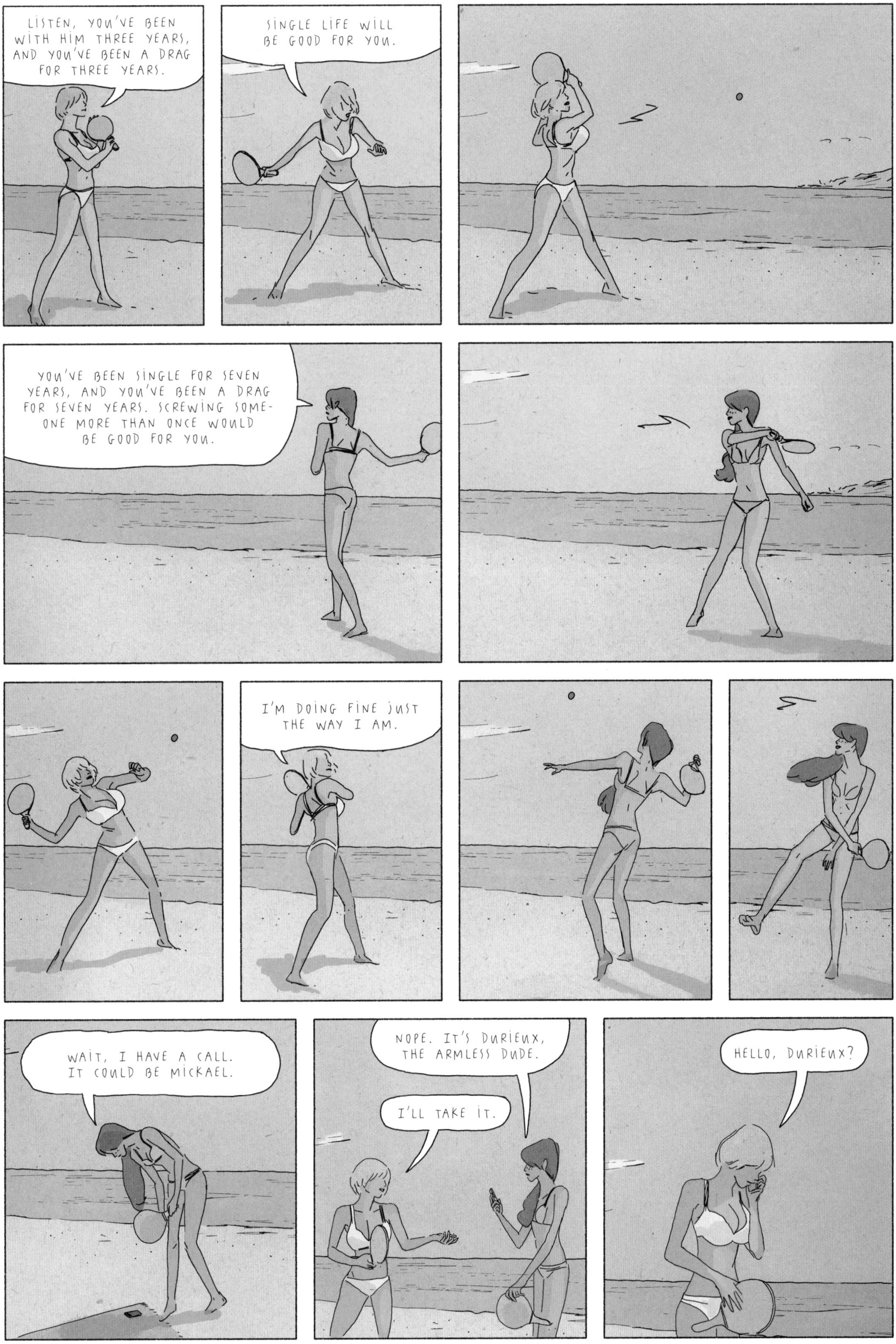
LISTEN, YOU'VE BEEN WITH HIM THREE YEARS, AND YOU'VE BEEN A DRAG FOR THREE YEARS.
SINGLE LIFE WILL BE GOOD FOR YOU.
YOU'VE BEEN SINGLE FOR SEVEN YEARS, AND YOU'VE BEEN A DRAG FOR SEVEN YEARS. SCREWING SOME-ONE MORE THAN ONCE WOULD BE GOOD FOR YOU.
I'M DOING FINE JUST THE WAY I AM.
WAIT, I HAVE A CALL. IT COULD BE MICKAEL.
NOPE. IT'S DURIEUX, THE ARMLESS DUDE.
I'LL TAKE IT.
HELLO, DURIEUX?

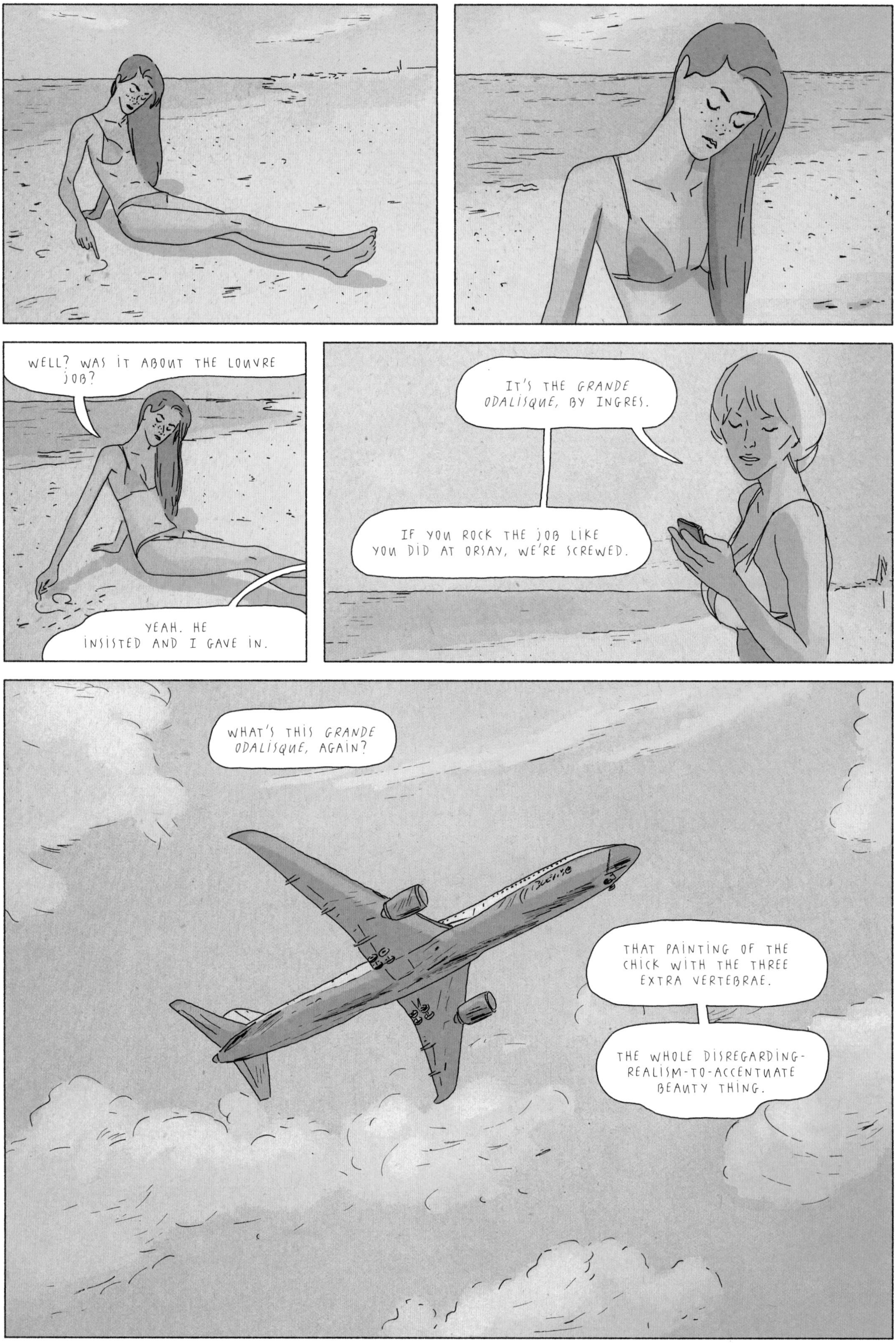
WELL? WAS IT ABOUT THE LOUVRE JOB?
YEAH. HE INSISTED AND I GAVE IN.
IT'S THE GRANDE ODALISQUE, BY INGRES.
IF YOU ROCK THE JOB LIKE YOU DID AT ORSAY, WE'RE SCREWED.
WHAT'S THIS GRANDE ODALISQUE, AGAIN?
THAT PAINTING OF THE CHICK WITH THE THREE EXTRA VERTEBRAE.
THE WHOLE DISREGARDING-REALISM-TO-ACCENTUATE BEAUTY THING.

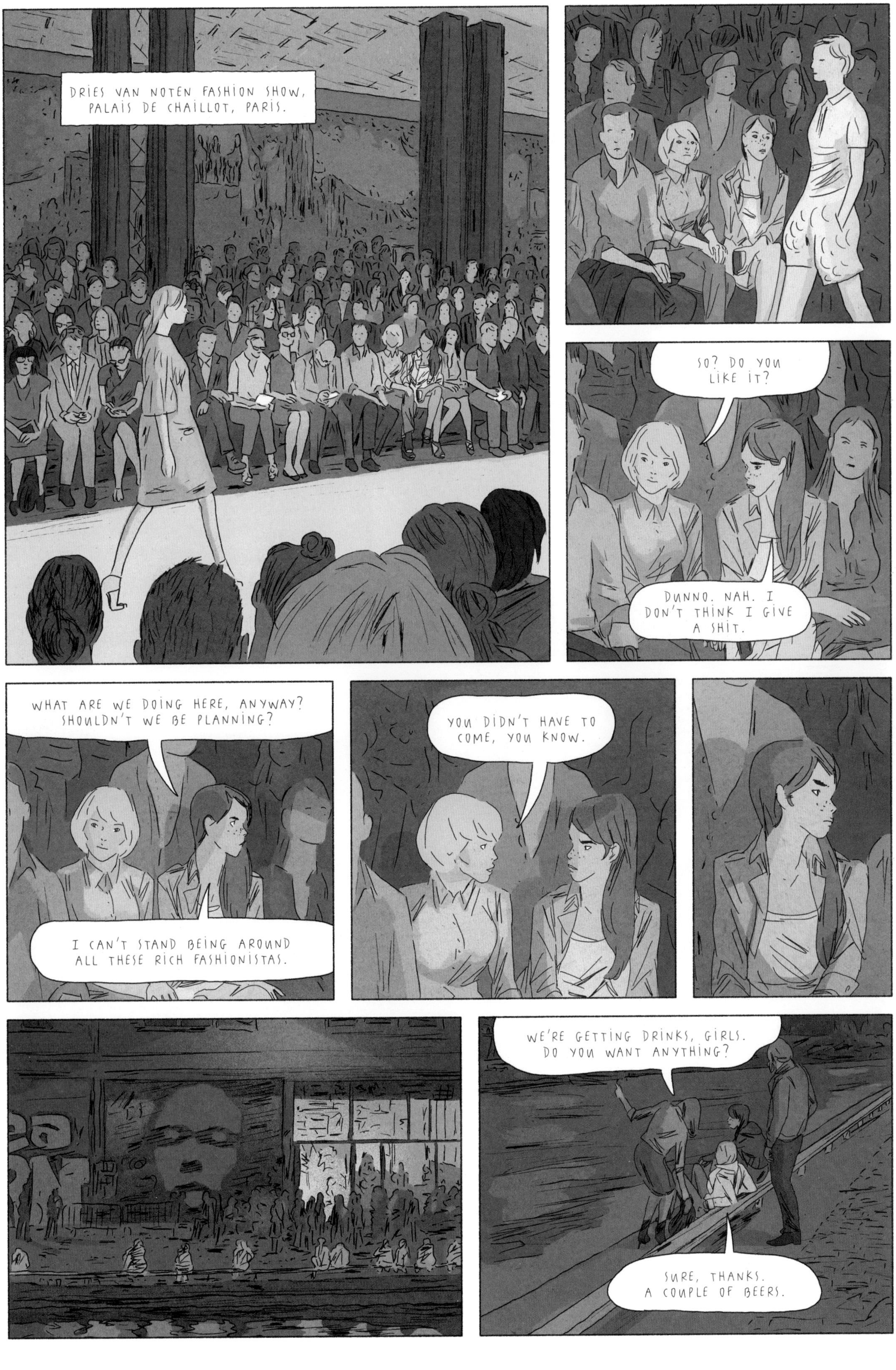
DRIES VAN NOTEN FASHION SHOW, PALAIS DE CHAILLOT, PARIS.
SO? DO YOU LIKE IT?
DUNNO. NAH. I DON'T THINK I GIVE A SHIT.
WHAT ARE WE DOING HERE, ANYWAY? SHOULDN'T WE BE PLANNING?
I CAN'T STAND BEING AROUND ALL THESE RICH FASHIONISTAS.
YOU DIDN'T HAVE TO COME, YOU KNOW.
WE'RE GETTING DRINKS, GIRLS. DO YOU WANT ANYTHING?
SURE, THANKS. A COUPLE OF BEERS.

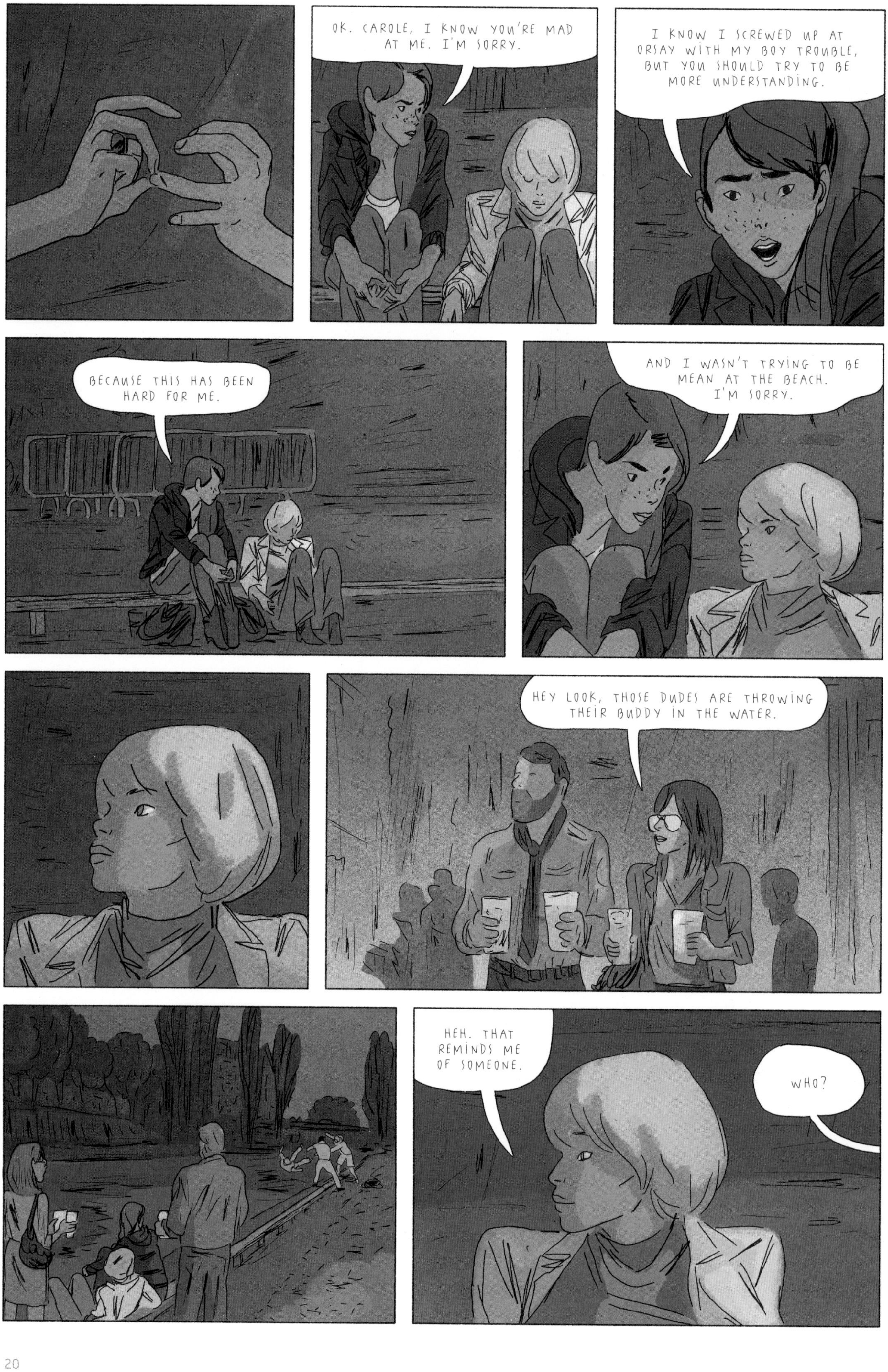
OK. CAROLE, I KNOW YOU'RE MAD AT ME. I'M SORRY.
I KNOW I SCREWED UP AT ORSAY WITH MY BOY TROUBLE, BUT YOU SHOULD TRY TO BE MORE UNDERSTANDING.
BECAUSE THIS HAS BEEN HARD FOR ME.
AND I WASN'T TRYING TO BE MEAN AT THE BEACH. I'M SORRY.
HEY LOOK, THOSE DUDES ARE THROWING THEIR BUDDY IN THE WATER.
HEH. THAT REMINDS ME OF SOMEONE.
WHO?

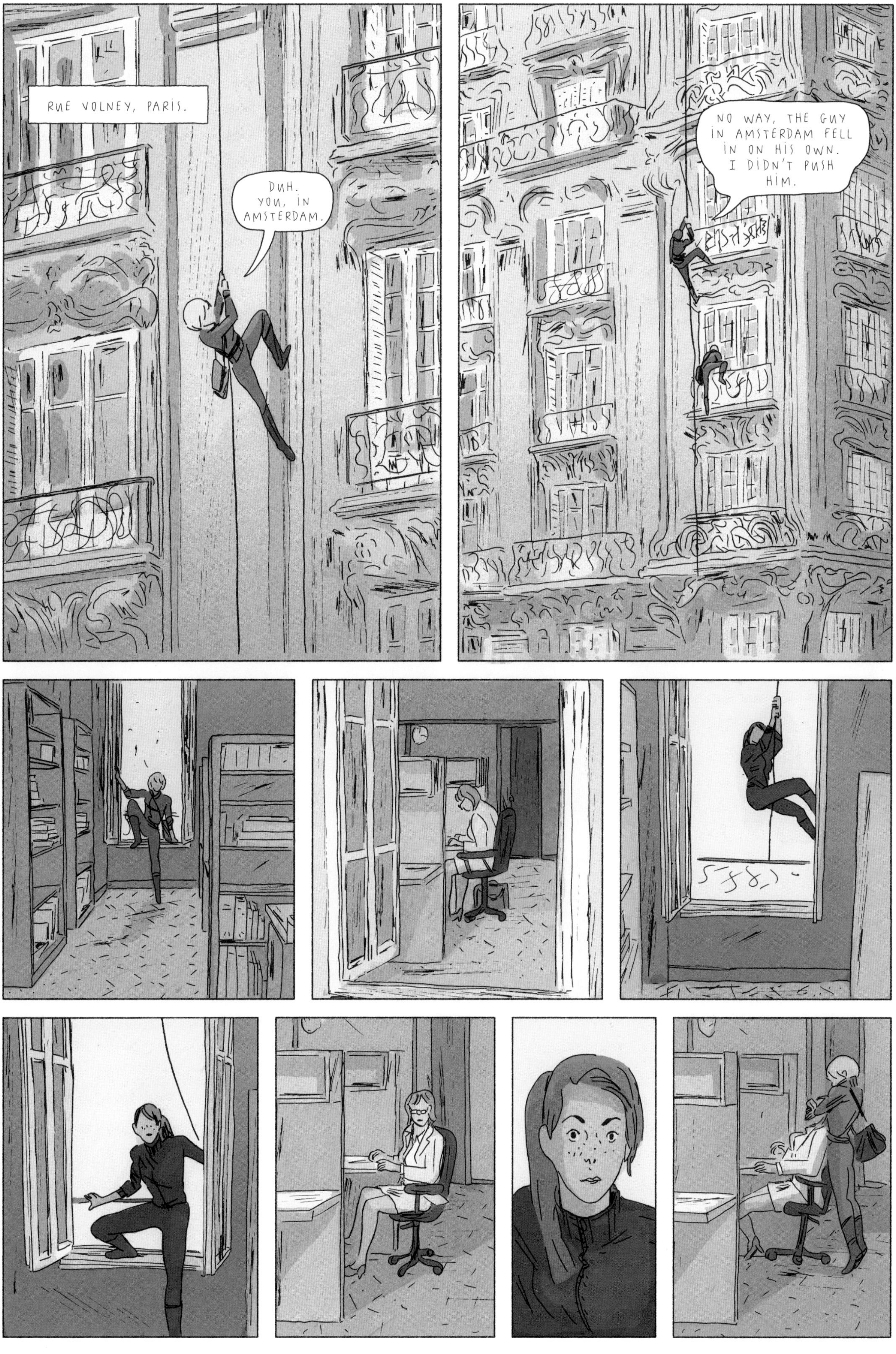

RUE VOLNEY, PARIS.
DUH. YOU, IN AMSTERDAM.
NO WAY, THE GUY IN AMSTERDAM FELL IN ON HIS OWN. I DIDN'T PUSH HIM.

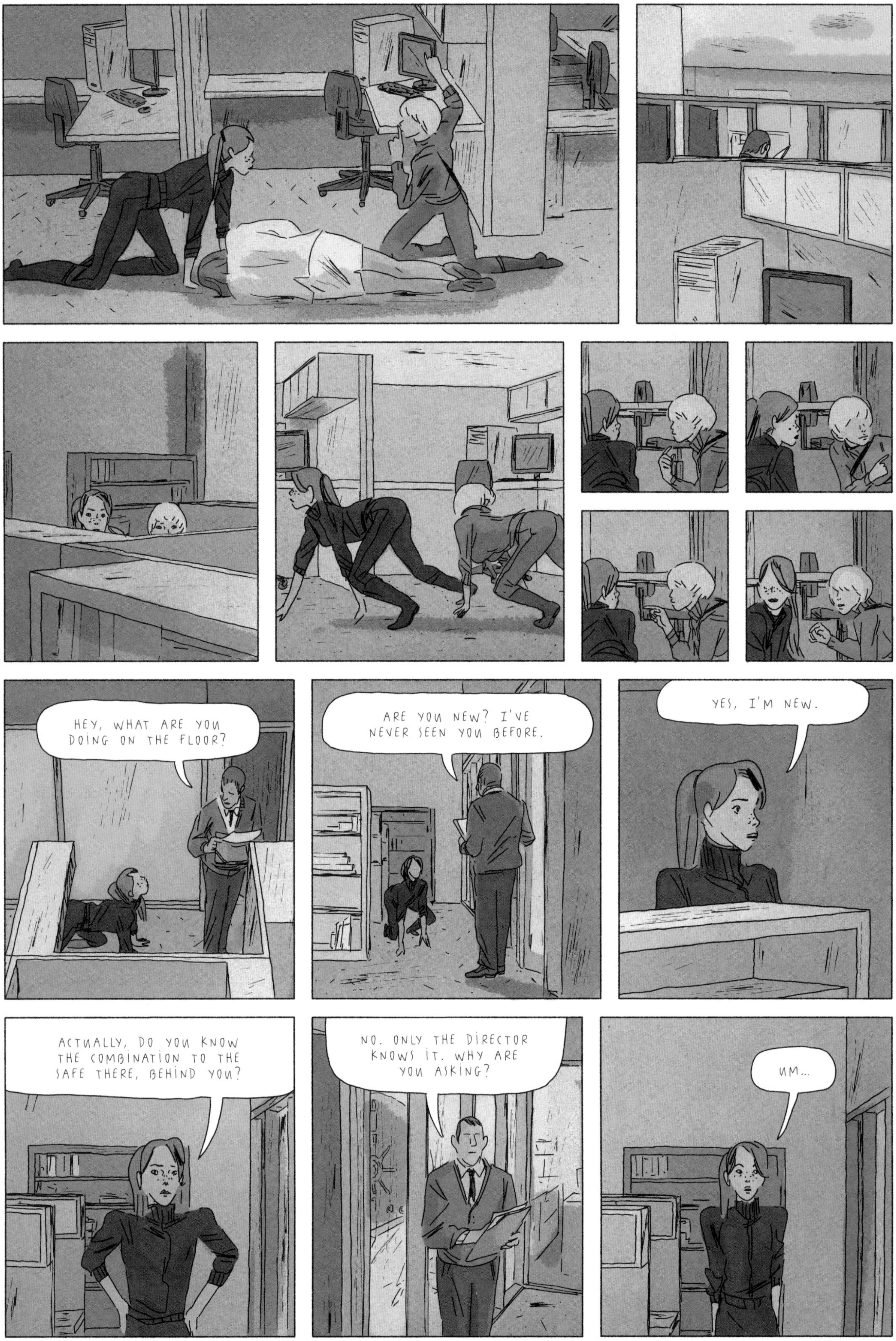
HEY, WHAT ARE YOU DOING ON THE FLOOR?
ARE YOU NEW? I'VE NEVER SEEN YOU BEFORE.
YES, I'M NEW.
ACTUALLY, DO YOU KNOW THE COMBINATION TO THE SAFE THERE, BEHIND YOU?
NO. ONLY THE DIRECTOR KNOWS IT. WHY ARE YOU ASKING?
UM...

SO I CAN RETRIEVE THE TECHNICAL FILE FOR THE ALARM SYSTEM WE DESIGNED FOR THE LOUVRE. I'M MAINLY INTERESTED IN THE PART COVERING THE *GRANDE ODALISQUE* PAINTING BY--

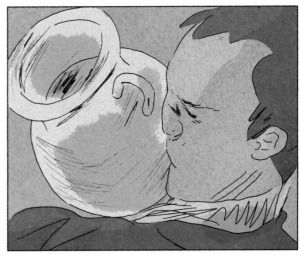

HELLO, SECURITY?

IT'S ODD, MY COLLEAGUE IS LYING ON THE FLOOR. SHE LOOKS LIKE SHE'S SLEEPING.

YES, THAT'S RIGHT, I THINK SHE WAS KNOCKED OUT.

LET'S GET OUTTA HERE!

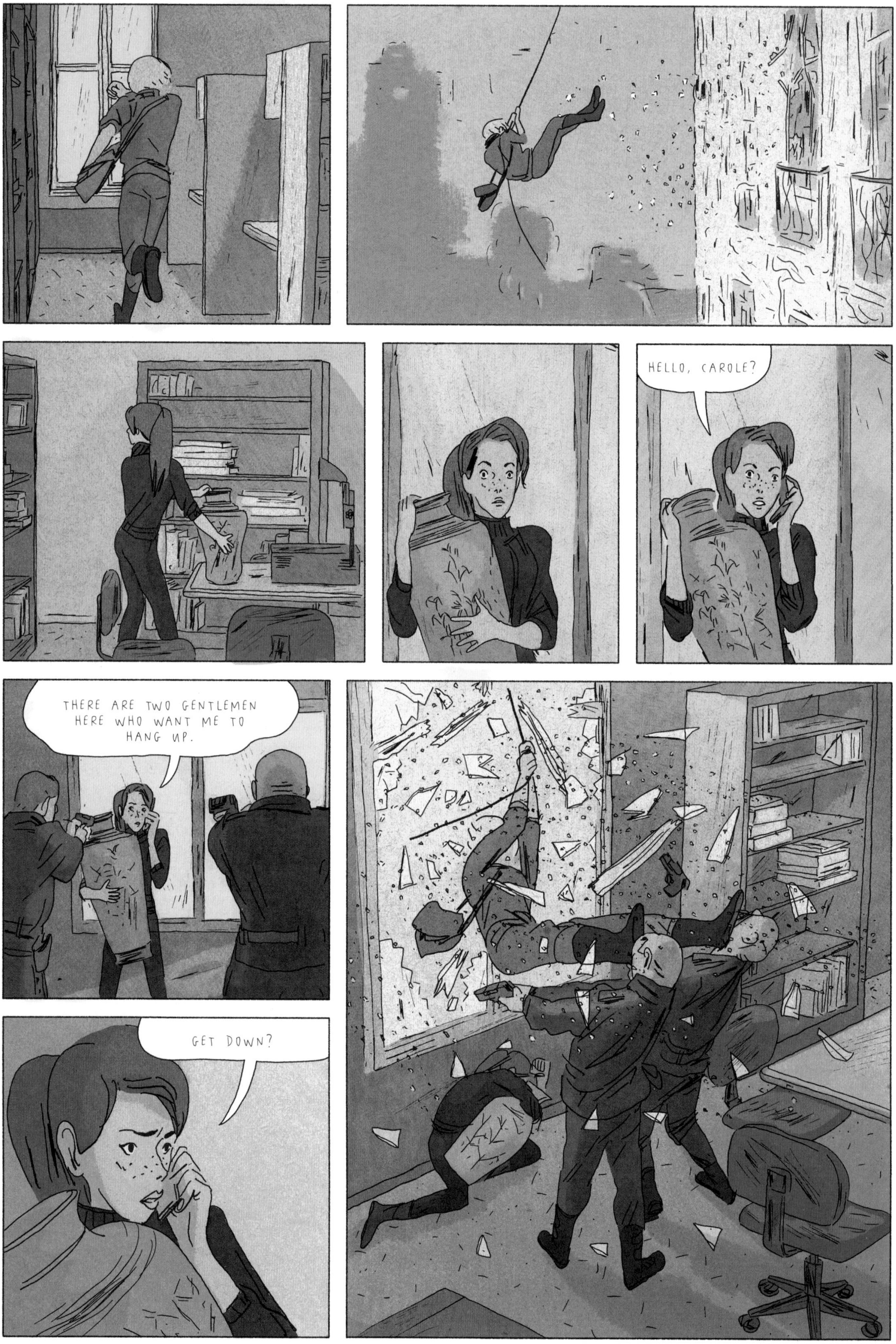
HELLO, CAROLE?
THERE ARE TWO GENTLEMEN HERE WHO WANT ME TO HANG UP.
GET DOWN?

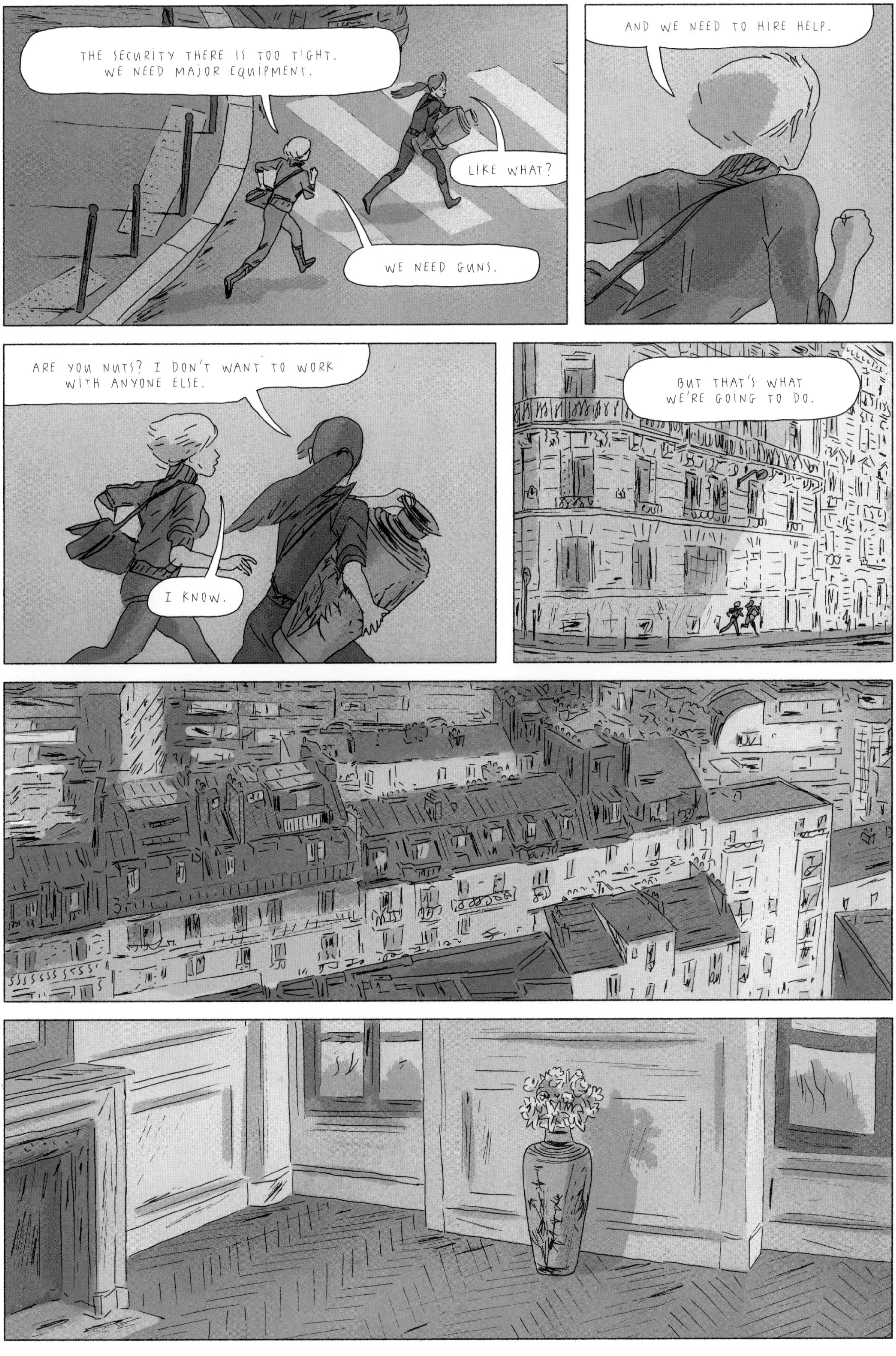
THE SECURITY THERE IS TOO TIGHT. WE NEED MAJOR EQUIPMENT.
LIKE WHAT?
WE NEED GUNS.
AND WE NEED TO HIRE HELP.
ARE YOU NUTS? I DON'T WANT TO WORK WITH ANYONE ELSE.
I KNOW.
BUT THAT'S WHAT WE'RE GOING TO DO.

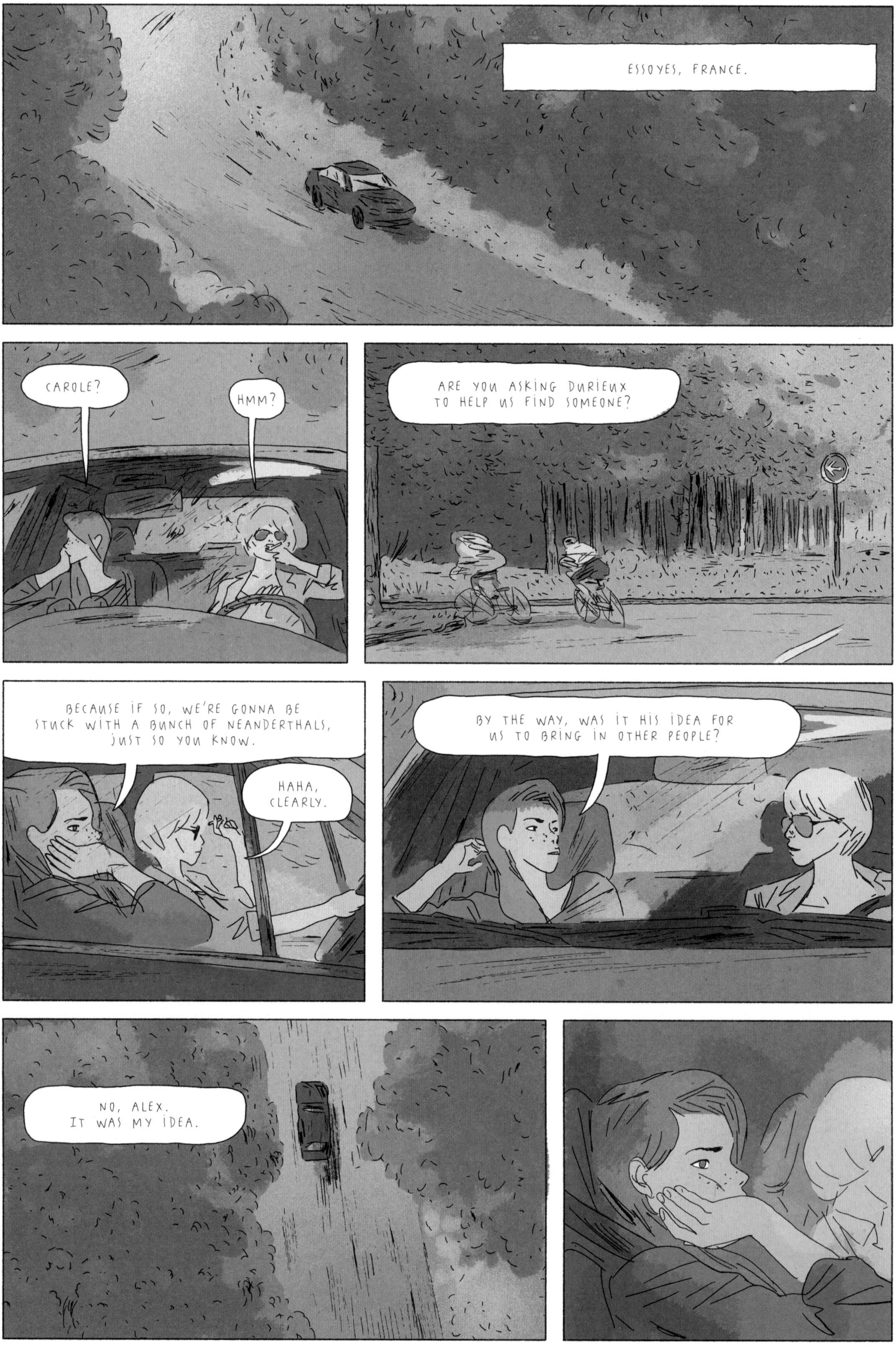
ESSOYES, FRANCE.
CAROLE?
HMM?
ARE YOU ASKING DURIEUX TO HELP US FIND SOMEONE?
BECAUSE IF SO, WE'RE GONNA BE STUCK WITH A BUNCH OF NEANDERTHALS, JUST SO YOU KNOW.
HAHA, CLEARLY.
BY THE WAY, WAS IT HIS IDEA FOR US TO BRING IN OTHER PEOPLE?
NO, ALEX. IT WAS MY IDEA.

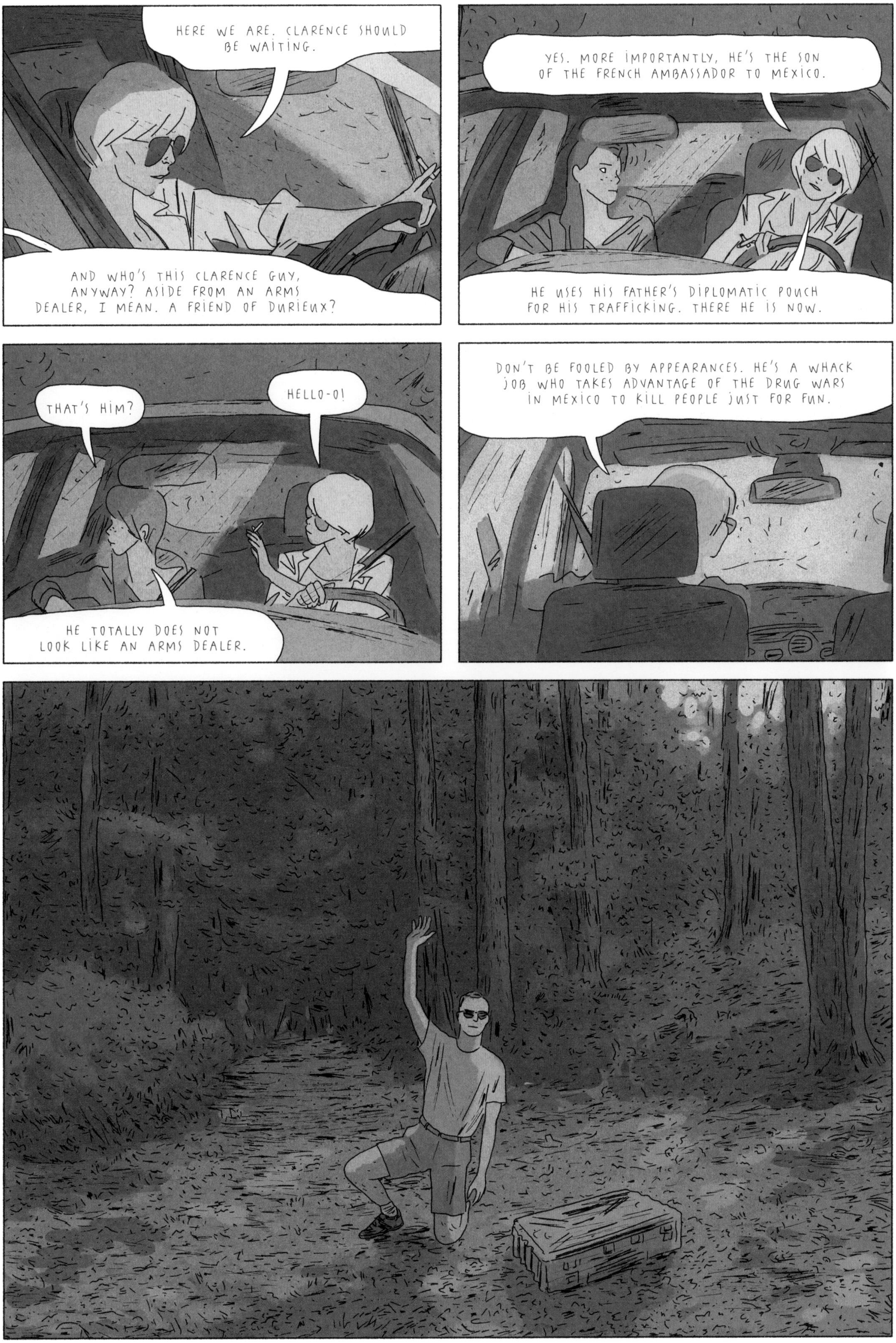
HERE WE ARE. CLARENCE SHOULD BE WAITING.
AND WHO'S THIS CLARENCE GUY, ANYWAY? ASIDE FROM AN ARMS DEALER, I MEAN. A FRIEND OF DURIEUX?
YES. MORE IMPORTANTLY, HE'S THE SON OF THE FRENCH AMBASSADOR TO MEXICO.
HE USES HIS FATHER'S DIPLOMATIC POUCH FOR HIS TRAFFICKING. THERE HE IS NOW.
THAT'S HIM?
HELLO-O!
HE TOTALLY DOES NOT LOOK LIKE AN ARMS DEALER.
DON'T BE FOOLED BY APPEARANCES. HE'S A WHACK JOB WHO TAKES ADVANTAGE OF THE DRUG WARS IN MEXICO TO KILL PEOPLE JUST FOR FUN.

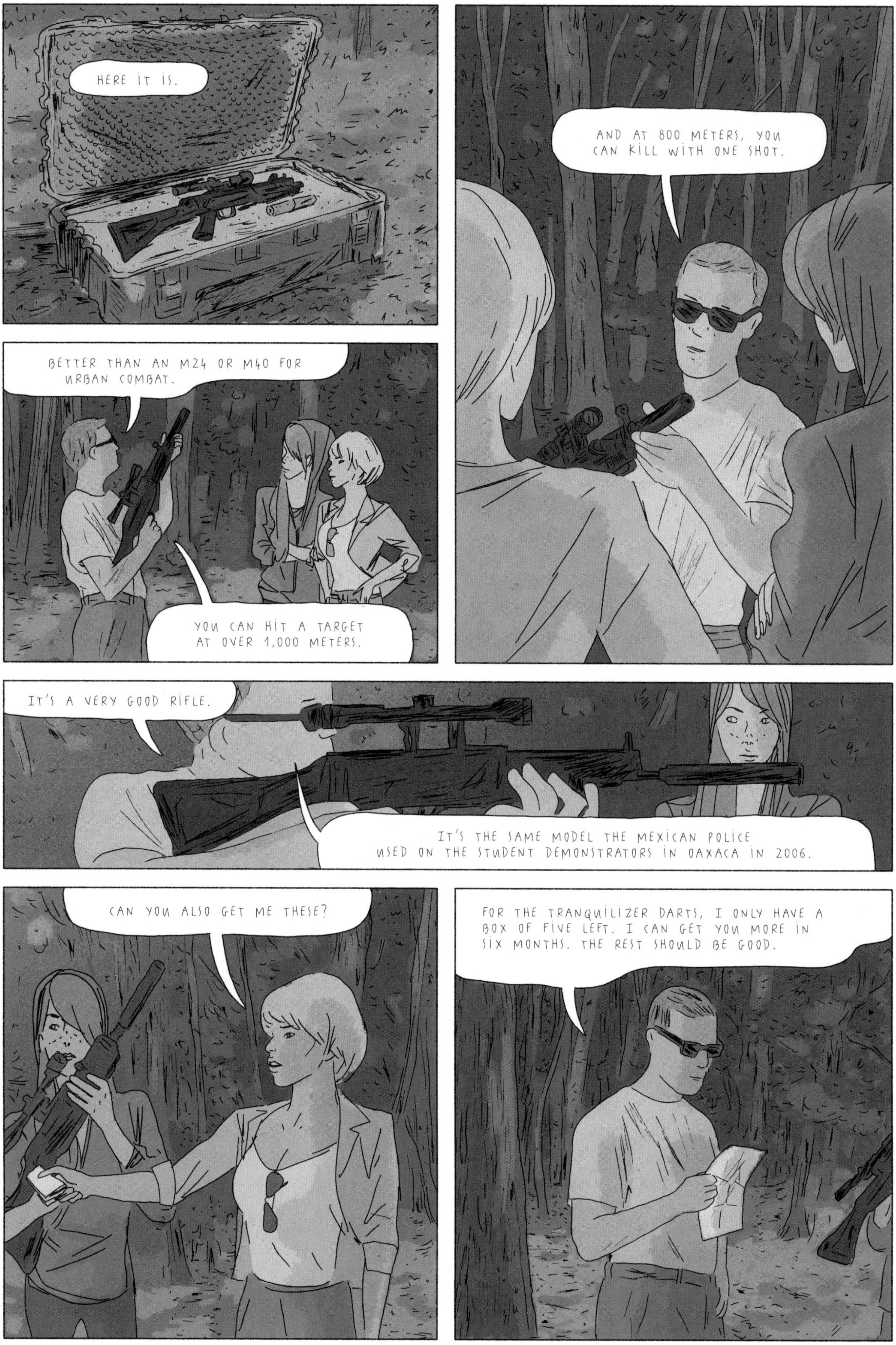
HERE IT IS.
AND AT 800 METERS, YOU CAN KILL WITH ONE SHOT.
BETTER THAN AN M24 OR M40 FOR URBAN COMBAT.
YOU CAN HIT A TARGET AT OVER 1,000 METERS.
IT'S A VERY GOOD RIFLE.
IT'S THE SAME MODEL THE MEXICAN POLICE USED ON THE STUDENT DEMONSTRATORS IN OAXACA IN 2006.
CAN YOU ALSO GET ME THESE?
FOR THE TRANQUILIZER DARTS, I ONLY HAVE A BOX OF FIVE LEFT. I CAN GET YOU MORE IN SIX MONTHS. THE REST SHOULD BE GOOD.

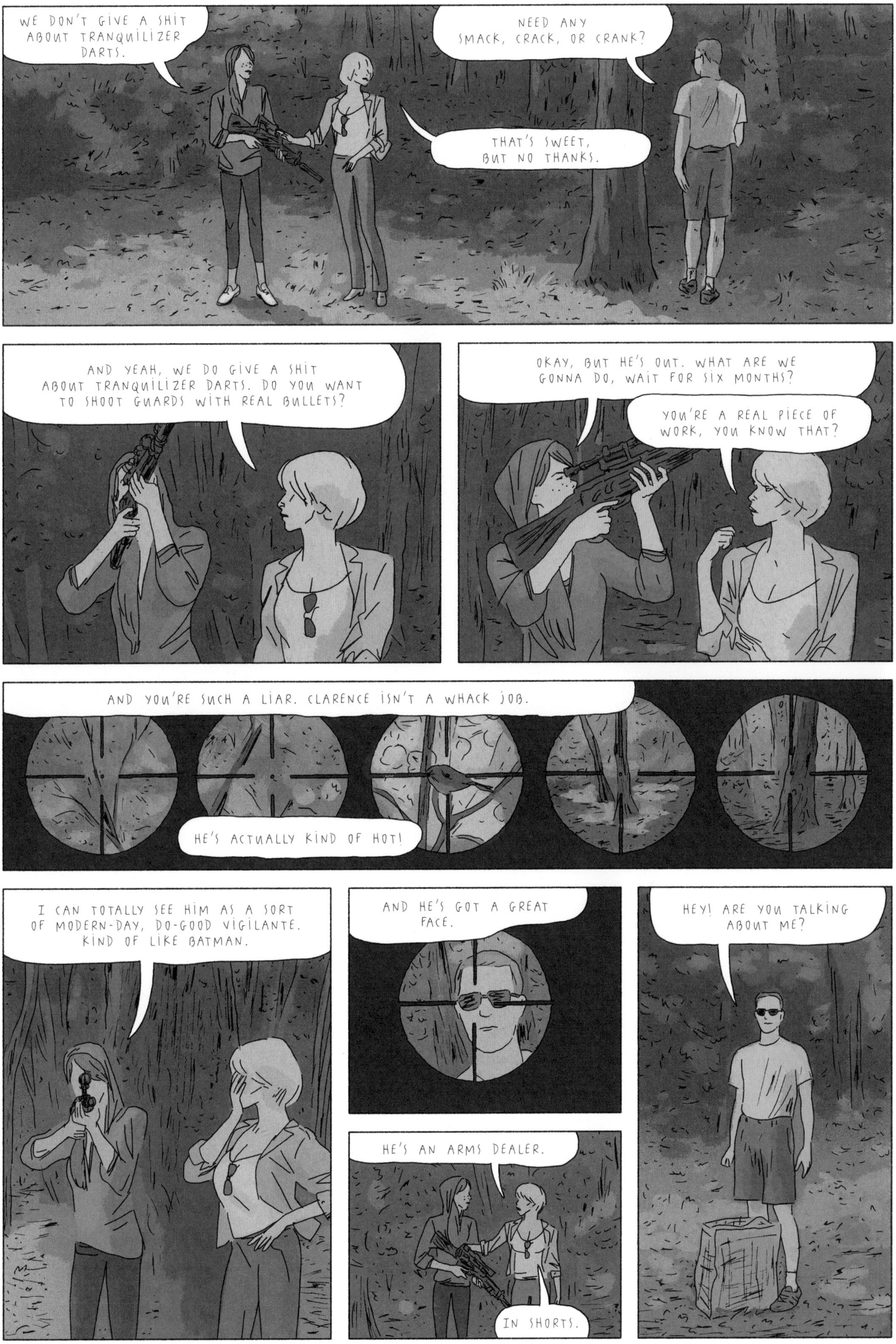
WE DON'T GIVE A SHIT ABOUT TRANQUILIZER DARTS.
NEED ANY SMACK, CRACK, OR CRANK?
THAT'S SWEET, BUT NO THANKS.
AND YEAH, WE DO GIVE A SHIT ABOUT TRANQUILIZER DARTS. DO YOU WANT TO SHOOT GUARDS WITH REAL BULLETS?
OKAY, BUT HE'S OUT. WHAT ARE WE GONNA DO, WAIT FOR SIX MONTHS?
YOU'RE A REAL PIECE OF WORK, YOU KNOW THAT?
AND YOU'RE SUCH A LIAR. CLARENCE ISN'T A WHACK JOB.
HE'S ACTUALLY KIND OF HOT!
I CAN TOTALLY SEE HIM AS A SORT OF MODERN-DAY, DO-GOOD VIGILANTE. KIND OF LIKE BATMAN.
AND HE'S GOT A GREAT FACE.
HE'S AN ARMS DEALER.
IN SHORTS.
HEY! ARE YOU TALKING ABOUT ME?

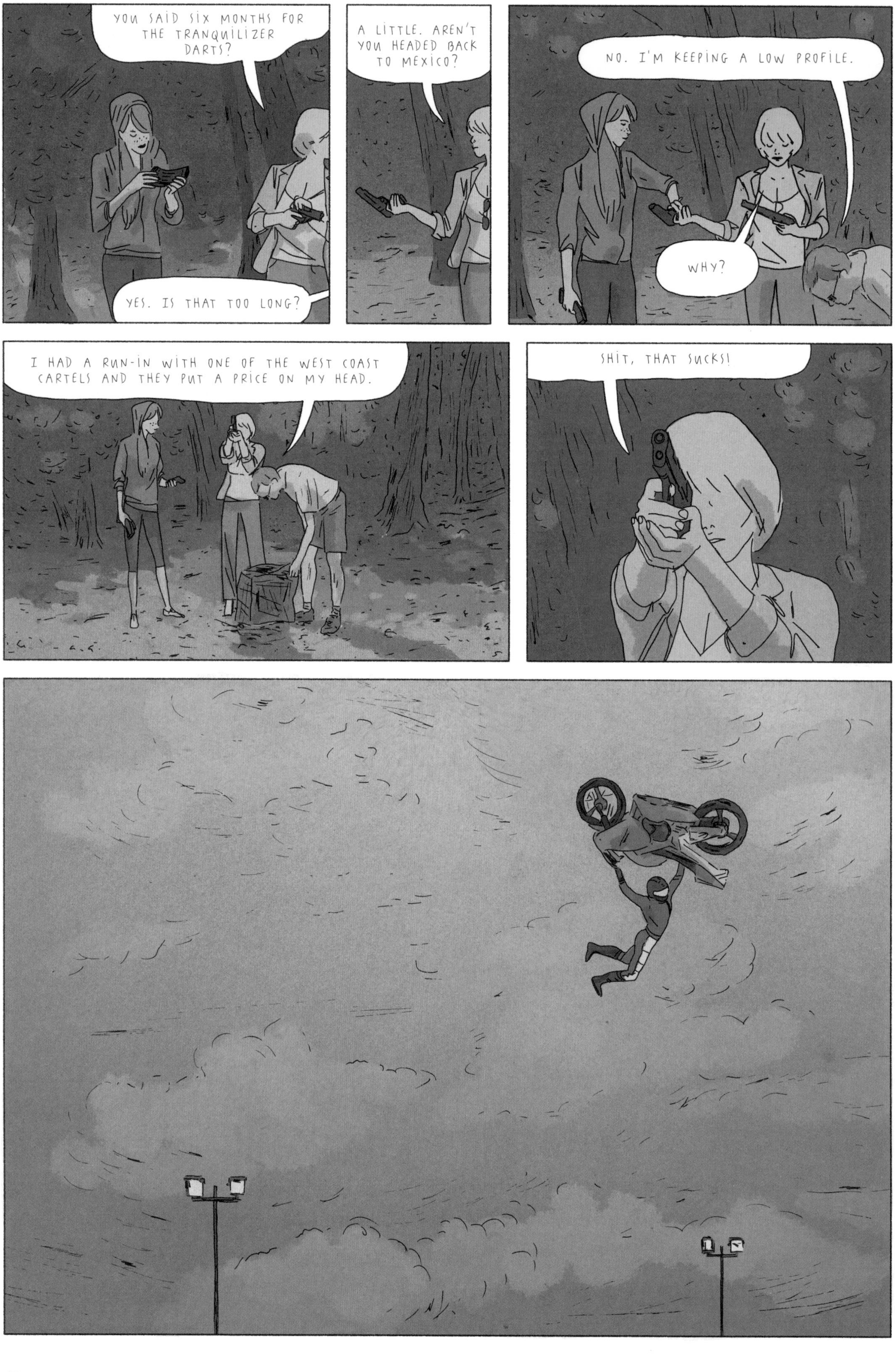
YOU SAID SIX MONTHS FOR THE TRANQUILIZER DARTS?
YES. IS THAT TOO LONG?
A LITTLE. AREN'T YOU HEADED BACK TO MEXICO?
NO. I'M KEEPING A LOW PROFILE.
WHY?
I HAD A RUN-IN WITH ONE OF THE WEST COAST CARTELS AND THEY PUT A PRICE ON MY HEAD.
SHIT, THAT SUCKS!

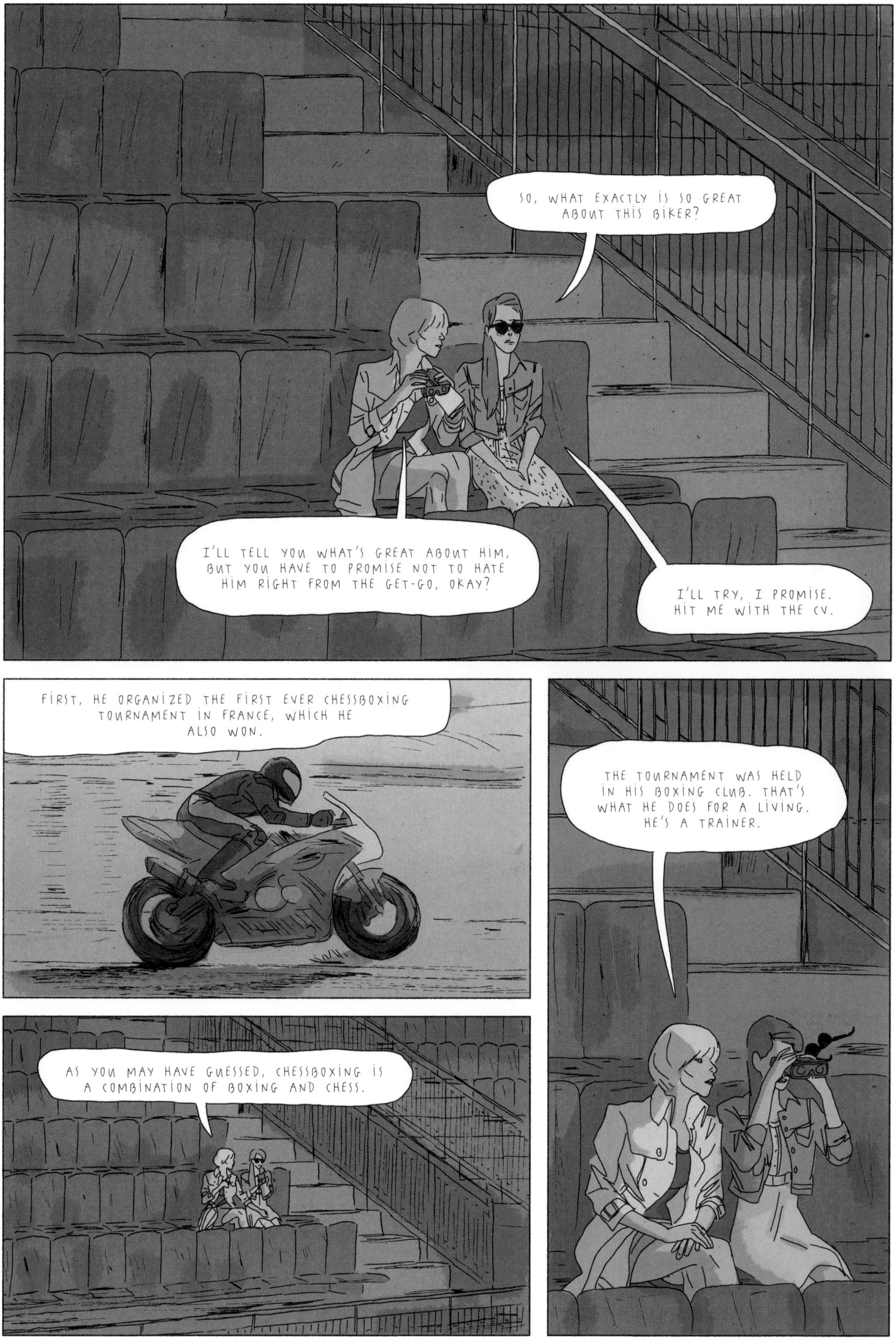

SO, WHAT EXACTLY IS SO GREAT ABOUT THIS BIKER?
I'LL TELL YOU WHAT'S GREAT ABOUT HIM, BUT YOU HAVE TO PROMISE NOT TO HATE HIM RIGHT FROM THE GET-GO, OKAY?
I'LL TRY, I PROMISE. HIT ME WITH THE CV.
FIRST, HE ORGANIZED THE FIRST EVER CHESSBOXING TOURNAMENT IN FRANCE, WHICH HE ALSO WON.
AS YOU MAY HAVE GUESSED, CHESSBOXING IS A COMBINATION OF BOXING AND CHESS.
THE TOURNAMENT WAS HELD IN HIS BOXING CLUB. THAT'S WHAT HE DOES FOR A LIVING. HE'S A TRAINER.

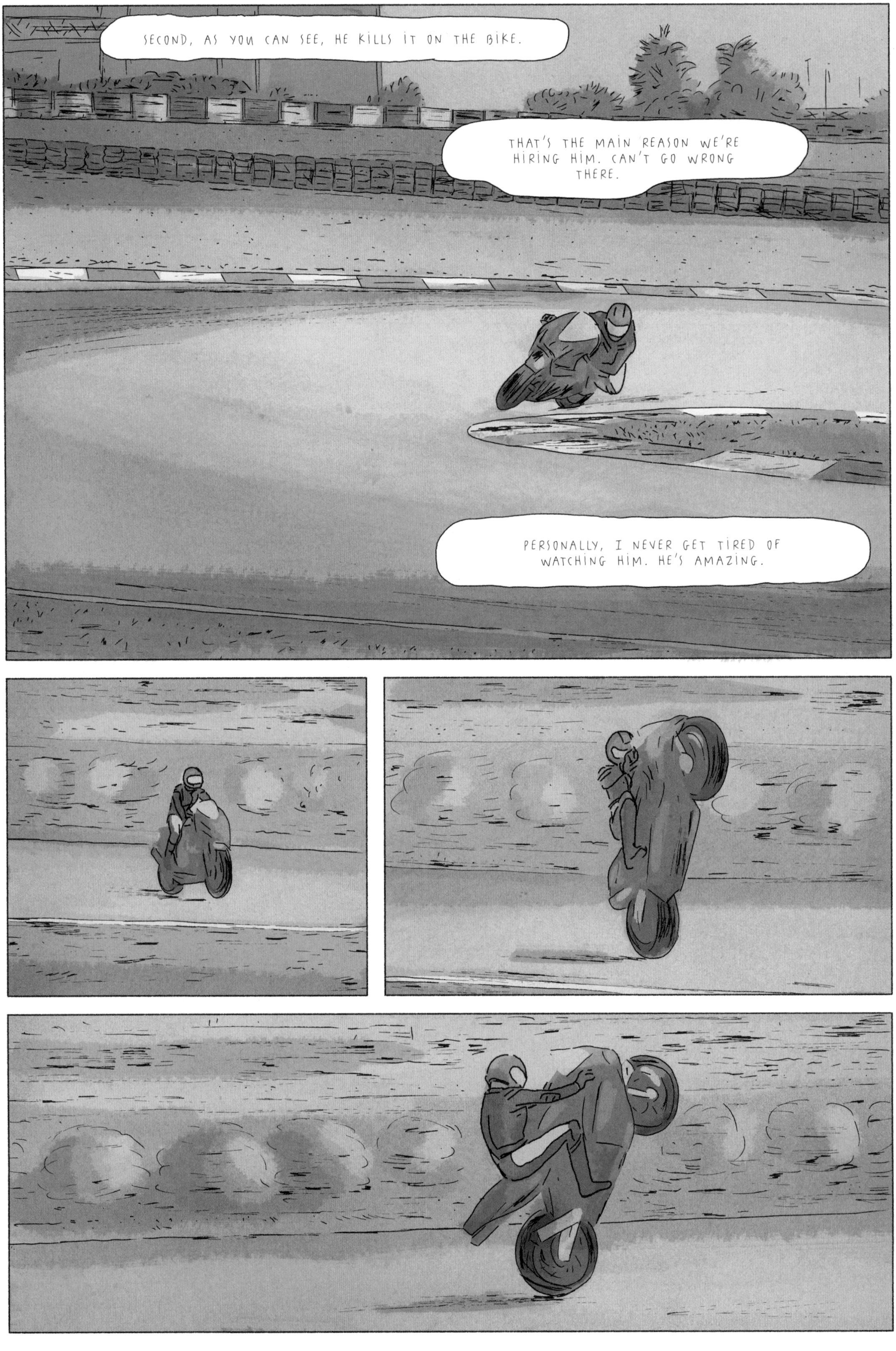
SECOND, AS YOU CAN SEE, HE KILLS IT ON THE BIKE.
THAT'S THE MAIN REASON WE'RE HIRING HIM. CAN'T GO WRONG THERE.
PERSONALLY, I NEVER GET TIRED OF WATCHING HIM. HE'S AMAZING.

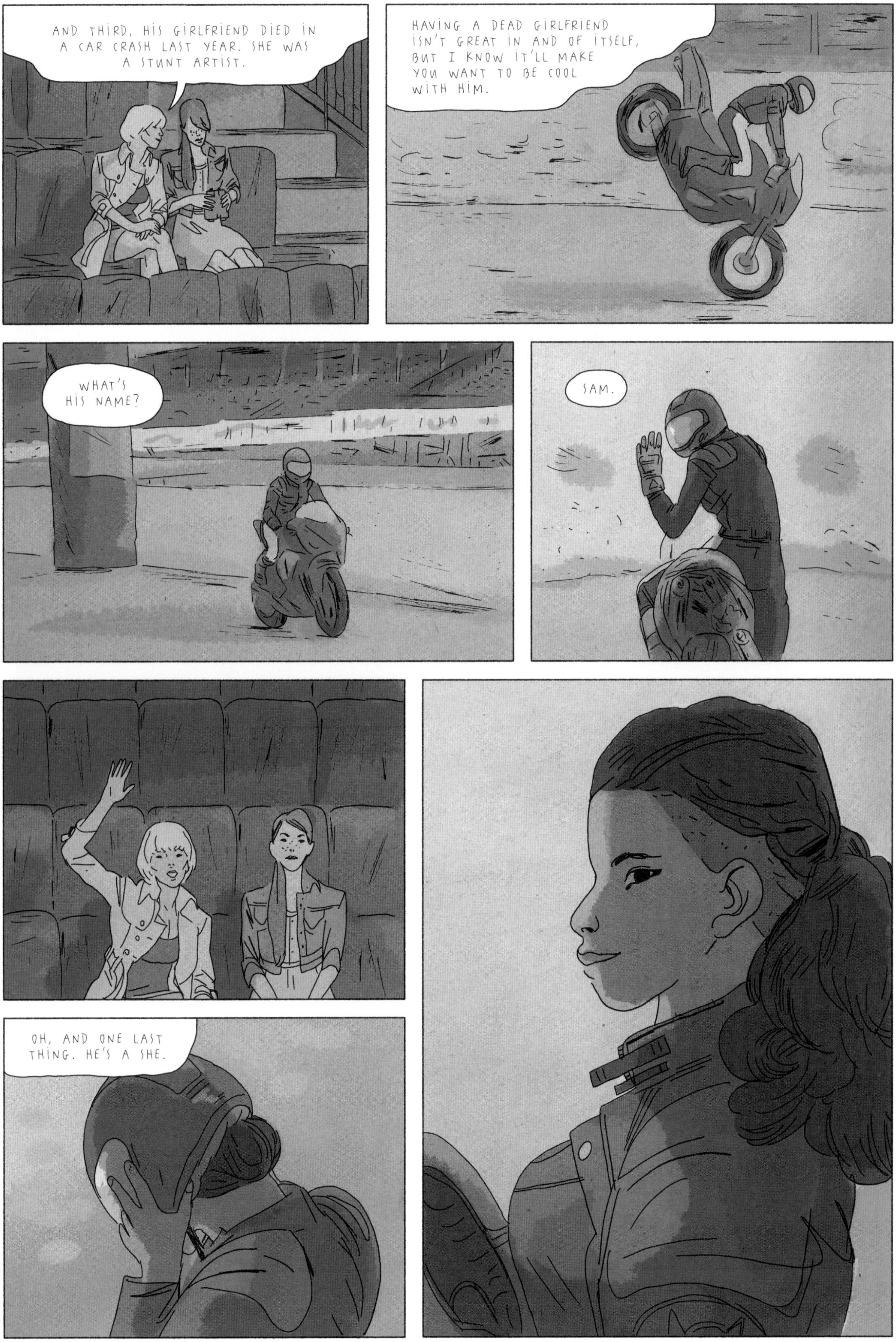
AND THIRD, HIS GIRLFRIEND DIED IN A CAR CRASH LAST YEAR. SHE WAS A STUNT ARTIST.
HAVING A DEAD GIRLFRIEND ISN'T GREAT IN AND OF ITSELF, BUT I KNOW IT'LL MAKE YOU WANT TO BE COOL WITH HIM.
WHAT'S HIS NAME?
SAM.
OH, AND ONE LAST THING. HE'S A SHE.

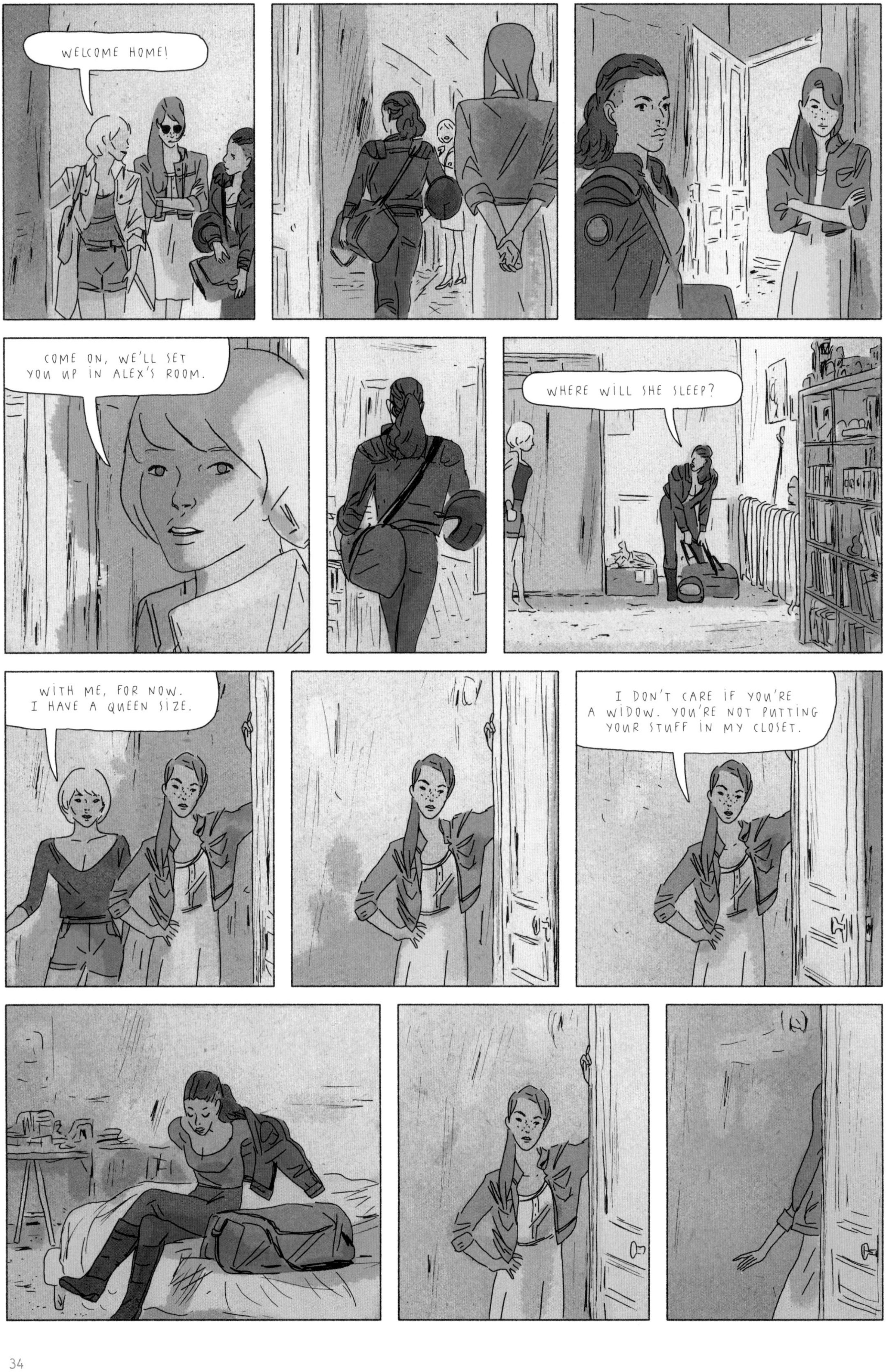
WELCOME HOME!
COME ON, WE'LL SET YOU UP IN ALEX'S ROOM.
WHERE WILL SHE SLEEP?
WITH ME, FOR NOW. I HAVE A QUEEN SIZE.
I DON'T CARE IF YOU'RE A WIDOW. YOU'RE NOT PUTTING YOUR STUFF IN MY CLOSET.

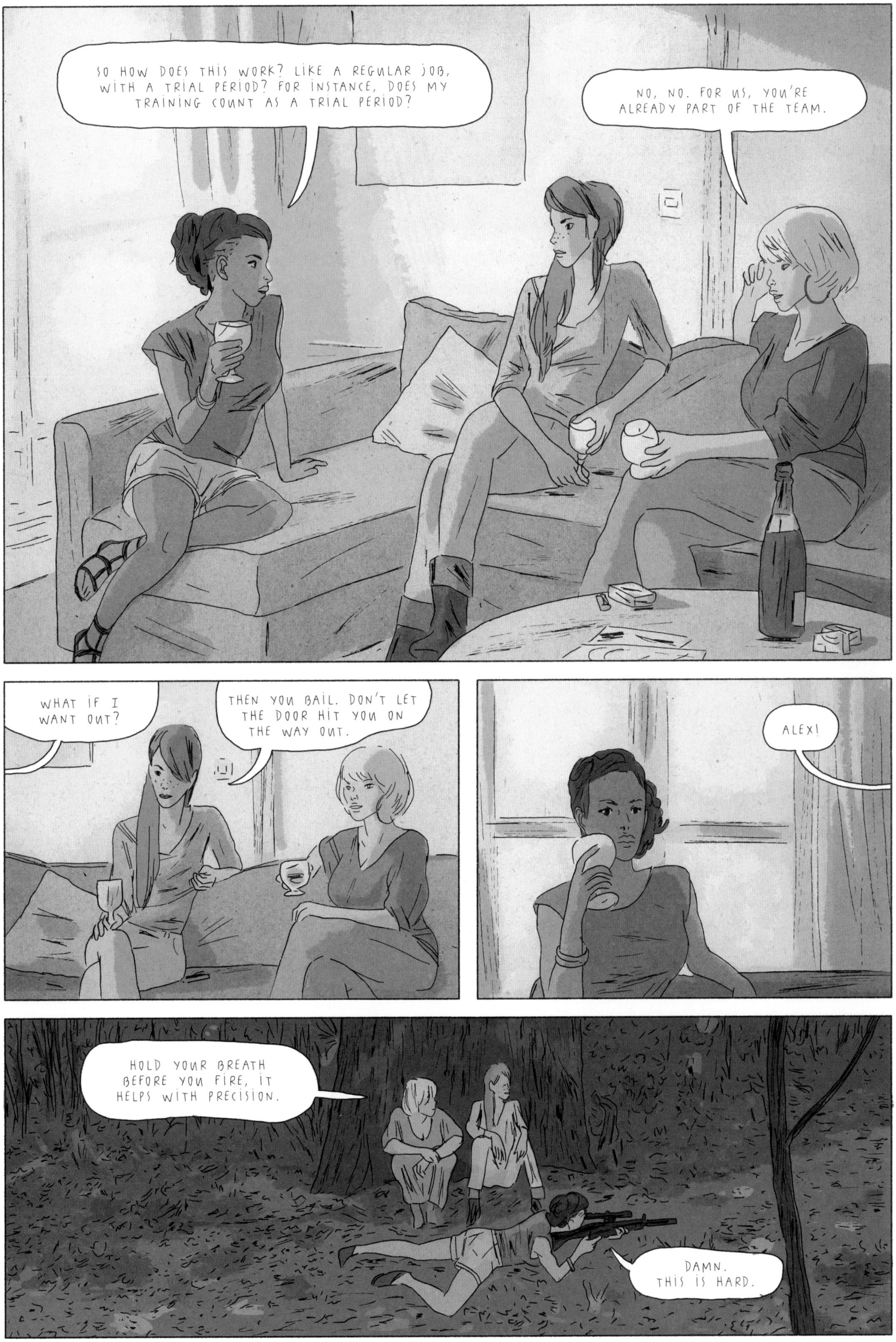
SO HOW DOES THIS WORK? LIKE A REGULAR JOB, WITH A TRIAL PERIOD? FOR INSTANCE, DOES MY TRAINING COUNT AS A TRIAL PERIOD?
NO, NO. FOR US, YOU'RE ALREADY PART OF THE TEAM.
WHAT IF I WANT OUT?
THEN YOU BAIL. DON'T LET THE DOOR HIT YOU ON THE WAY OUT.
ALEX!
HOLD YOUR BREATH BEFORE YOU FIRE, IT HELPS WITH PRECISION.
DAMN. THIS IS HARD.

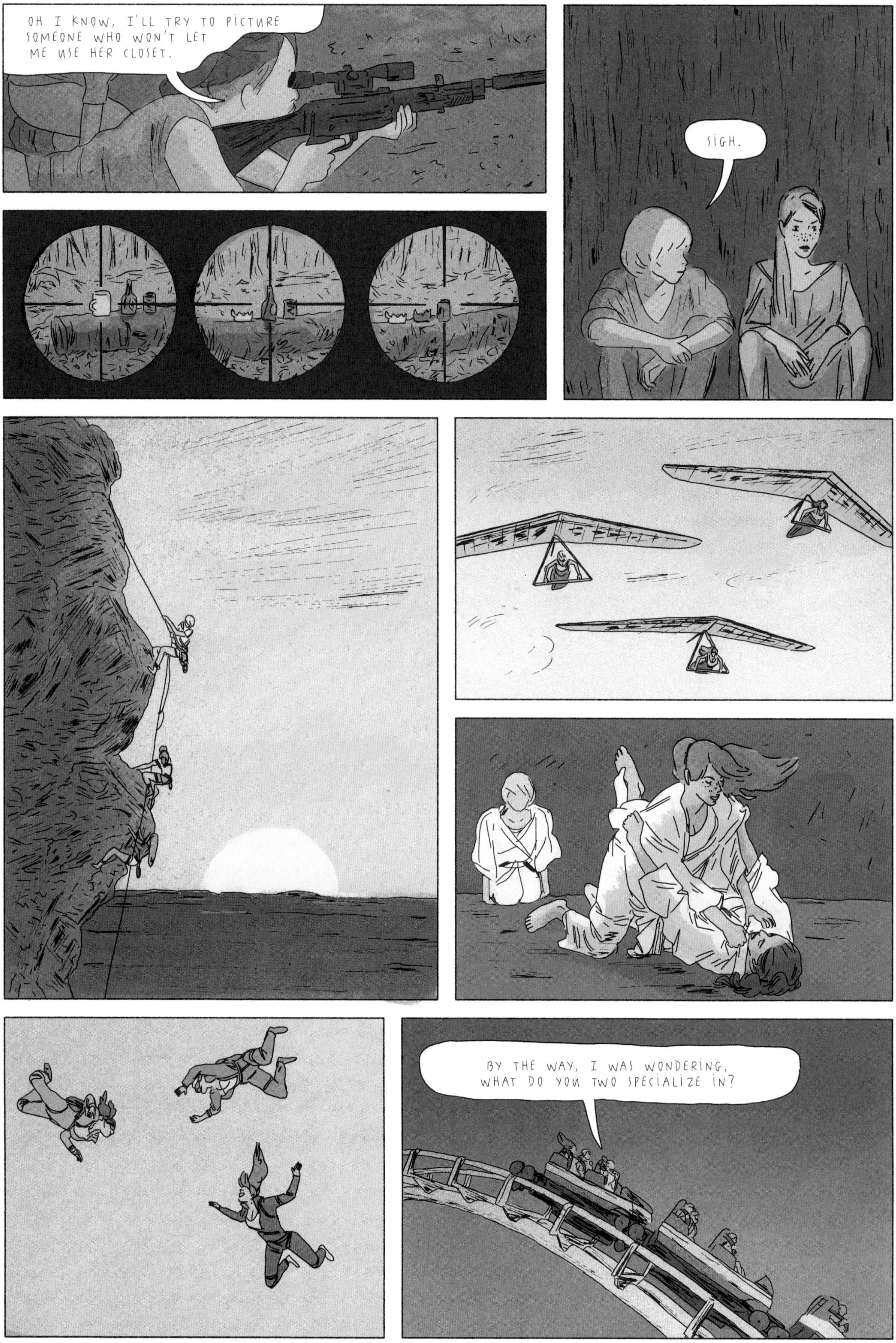
OH I KNOW, I'LL TRY TO PICTURE SOMEONE WHO WON'T LET ME USE HER CLOSET.
SIGH.
BY THE WAY, I WAS WONDERING, WHAT DO YOU TWO SPECIALIZE IN?

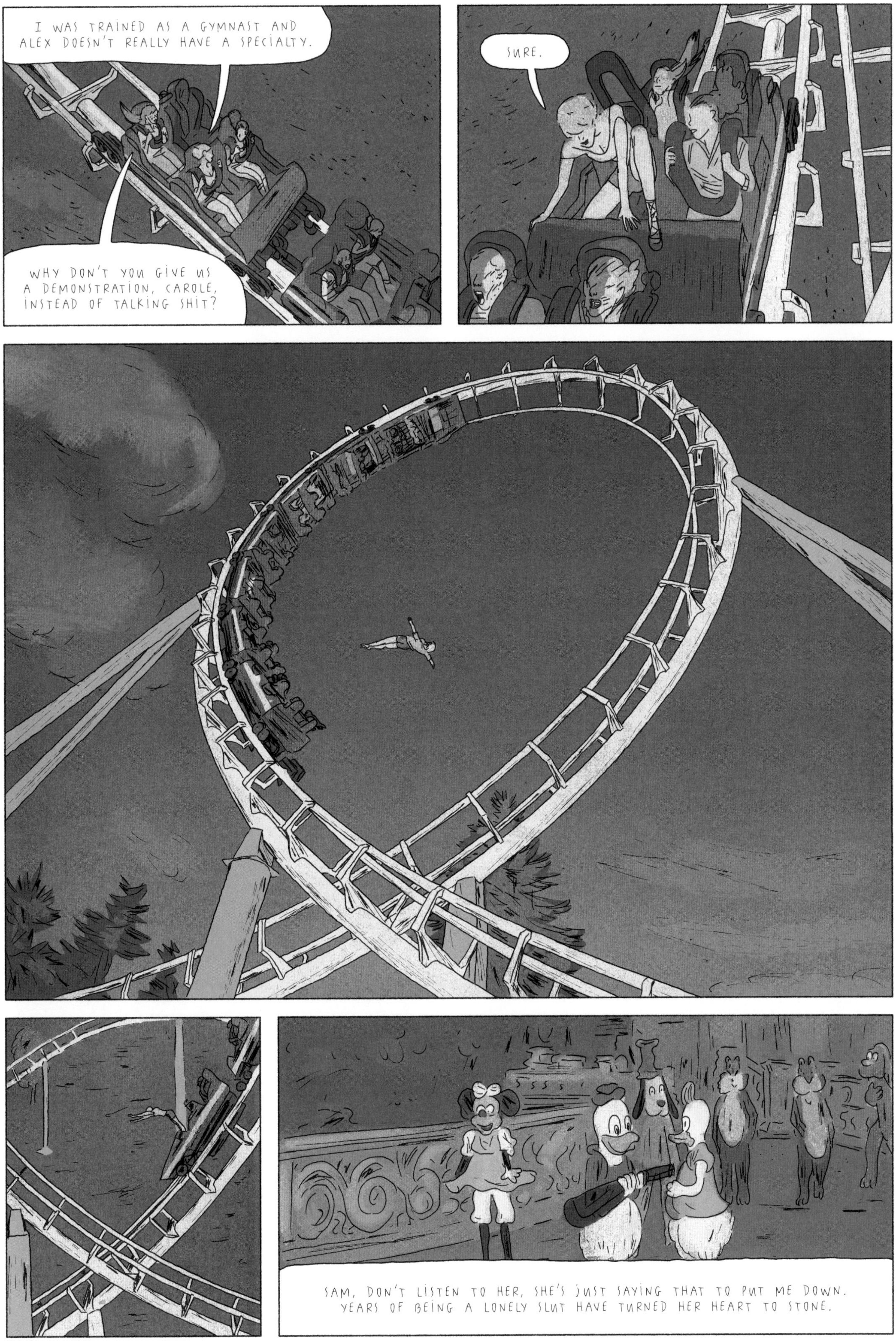
I WAS TRAINED AS A GYMNAST AND ALEX DOESN'T REALLY HAVE A SPECIALTY.
WHY DON'T YOU GIVE US A DEMONSTRATION, CAROLE, INSTEAD OF TALKING SHIT?
SURE.
SAM, DON'T LISTEN TO HER, SHE'S JUST SAYING THAT TO PUT ME DOWN. YEARS OF BEING A LONELY SLUT HAVE TURNED HER HEART TO STONE.

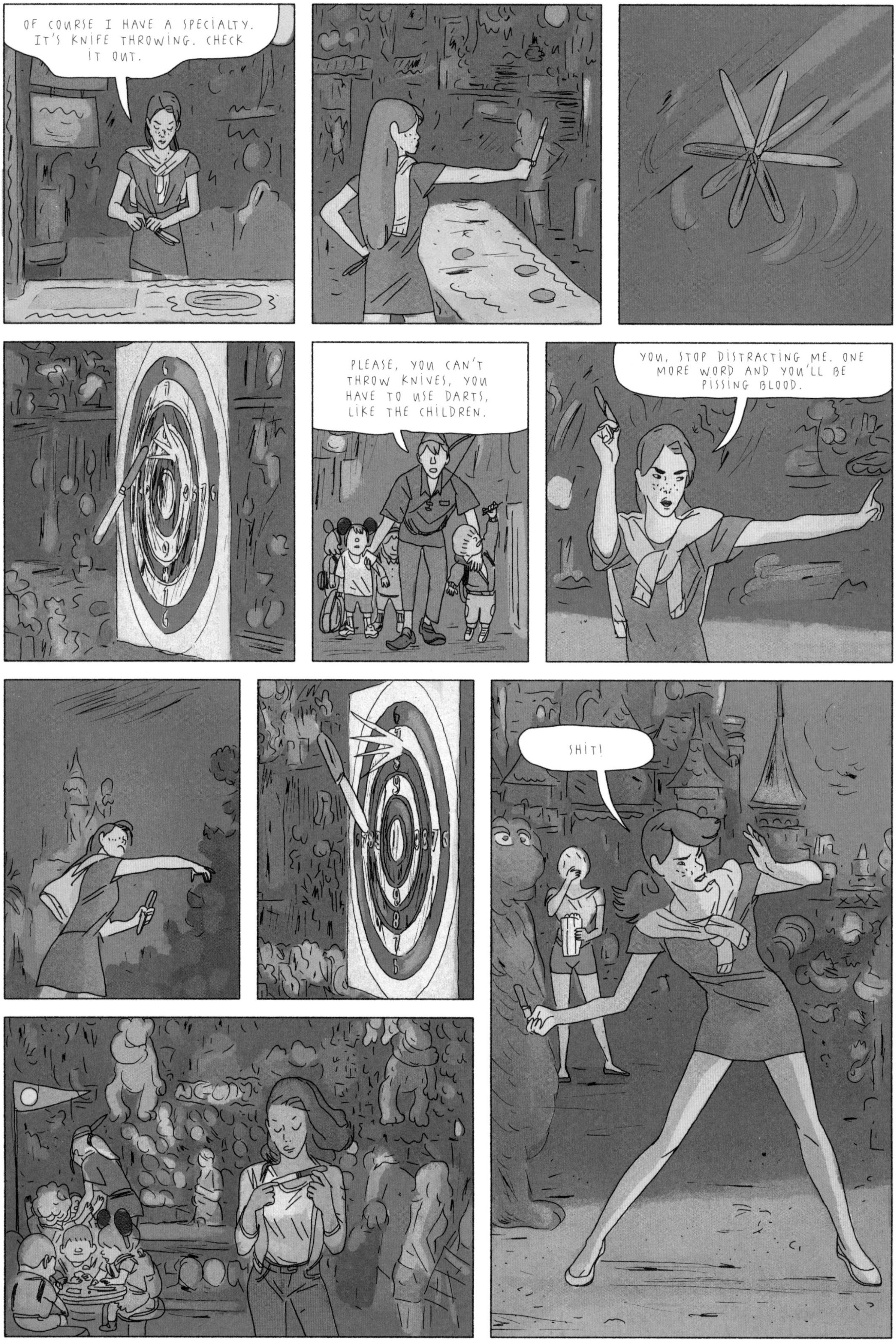
OF COURSE I HAVE A SPECIALTY. IT'S KNIFE THROWING. CHECK IT OUT.
PLEASE, YOU CAN'T THROW KNIVES, YOU HAVE TO USE DARTS, LIKE THE CHILDREN.
YOU, STOP DISTRACTING ME. ONE MORE WORD AND YOU'LL BE PISSING BLOOD.
SHIT!

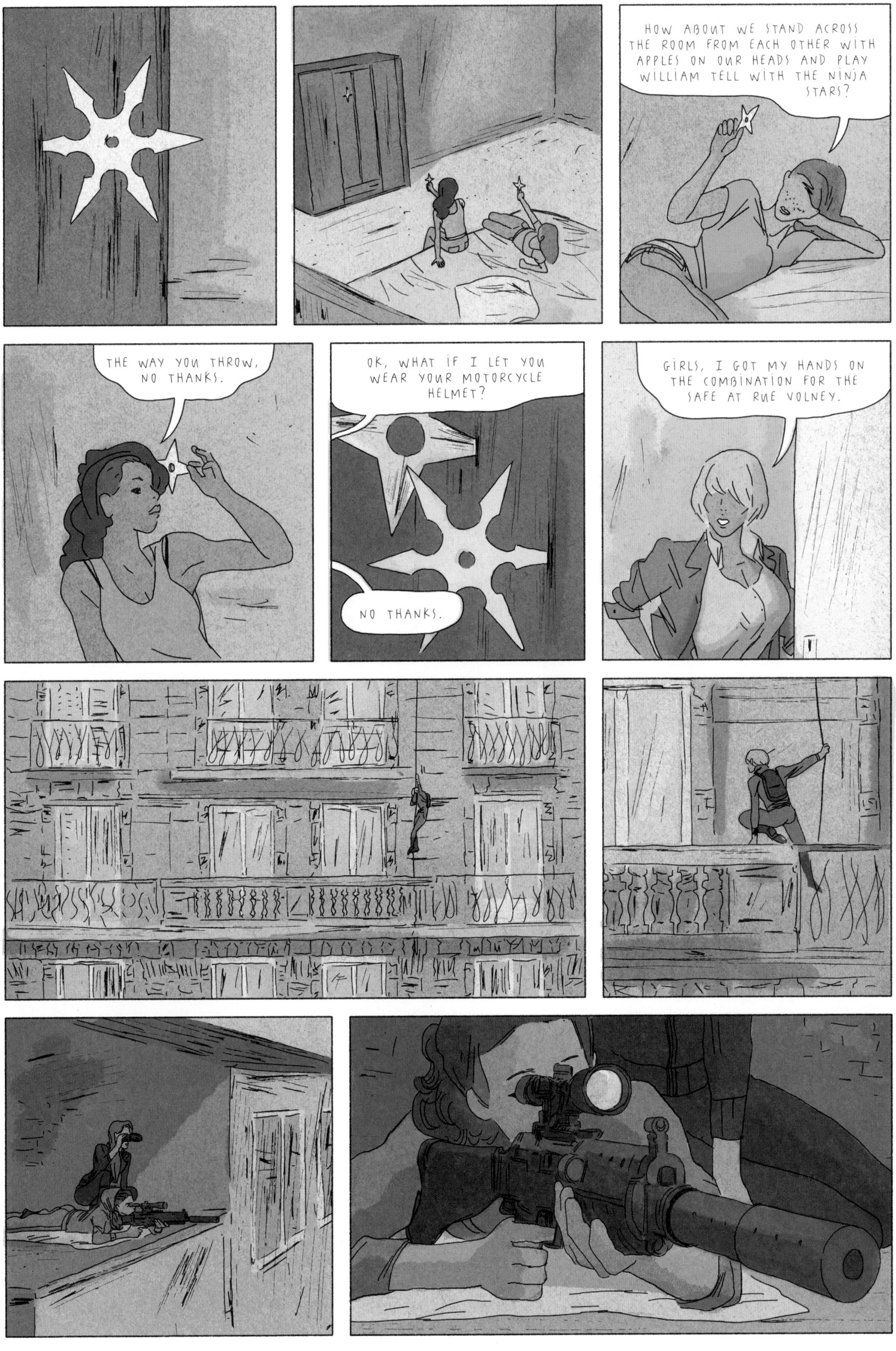
HOW ABOUT WE STAND ACROSS THE ROOM FROM EACH OTHER WITH APPLES ON OUR HEADS AND PLAY WILLIAM TELL WITH THE NINJA STARS?
THE WAY YOU THROW, NO THANKS.
OK, WHAT IF I LET YOU WEAR YOUR MOTORCYCLE HELMET?
NO THANKS.
GIRLS, I GOT MY HANDS ON THE COMBINATION FOR THE SAFE AT RUE VOLNEY.

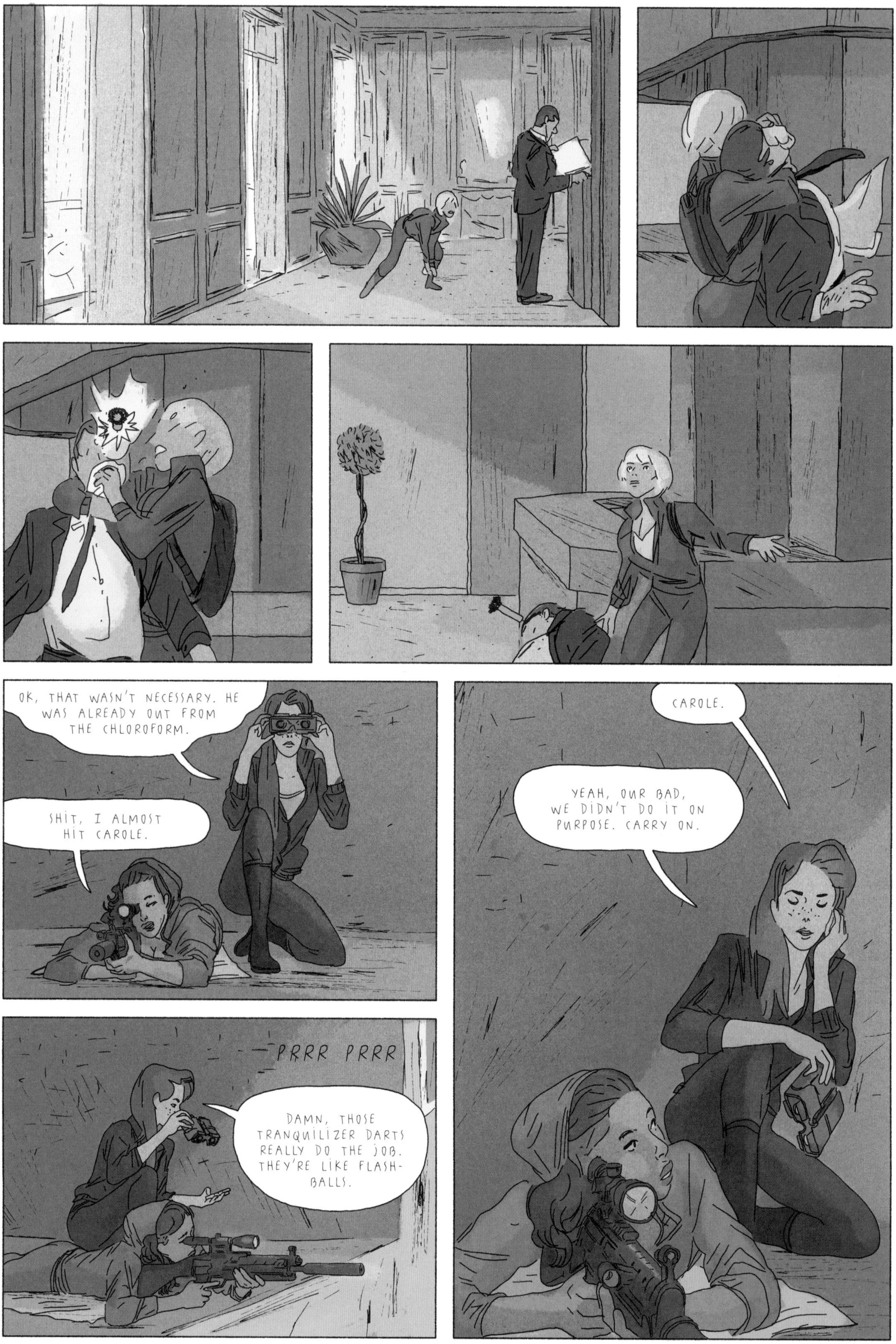
OK, THAT WASN'T NECESSARY. HE WAS ALREADY OUT FROM THE CHLOROFORM.
SHIT, I ALMOST HIT CAROLE.
CAROLE.
YEAH, OUR BAD, WE DIDN'T DO IT ON PURPOSE. CARRY ON.
PRRR PRRR
DAMN, THOSE TRANQUILIZER DARTS REALLY DO THE JOB. THEY'RE LIKE FLASH-BALLS.

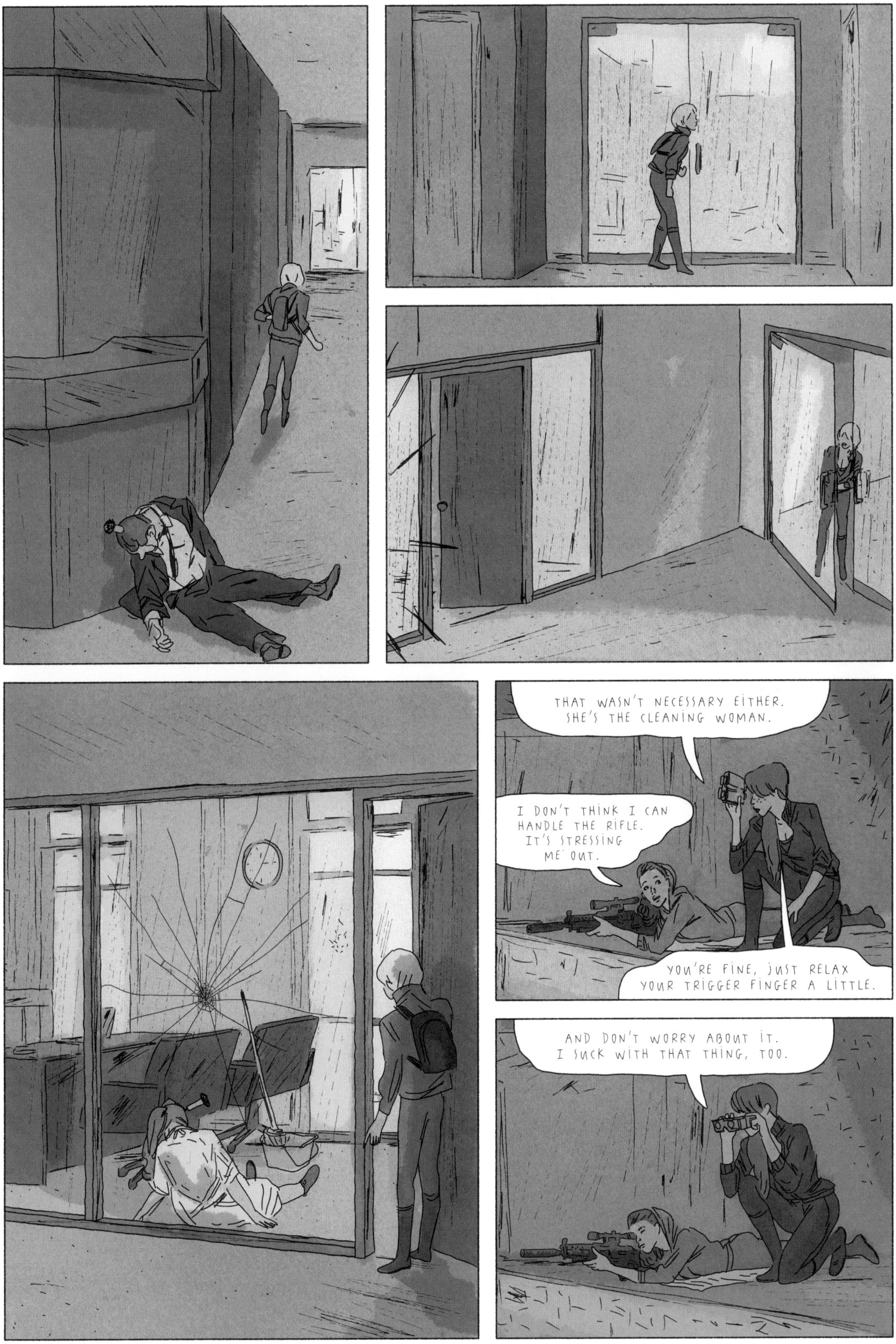
THAT WASN'T NECESSARY EITHER. SHE'S THE CLEANING WOMAN.
I DON'T THINK I CAN HANDLE THE RIFLE. IT'S STRESSING ME OUT.
YOU'RE FINE, JUST RELAX YOUR TRIGGER FINGER A LITTLE.
AND DON'T WORRY ABOUT IT. I SUCK WITH THAT THING, TOO.

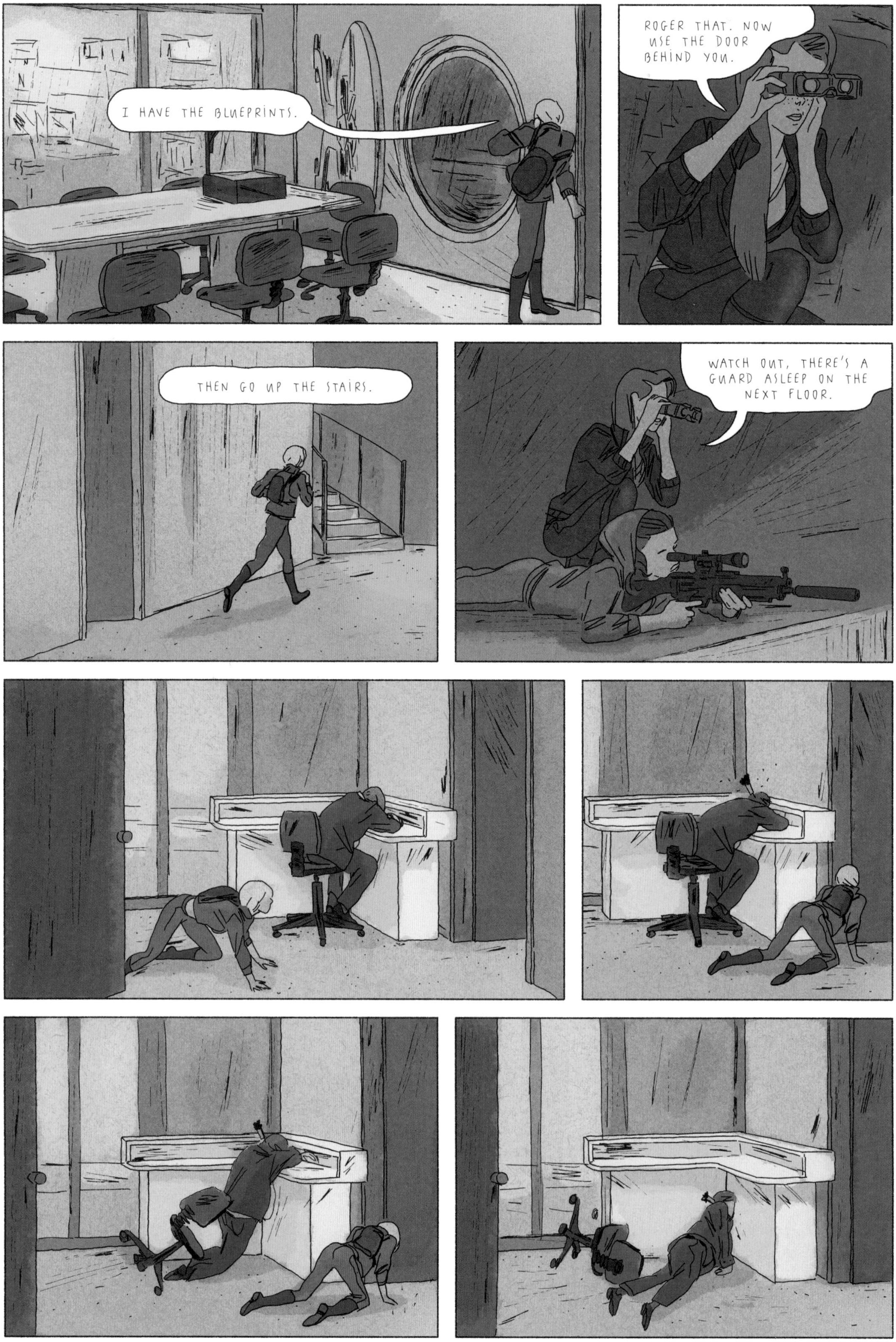
I HAVE THE BLUEPRINTS.
ROGER THAT. NOW USE THE DOOR BEHIND YOU.
THEN GO UP THE STAIRS.
WATCH OUT, THERE'S A GUARD ASLEEP ON THE NEXT FLOOR.

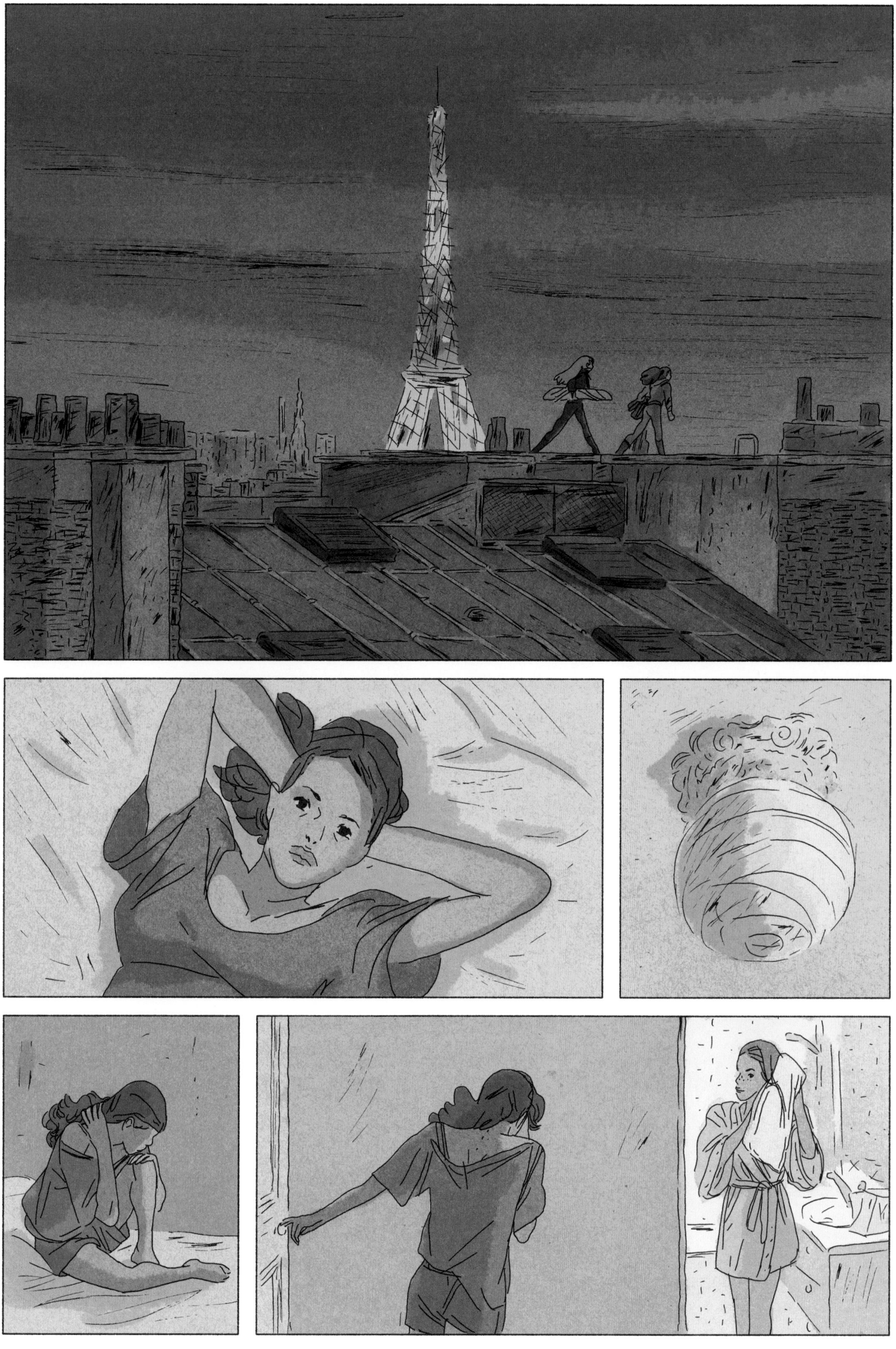

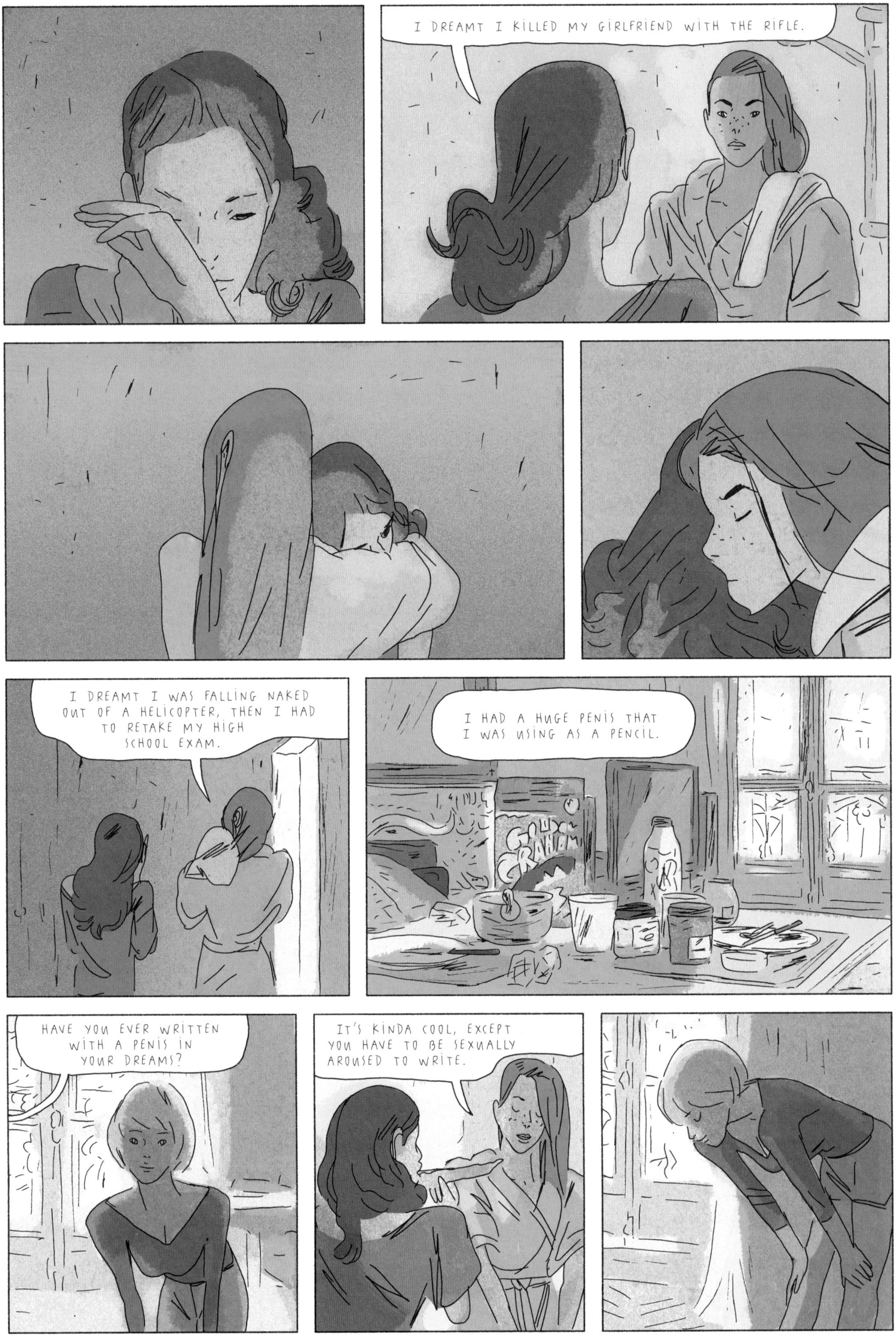
I DREAMT I KILLED MY GIRLFRIEND WITH THE RIFLE.
I DREAMT I WAS FALLING NAKED OUT OF A HELICOPTER, THEN I HAD TO RETAKE MY HIGH SCHOOL EXAM.
I HAD A HUGE PENIS THAT I WAS USING AS A PENCIL.
GOLDEN GRAHAMS
HAVE YOU EVER WRITTEN WITH A PENIS IN YOUR DREAMS?
IT'S KINDA COOL, EXCEPT YOU HAVE TO BE SEXUALLY AROUSED TO WRITE.

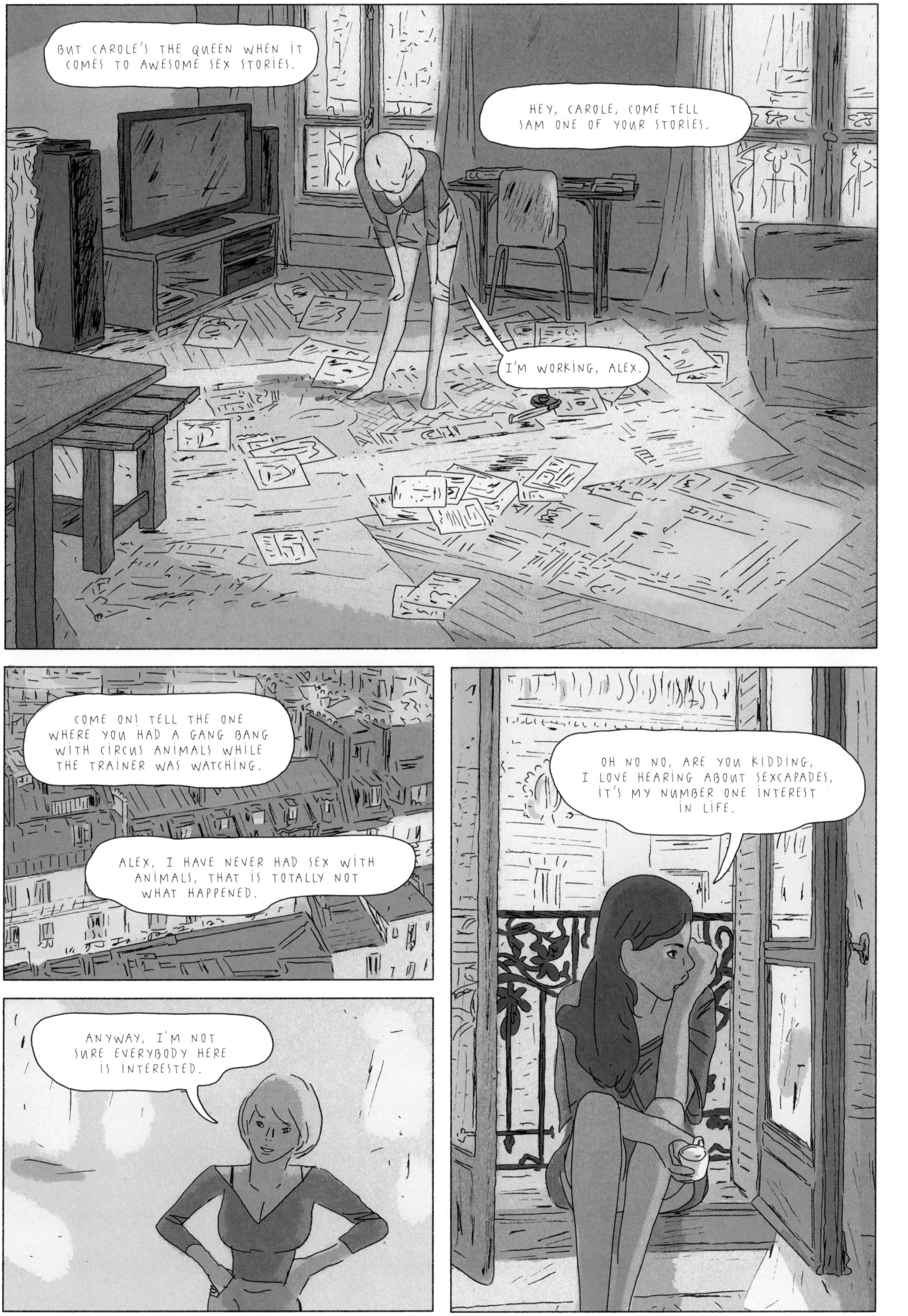
BUT CAROLE'S THE QUEEN WHEN IT COMES TO AWESOME SEX STORIES.
HEY, CAROLE, COME TELL SAM ONE OF YOUR STORIES.
I'M WORKING, ALEX.
COME ON! TELL THE ONE WHERE YOU HAD A GANG BANG WITH CIRCUS ANIMALS WHILE THE TRAINER WAS WATCHING.
ALEX, I HAVE NEVER HAD SEX WITH ANIMALS, THAT IS TOTALLY NOT WHAT HAPPENED.
ANYWAY, I'M NOT SURE EVERYBODY HERE IS INTERESTED.
OH NO NO, ARE YOU KIDDING, I LOVE HEARING ABOUT SEXCAPADES, IT'S MY NUMBER ONE INTEREST IN LIFE.

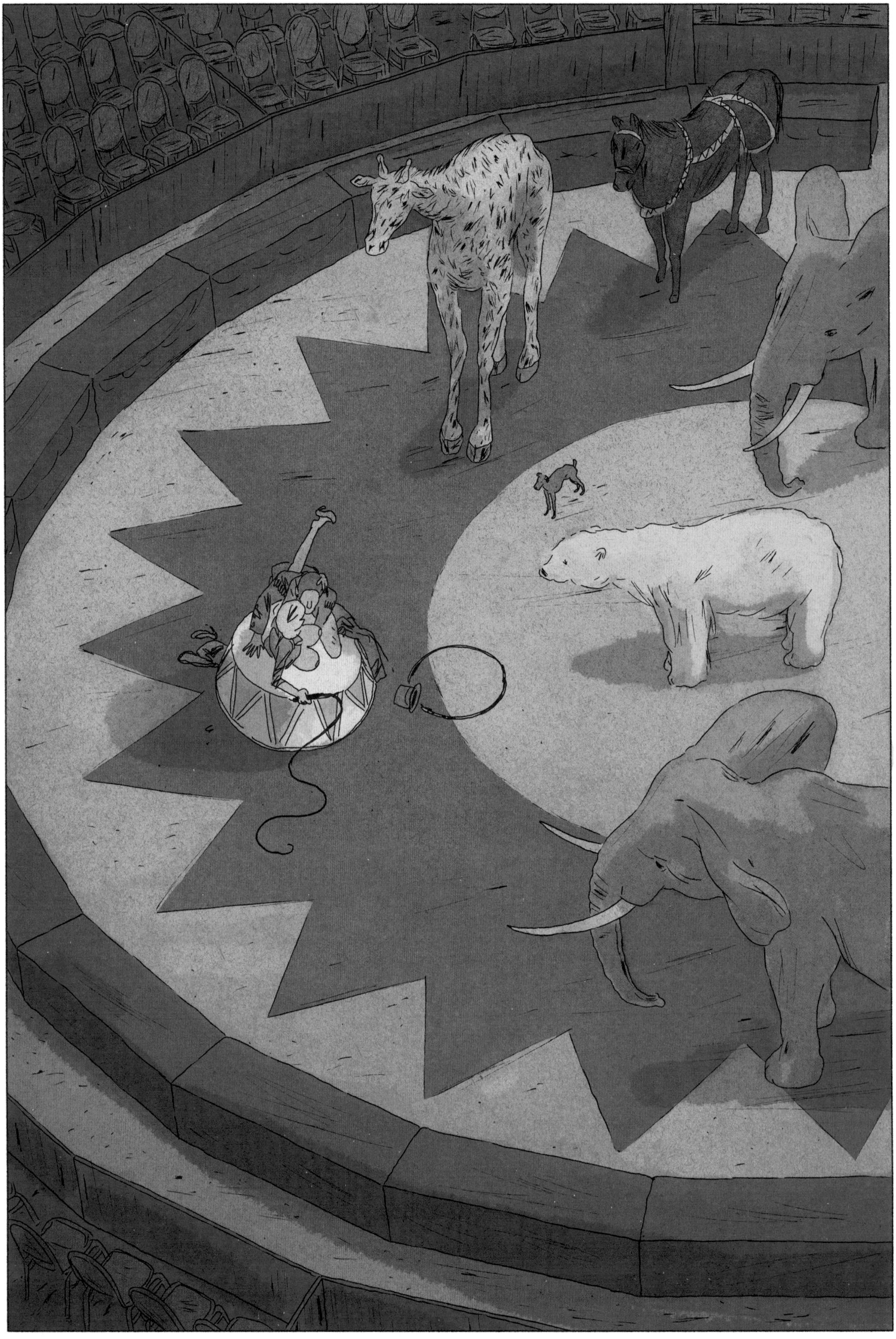

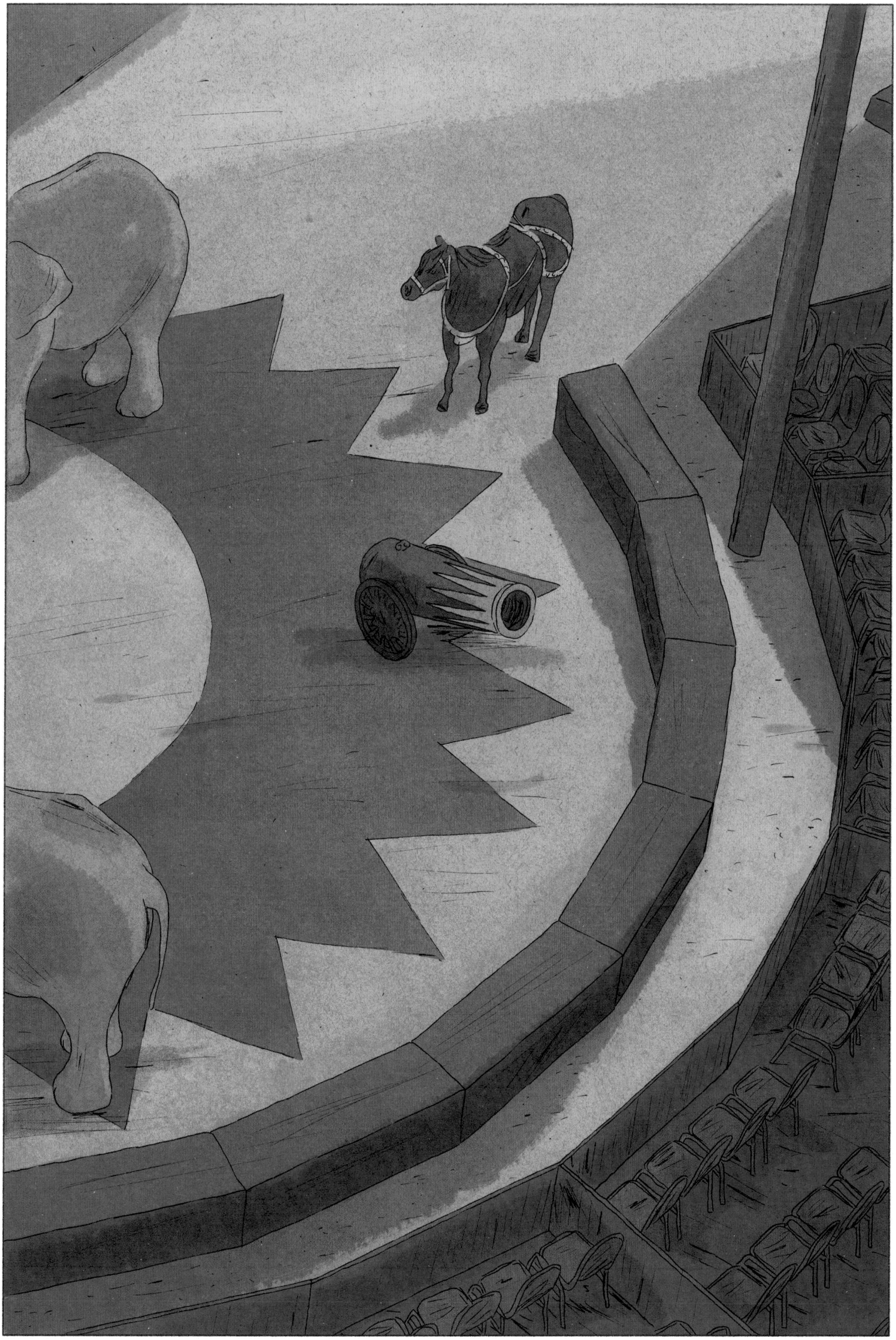

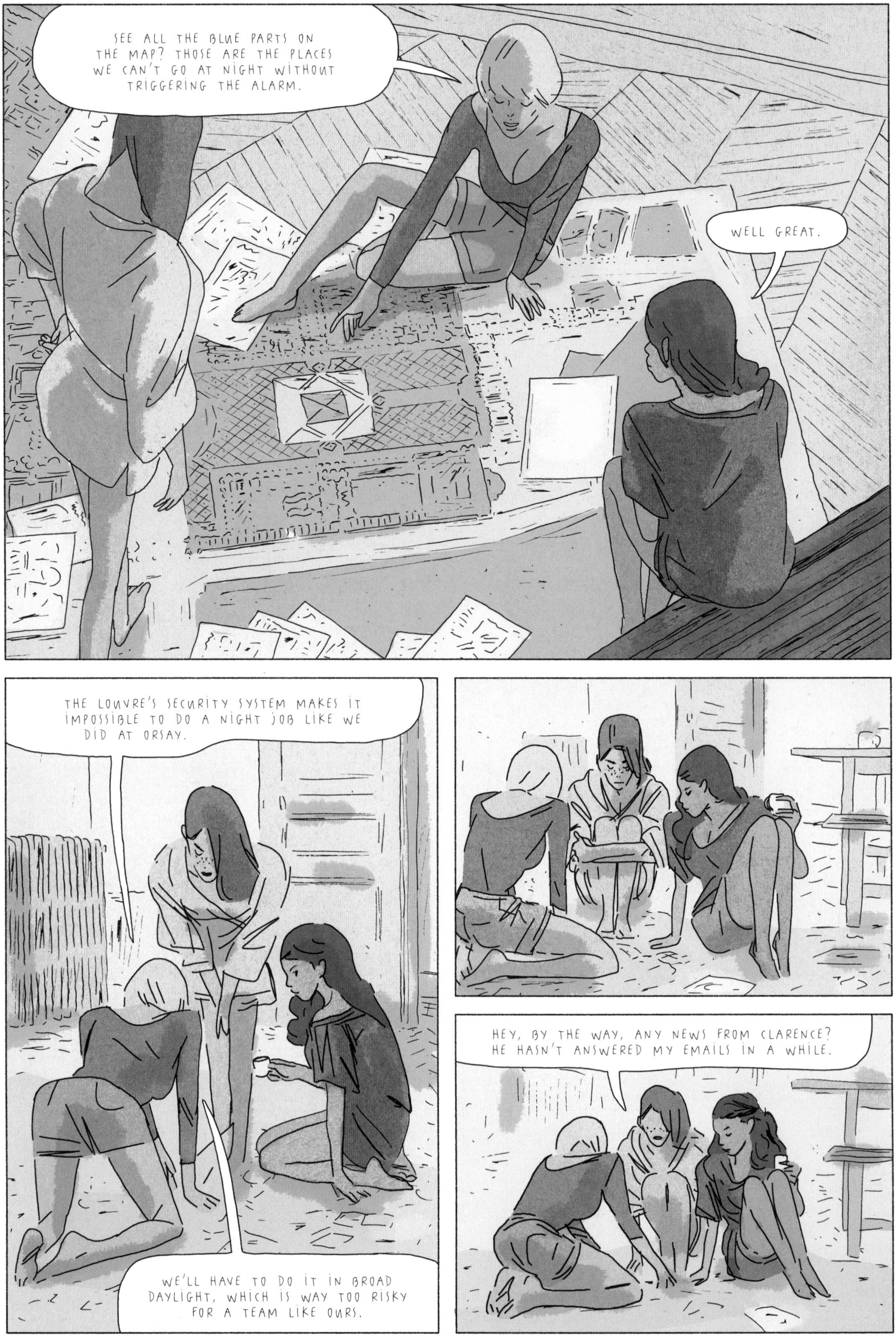
SEE ALL THE BLUE PARTS ON THE MAP? THOSE ARE THE PLACES WE CAN'T GO AT NIGHT WITHOUT TRIGGERING THE ALARM.
WELL GREAT.
THE LOUVRE'S SECURITY SYSTEM MAKES IT IMPOSSIBLE TO DO A NIGHT JOB LIKE WE DID AT ORSAY.
WE'LL HAVE TO DO IT IN BROAD DAYLIGHT, WHICH IS WAY TOO RISKY FOR A TEAM LIKE OURS.
HEY, BY THE WAY, ANY NEWS FROM CLARENCE? HE HASN'T ANSWERED MY EMAILS IN A WHILE.

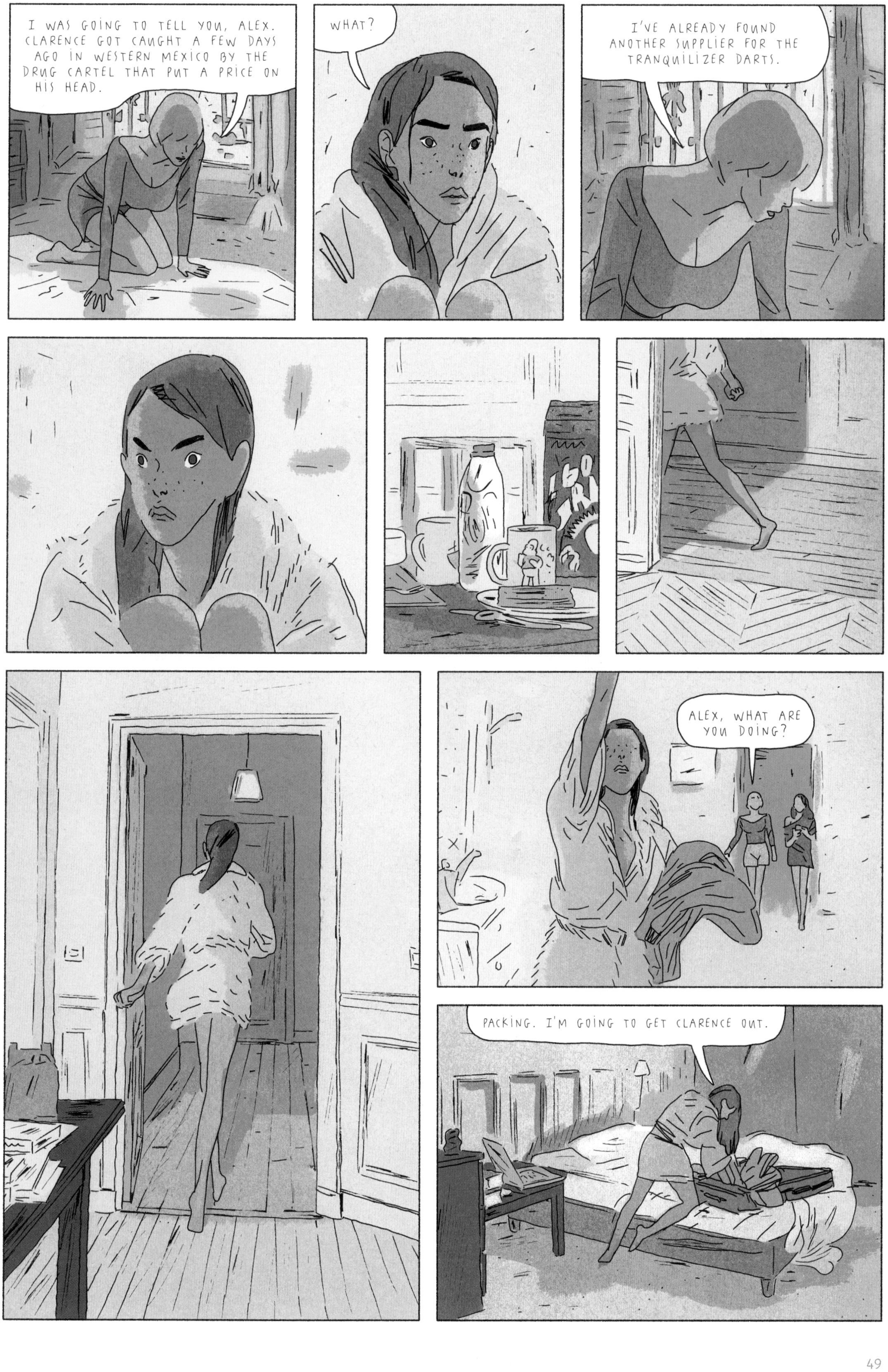
I WAS GOING TO TELL YOU, ALEX. CLARENCE GOT CAUGHT A FEW DAYS AGO IN WESTERN MEXICO BY THE DRUG CARTEL THAT PUT A PRICE ON HIS HEAD.
WHAT?
I'VE ALREADY FOUND ANOTHER SUPPLIER FOR THE TRANQUILIZER DARTS.
ALEX, WHAT ARE YOU DOING?
PACKING. I'M GOING TO GET CLARENCE OUT.

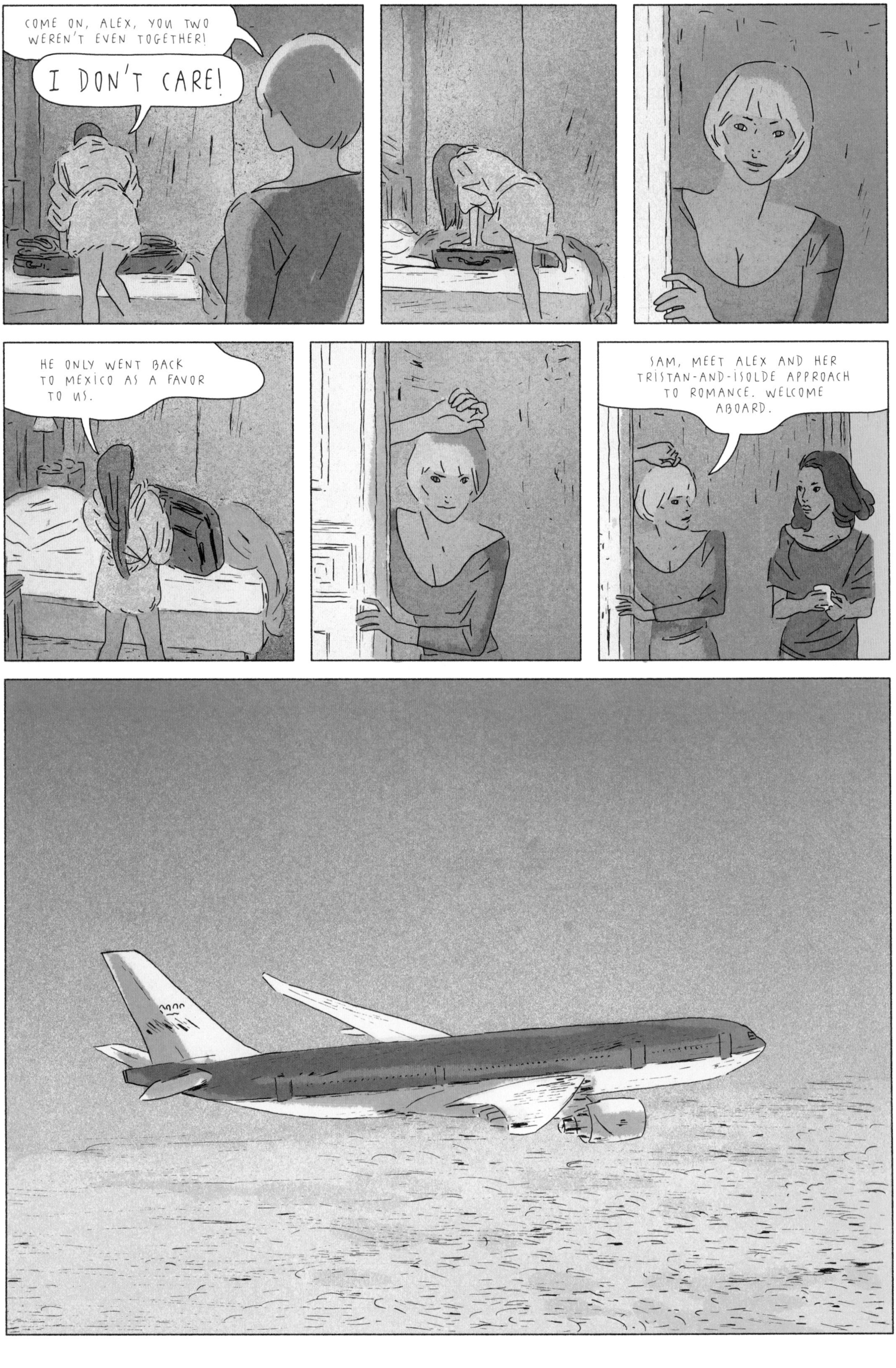
COME ON, ALEX, YOU TWO WEREN'T EVEN TOGETHER!
I DON'T CARE!
HE ONLY WENT BACK TO MEXICO AS A FAVOR TO US.
SAM, MEET ALEX AND HER TRISTAN-AND-ISOLDE APPROACH TO ROMANCE. WELCOME ABOARD.

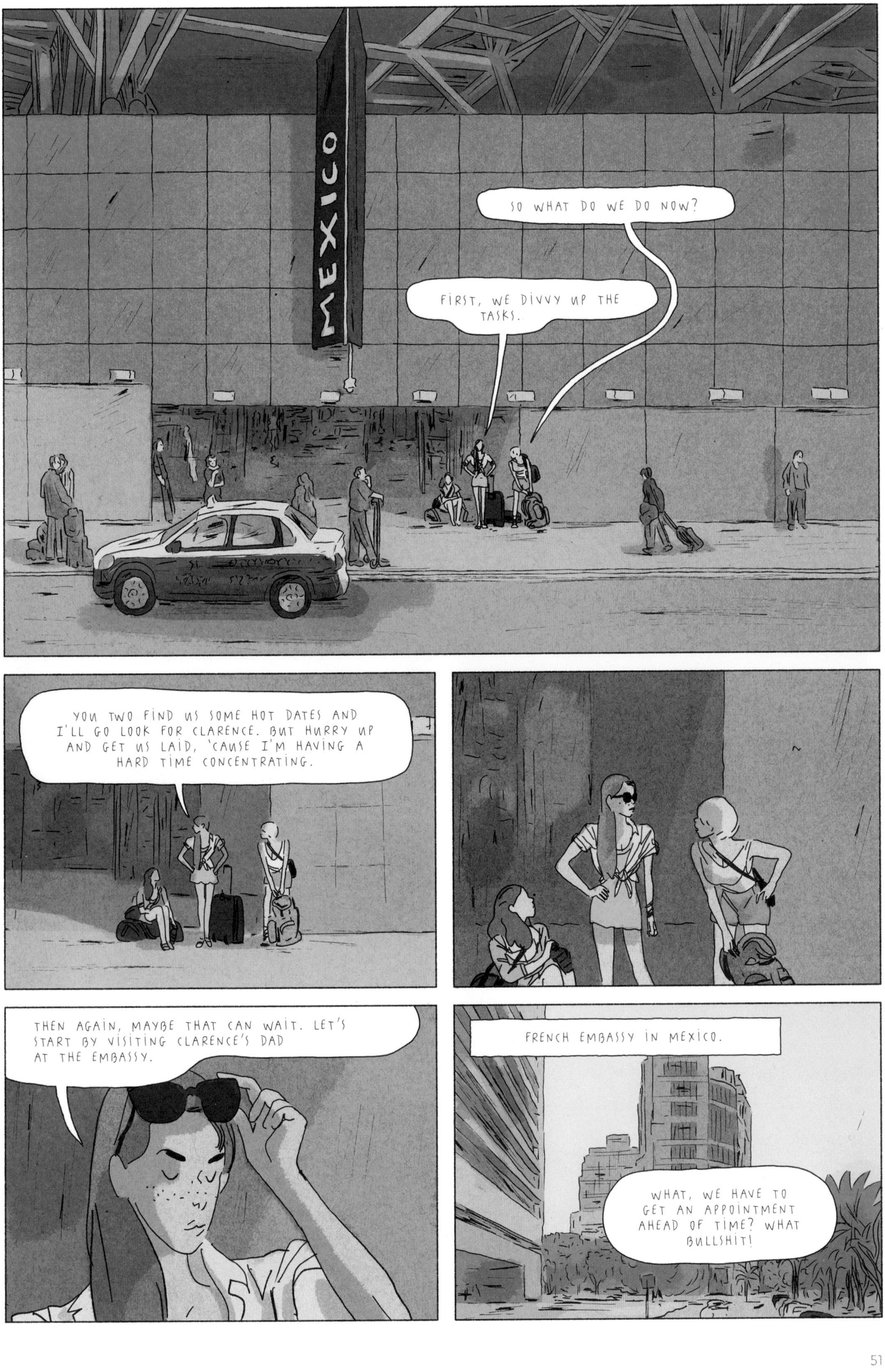
MEXICO
SO WHAT DO WE DO NOW?
FIRST, WE DIVVY UP THE TASKS.
YOU TWO FIND US SOME HOT DATES AND I'LL GO LOOK FOR CLARENCE. BUT HURRY UP AND GET US LAID, 'CAUSE I'M HAVING A HARD TIME CONCENTRATING.
THEN AGAIN, MAYBE THAT CAN WAIT. LET'S START BY VISITING CLARENCE'S DAD AT THE EMBASSY.
FRENCH EMBASSY IN MEXICO.
WHAT, WE HAVE TO GET AN APPOINTMENT AHEAD OF TIME? WHAT BULLSHIT!

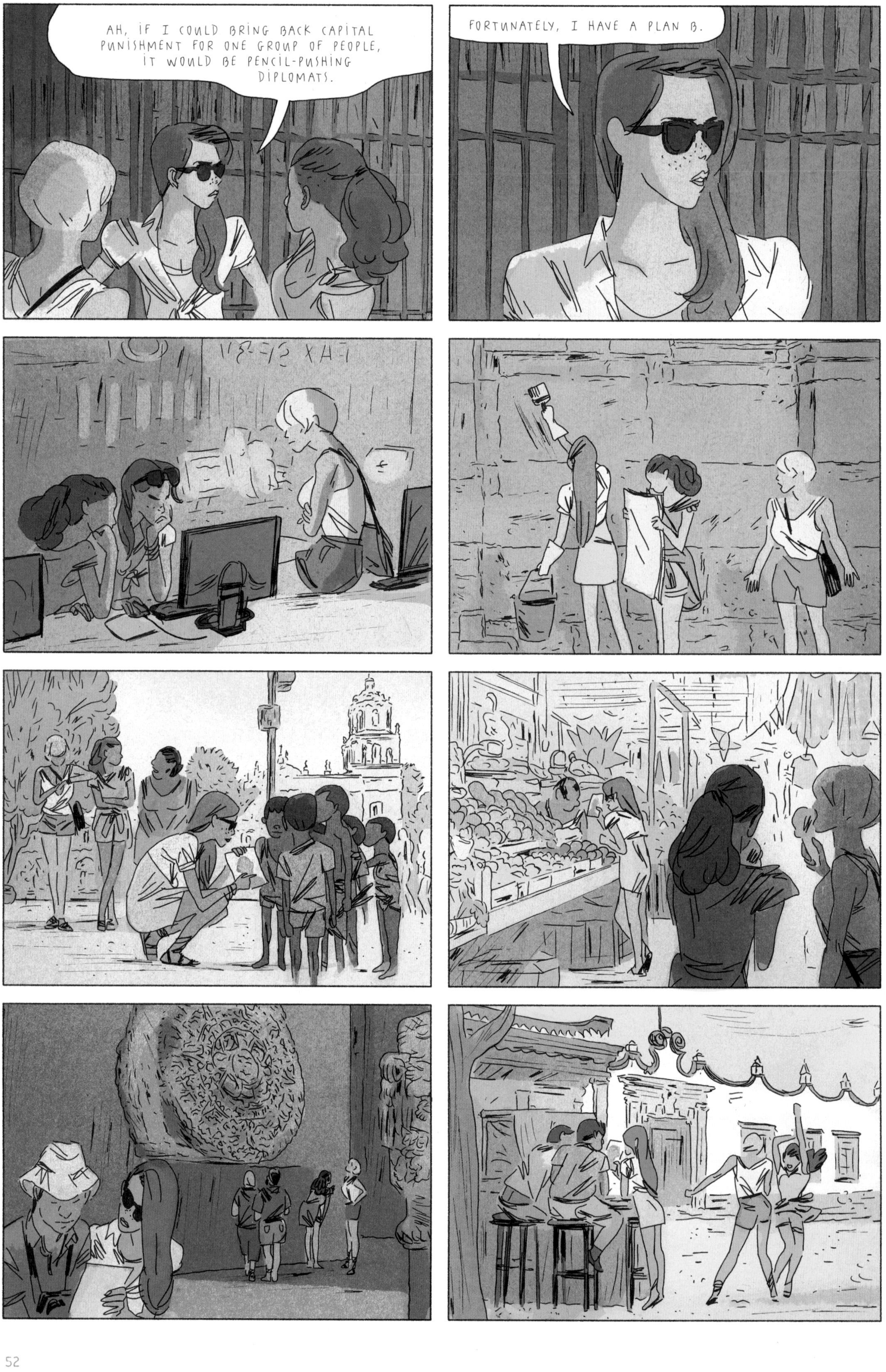
AH, IF I COULD BRING BACK CAPITAL PUNISHMENT FOR ONE GROUP OF PEOPLE, IT WOULD BE PENCIL-PUSHING DIPLOMATS.
FORTUNATELY, I HAVE A PLAN B.

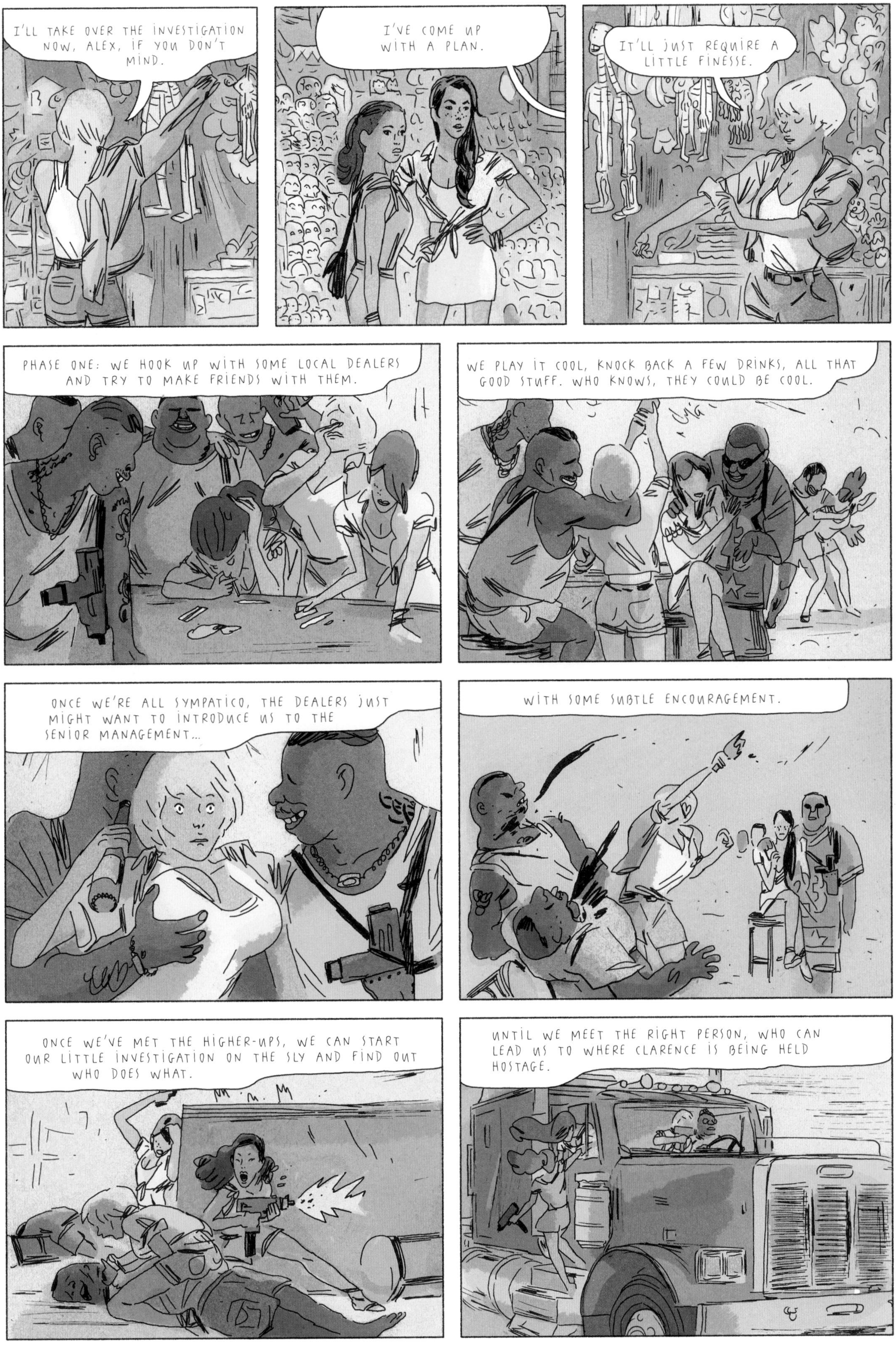
I'LL TAKE OVER THE INVESTIGATION NOW, ALEX, IF YOU DON'T MIND.
I'VE COME UP WITH A PLAN.
IT'LL JUST REQUIRE A LITTLE FINESSE.
PHASE ONE: WE HOOK UP WITH SOME LOCAL DEALERS AND TRY TO MAKE FRIENDS WITH THEM.
WE PLAY IT COOL, KNOCK BACK A FEW DRINKS, ALL THAT GOOD STUFF. WHO KNOWS, THEY COULD BE COOL.
ONCE WE'RE ALL SYMPATICO, THE DEALERS JUST MIGHT WANT TO INTRODUCE US TO THE SENIOR MANAGEMENT...
WITH SOME SUBTLE ENCOURAGEMENT.
ONCE WE'VE MET THE HIGHER-UPS, WE CAN START OUR LITTLE INVESTIGATION ON THE SLY AND FIND OUT WHO DOES WHAT.
UNTIL WE MEET THE RIGHT PERSON, WHO CAN LEAD US TO WHERE CLARENCE IS BEING HELD HOSTAGE.

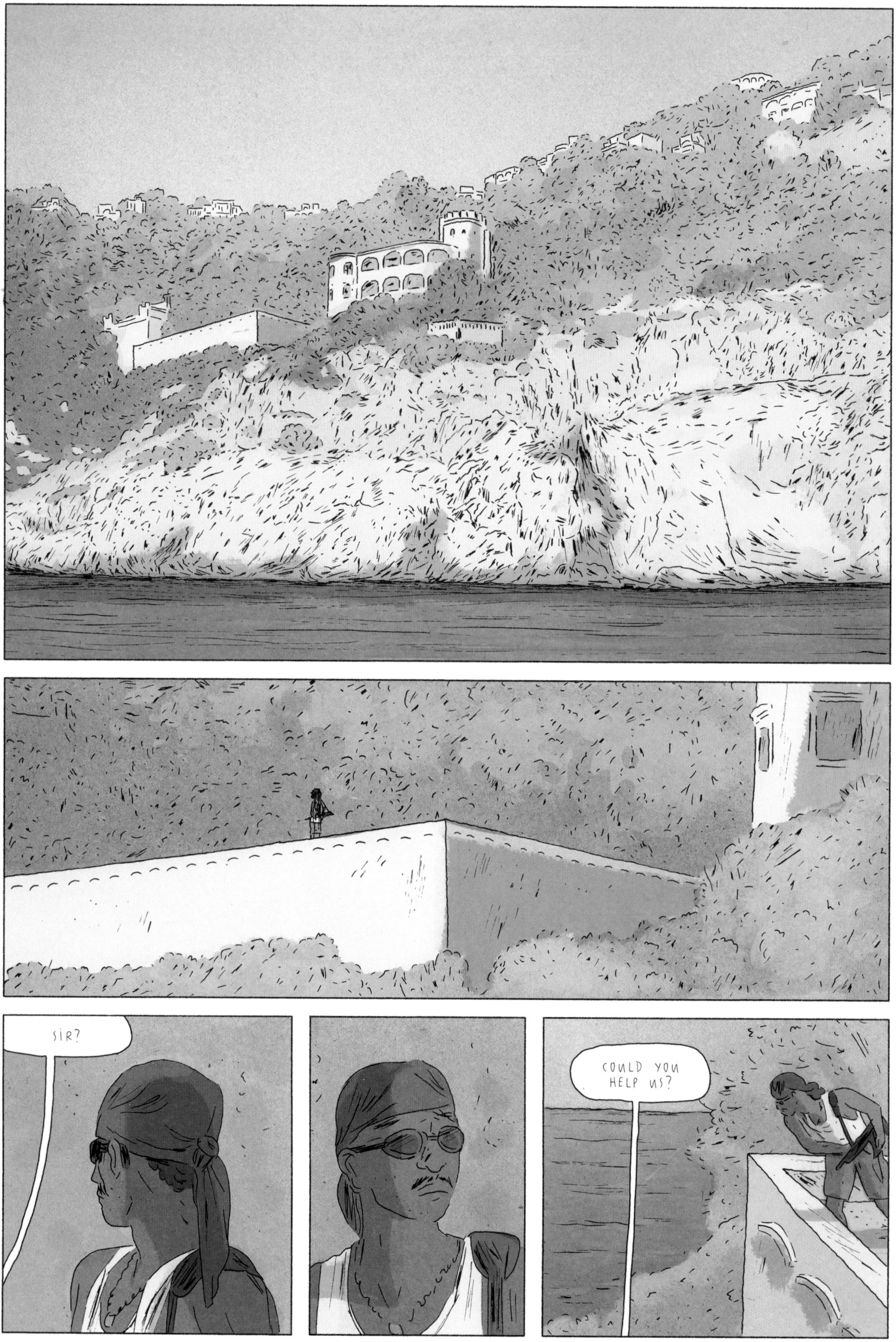
SIR?
COULD YOU HELP US?

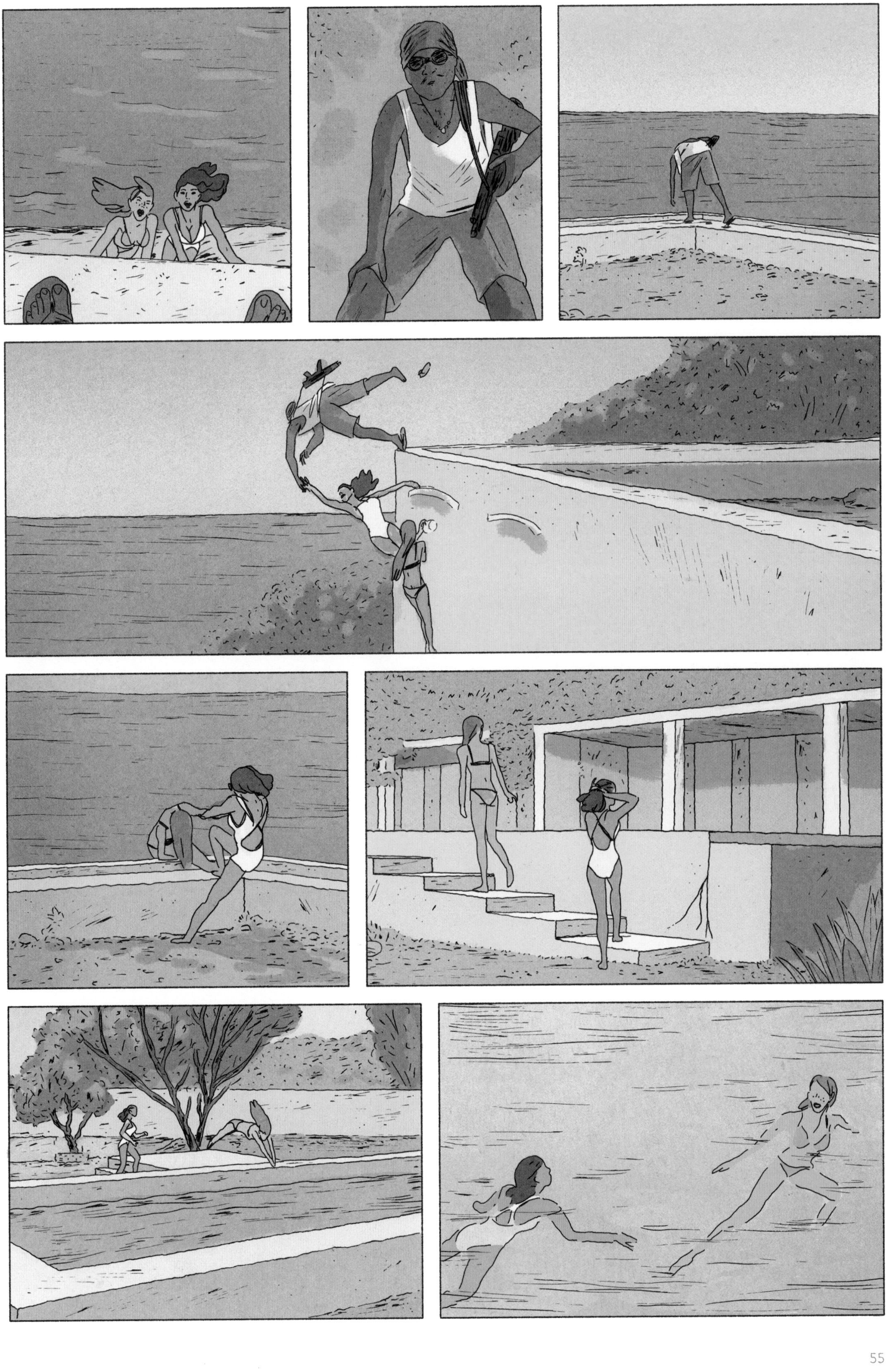

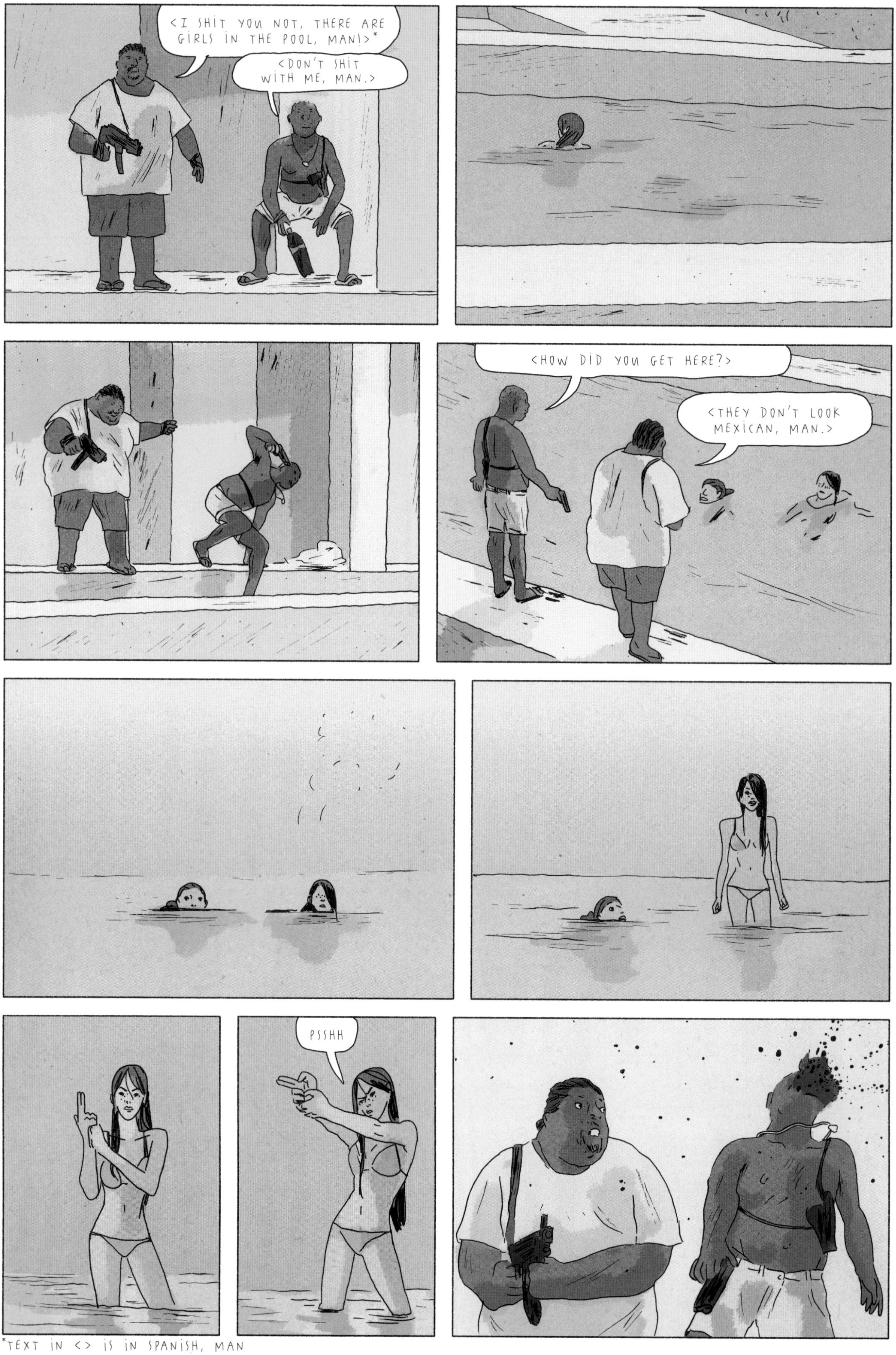
<I SHIT YOU NOT, THERE ARE GIRLS IN THE POOL, MAN!>*
<DON'T SHIT WITH ME, MAN.>
<HOW DID YOU GET HERE?>
<THEY DON'T LOOK MEXICAN, MAN.>
PSSHH

*TEXT IN <> IS IN SPANISH, MAN

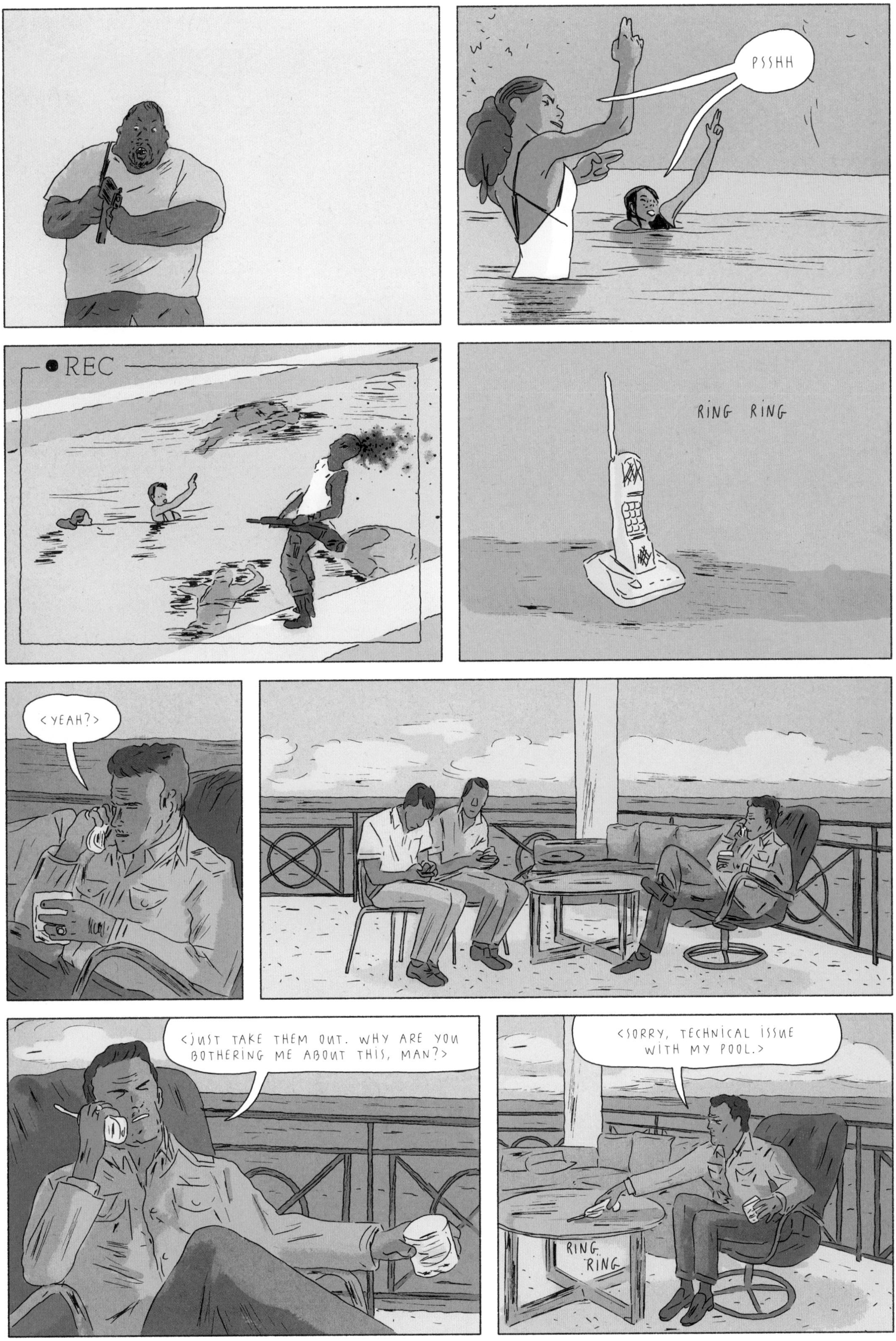
PSSHH
REC
RING RING
<YEAH?>
<JUST TAKE THEM OUT. WHY ARE YOU BOTHERING ME ABOUT THIS, MAN?>
<SORRY, TECHNICAL ISSUE WITH MY POOL.>
RING RING

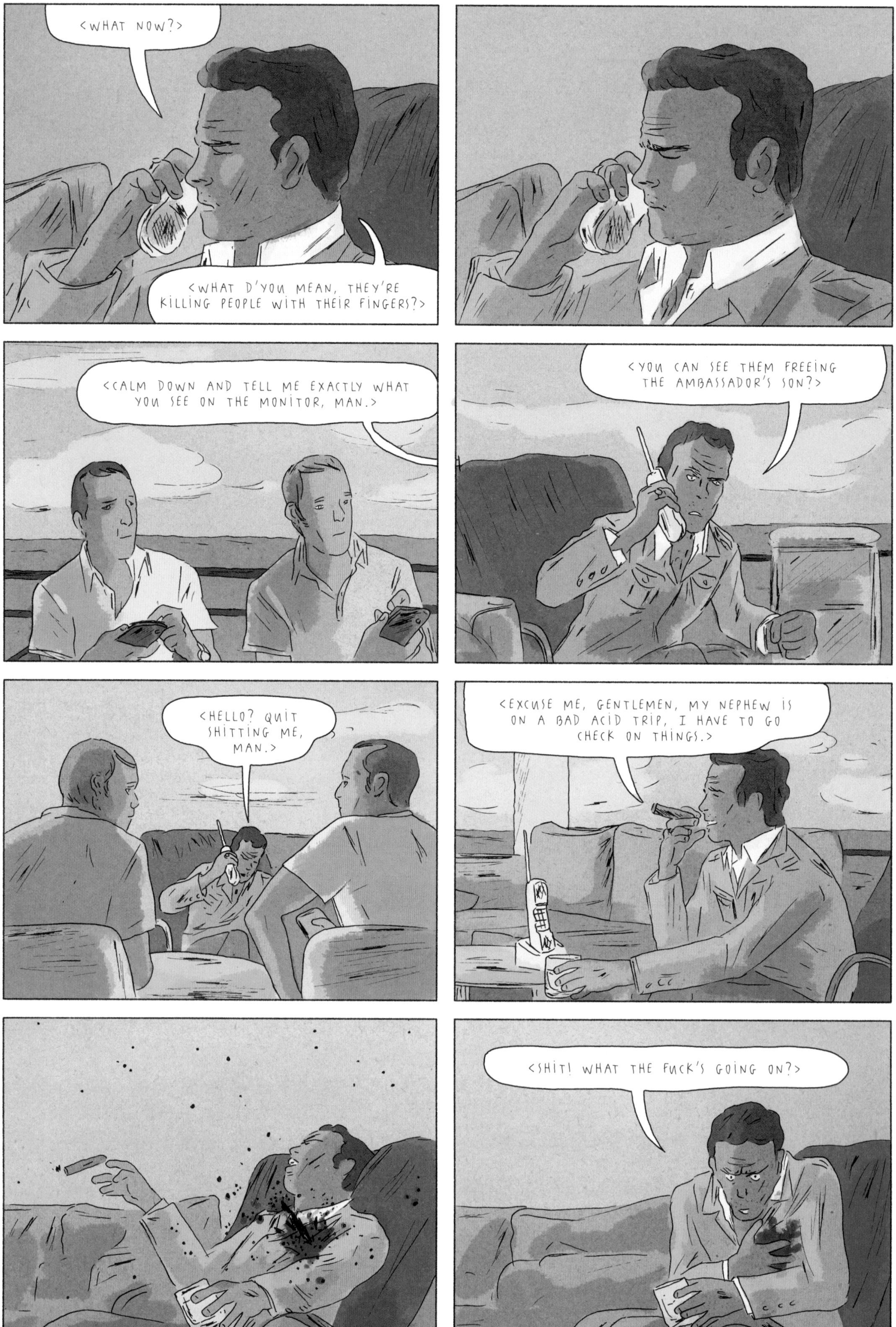
<WHAT NOW?>
<WHAT D'YOU MEAN, THEY'RE KILLING PEOPLE WITH THEIR FINGERS?>
<CALM DOWN AND TELL ME EXACTLY WHAT YOU SEE ON THE MONITOR, MAN.>
<YOU CAN SEE THEM FREEING THE AMBASSADOR'S SON?>
<HELLO? QUIT SHITTING ME, MAN.>
<EXCUSE ME, GENTLEMEN, MY NEPHEW IS ON A BAD ACID TRIP, I HAVE TO GO CHECK ON THINGS.>
<SHIT! WHAT THE FUCK'S GOING ON?>

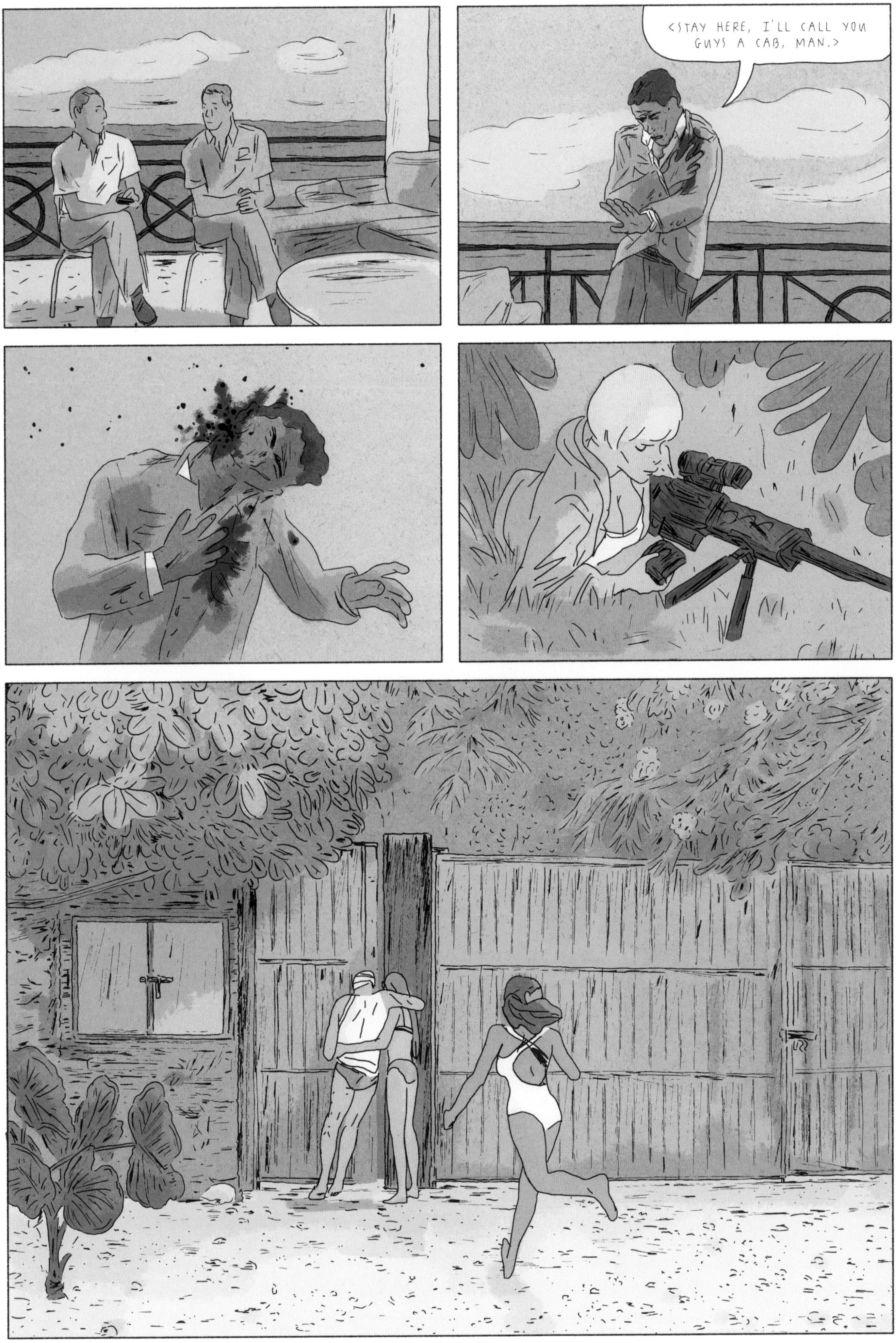
<STAY HERE, I'LL CALL YOU GUYS A CAB, MAN.>

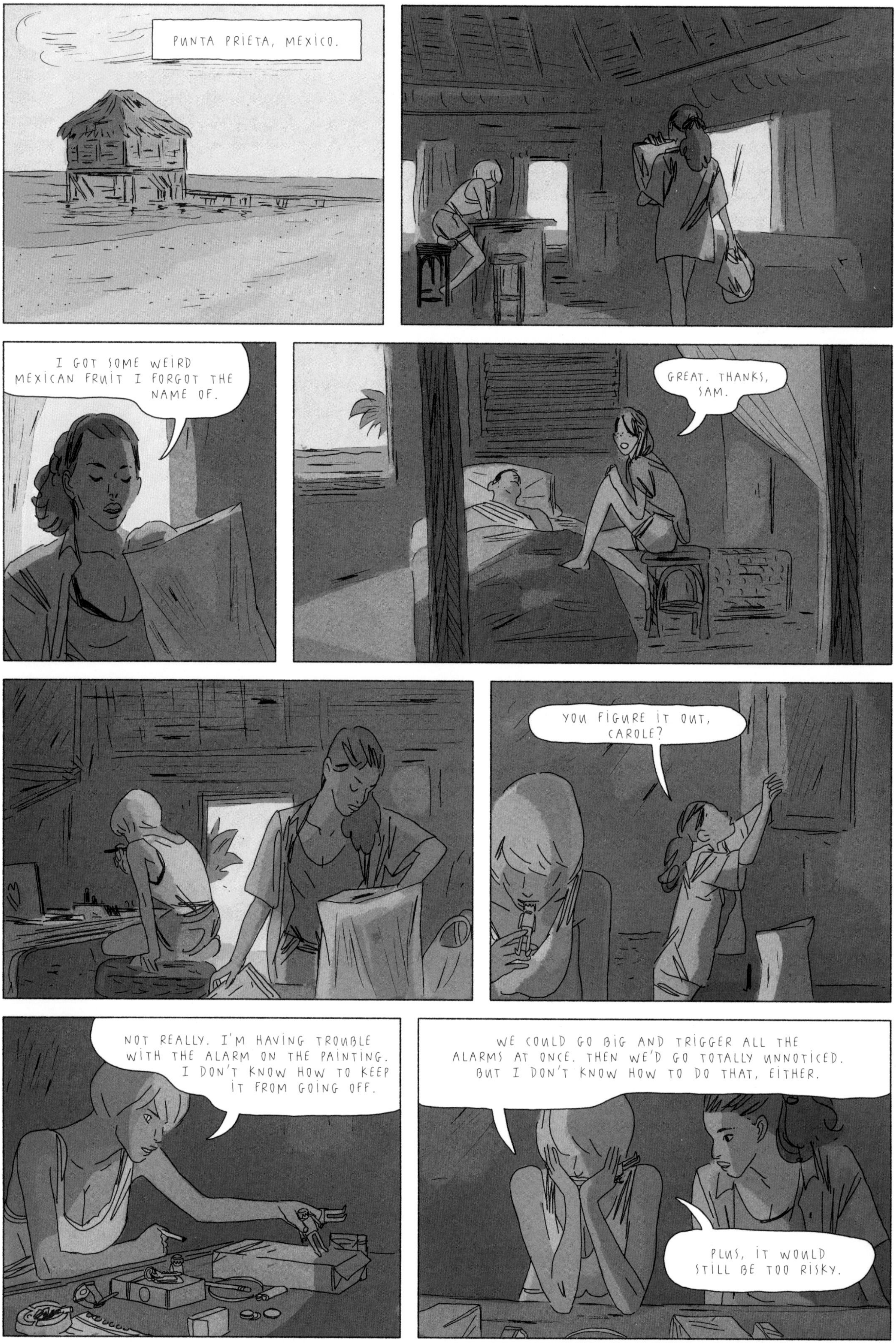
PUNTA PRIETA, MEXICO.
I GOT SOME WEIRD MEXICAN FRUIT I FORGOT THE NAME OF.
GREAT. THANKS, SAM.
YOU FIGURE IT OUT, CAROLE?
NOT REALLY. I'M HAVING TROUBLE WITH THE ALARM ON THE PAINTING. I DON'T KNOW HOW TO KEEP IT FROM GOING OFF.
WE COULD GO BIG AND TRIGGER ALL THE ALARMS AT ONCE. THEN WE'D GO TOTALLY UNNOTICED. BUT I DON'T KNOW HOW TO DO THAT, EITHER.
PLUS, IT WOULD STILL BE TOO RISKY.

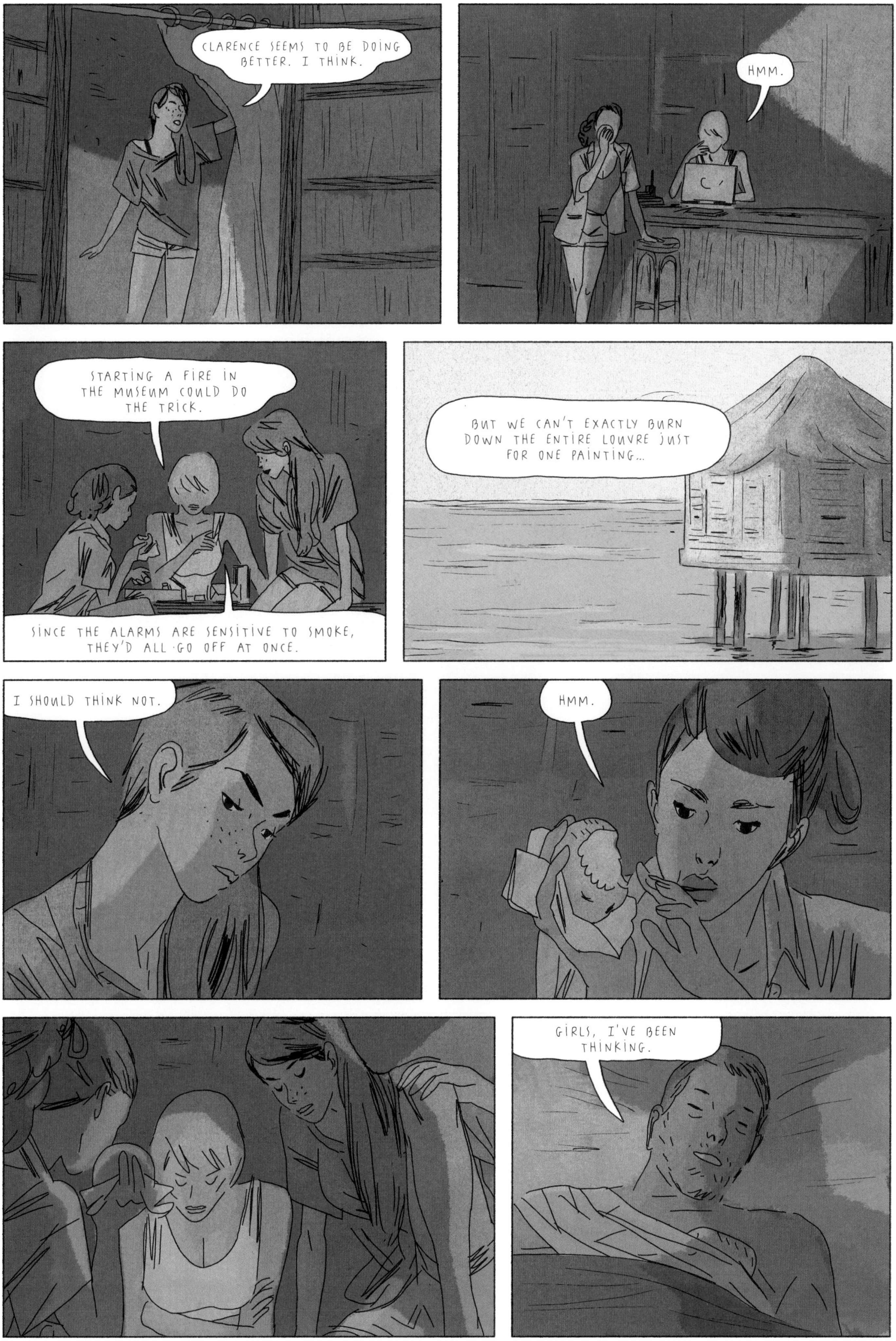
CLARENCE SEEMS TO BE DOING BETTER. I THINK.
HMM.
STARTING A FIRE IN THE MUSEUM COULD DO THE TRICK.
SINCE THE ALARMS ARE SENSITIVE TO SMOKE, THEY'D ALL GO OFF AT ONCE.
BUT WE CAN'T EXACTLY BURN DOWN THE ENTIRE LOUVRE JUST FOR ONE PAINTING...
I SHOULD THINK NOT.
HMM.
GIRLS, I'VE BEEN THINKING.

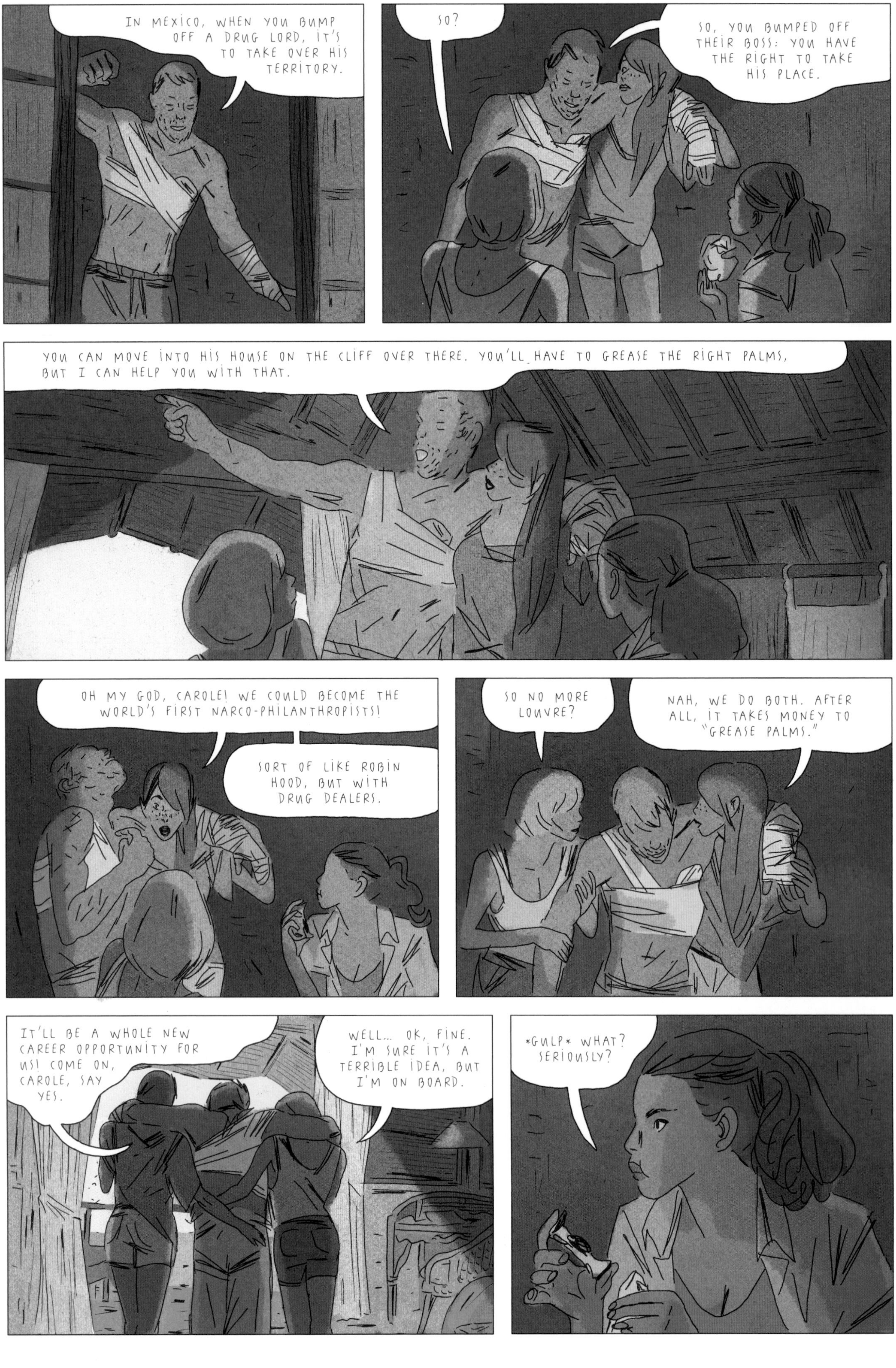

IN MEXICO, WHEN YOU BUMP OFF A DRUG LORD, IT'S TO TAKE OVER HIS TERRITORY.
SO?
SO, YOU BUMPED OFF THEIR BOSS: YOU HAVE THE RIGHT TO TAKE HIS PLACE.
YOU CAN MOVE INTO HIS HOUSE ON THE CLIFF OVER THERE. YOU'LL HAVE TO GREASE THE RIGHT PALMS, BUT I CAN HELP YOU WITH THAT.
OH MY GOD, CAROLE! WE COULD BECOME THE WORLD'S FIRST NARCO-PHILANTHROPISTS!
SORT OF LIKE ROBIN HOOD, BUT WITH DRUG DEALERS.
SO NO MORE LOUVRE?
NAH, WE DO BOTH. AFTER ALL, IT TAKES MONEY TO "GREASE PALMS."
IT'LL BE A WHOLE NEW CAREER OPPORTUNITY FOR US! COME ON, CAROLE, SAY YES.
WELL... OK, FINE. I'M SURE IT'S A TERRIBLE IDEA, BUT I'M ON BOARD.
GULP WHAT? SERIOUSLY?

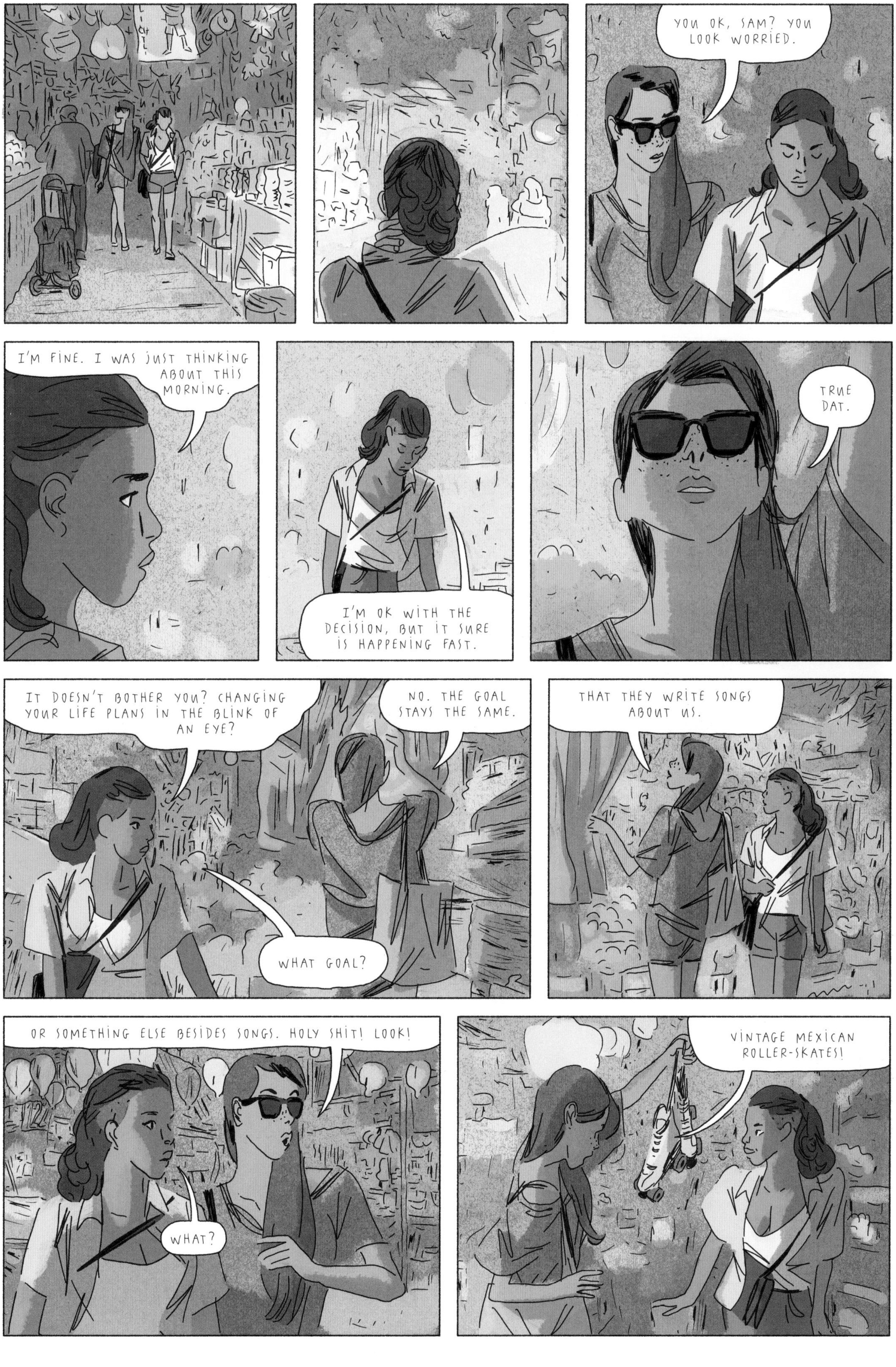
YOU OK, SAM? YOU LOOK WORRIED.
I'M FINE. I WAS JUST THINKING ABOUT THIS MORNING.
I'M OK WITH THE DECISION, BUT IT SURE IS HAPPENING FAST.
TRUE DAT.
IT DOESN'T BOTHER YOU? CHANGING YOUR LIFE PLANS IN THE BLINK OF AN EYE?
NO. THE GOAL STAYS THE SAME.
WHAT GOAL?
THAT THEY WRITE SONGS ABOUT US.
OR SOMETHING ELSE BESIDES SONGS. HOLY SHIT! LOOK!
WHAT?
VINTAGE MEXICAN ROLLER-SKATES!

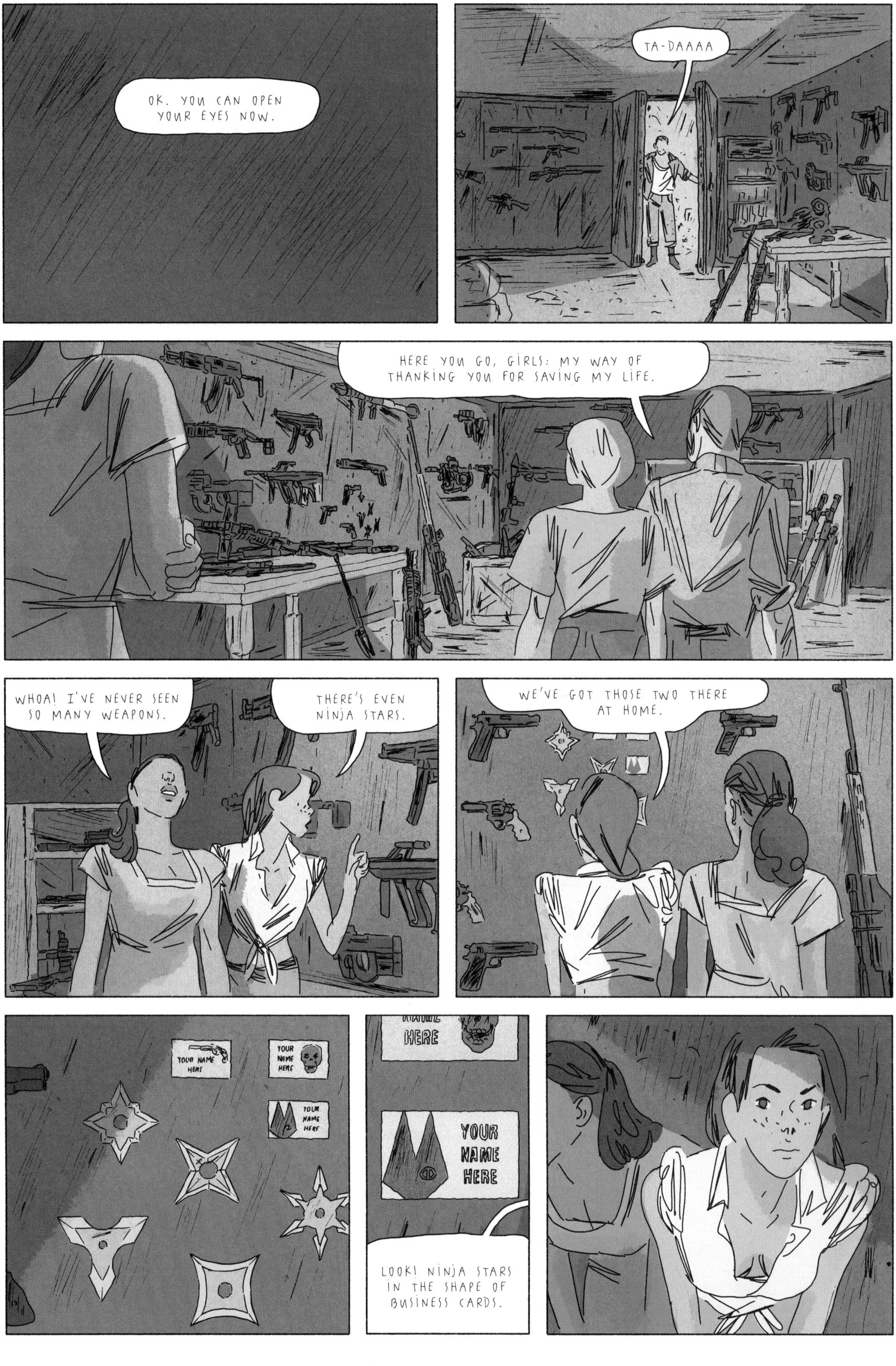
OK. YOU CAN OPEN YOUR EYES NOW.
TA-DAAAA
HERE YOU GO, GIRLS: MY WAY OF THANKING YOU FOR SAVING MY LIFE.
WHOA! I'VE NEVER SEEN SO MANY WEAPONS.
THERE'S EVEN NINJA STARS.
WE'VE GOT THOSE TWO THERE AT HOME.
YOUR NAME HERE
YOUR NAME HERE
YOUR NAME HERE
HERE
YOUR NAME HERE
LOOK! NINJA STARS IN THE SHAPE OF BUSINESS CARDS.

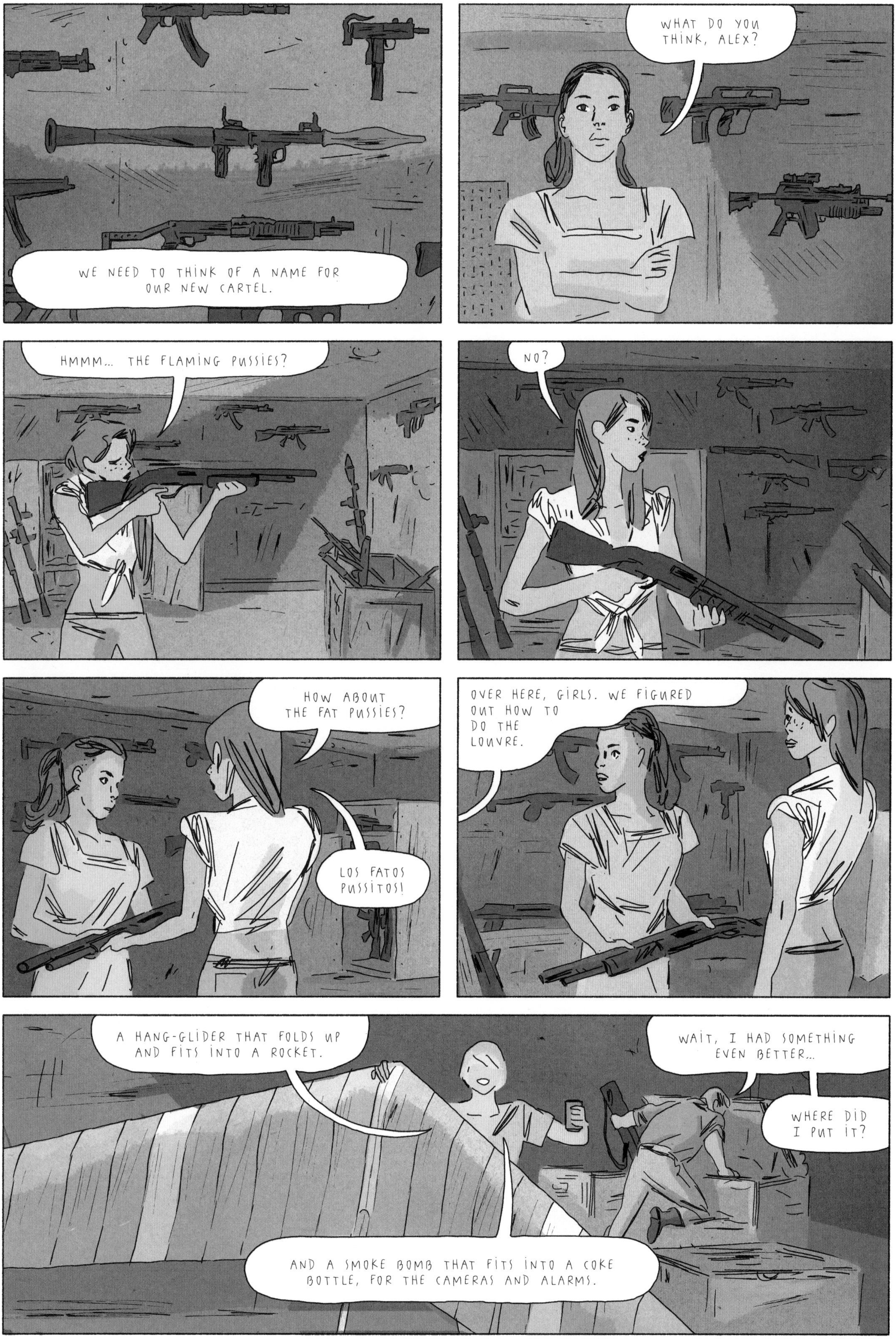
WE NEED TO THINK OF A NAME FOR OUR NEW CARTEL.
WHAT DO YOU THINK, ALEX?
HMMM... THE FLAMING PUSSIES?
NO?
HOW ABOUT THE FAT PUSSIES?
LOS FATOS PUSSITOS!
OVER HERE, GIRLS. WE FIGURED OUT HOW TO DO THE LOUVRE.
A HANG-GLIDER THAT FOLDS UP AND FITS INTO A ROCKET.
WAIT, I HAD SOMETHING EVEN BETTER...
WHERE DID I PUT IT?
AND A SMOKE BOMB THAT FITS INTO A COKE BOTTLE, FOR THE CAMERAS AND ALARMS.

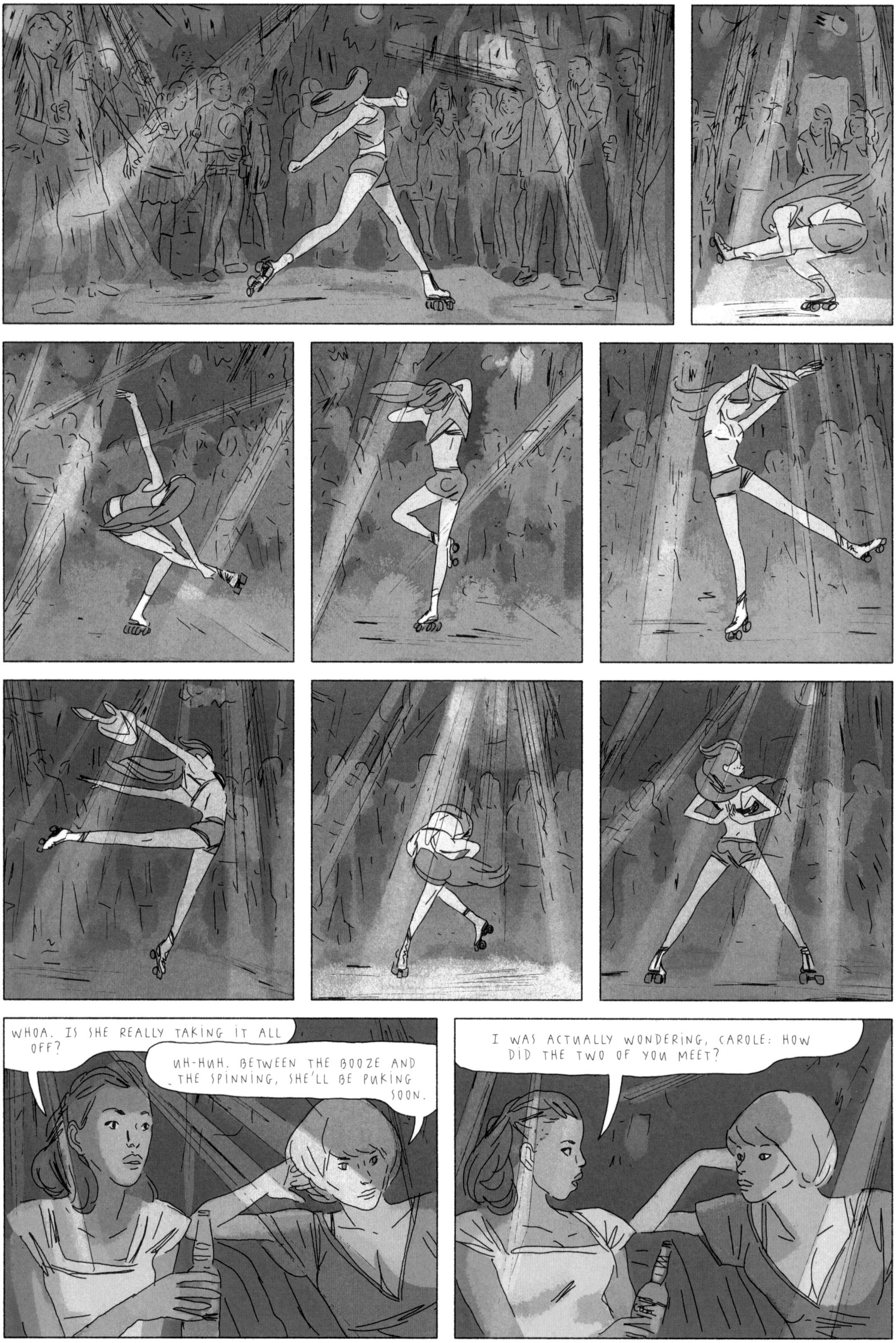
WHOA. IS SHE REALLY TAKING IT ALL OFF?
UH-HUH. BETWEEN THE BOOZE AND THE SPINNING, SHE'LL BE PUKING SOON.
I WAS ACTUALLY WONDERING, CAROLE: HOW DID THE TWO OF YOU MEET?

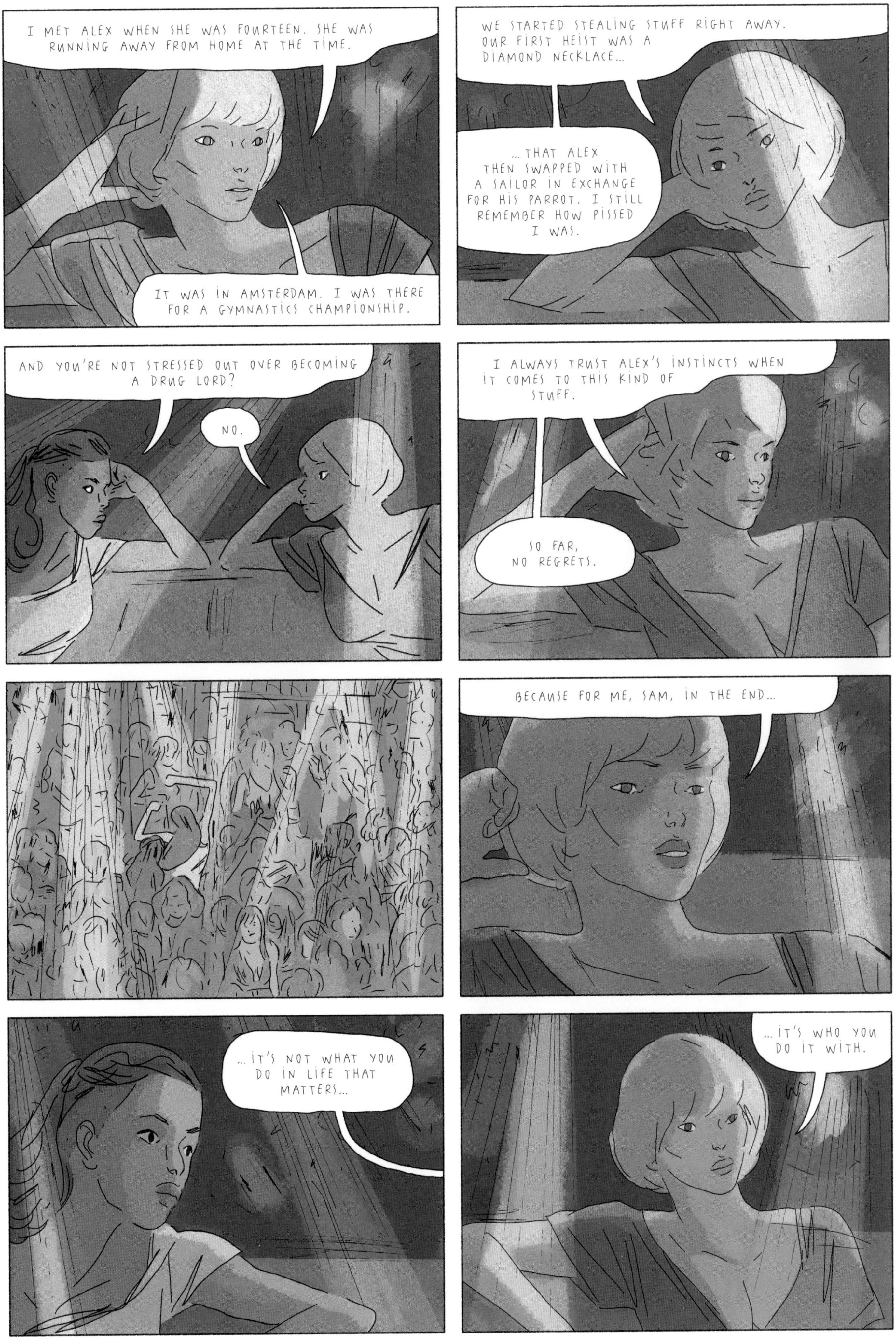
I MET ALEX WHEN SHE WAS FOURTEEN. SHE WAS RUNNING AWAY FROM HOME AT THE TIME.
IT WAS IN AMSTERDAM. I WAS THERE FOR A GYMNASTICS CHAMPIONSHIP.
WE STARTED STEALING STUFF RIGHT AWAY. OUR FIRST HEIST WAS A DIAMOND NECKLACE...
...THAT ALEX THEN SWAPPED WITH A SAILOR IN EXCHANGE FOR HIS PARROT. I STILL REMEMBER HOW PISSED I WAS.
AND YOU'RE NOT STRESSED OUT OVER BECOMING A DRUG LORD?
NO.
I ALWAYS TRUST ALEX'S INSTINCTS WHEN IT COMES TO THIS KIND OF STUFF.
SO FAR, NO REGRETS.
BECAUSE FOR ME, SAM, IN THE END...
...IT'S NOT WHAT YOU DO IN LIFE THAT MATTERS...
...IT'S WHO YOU DO IT WITH.

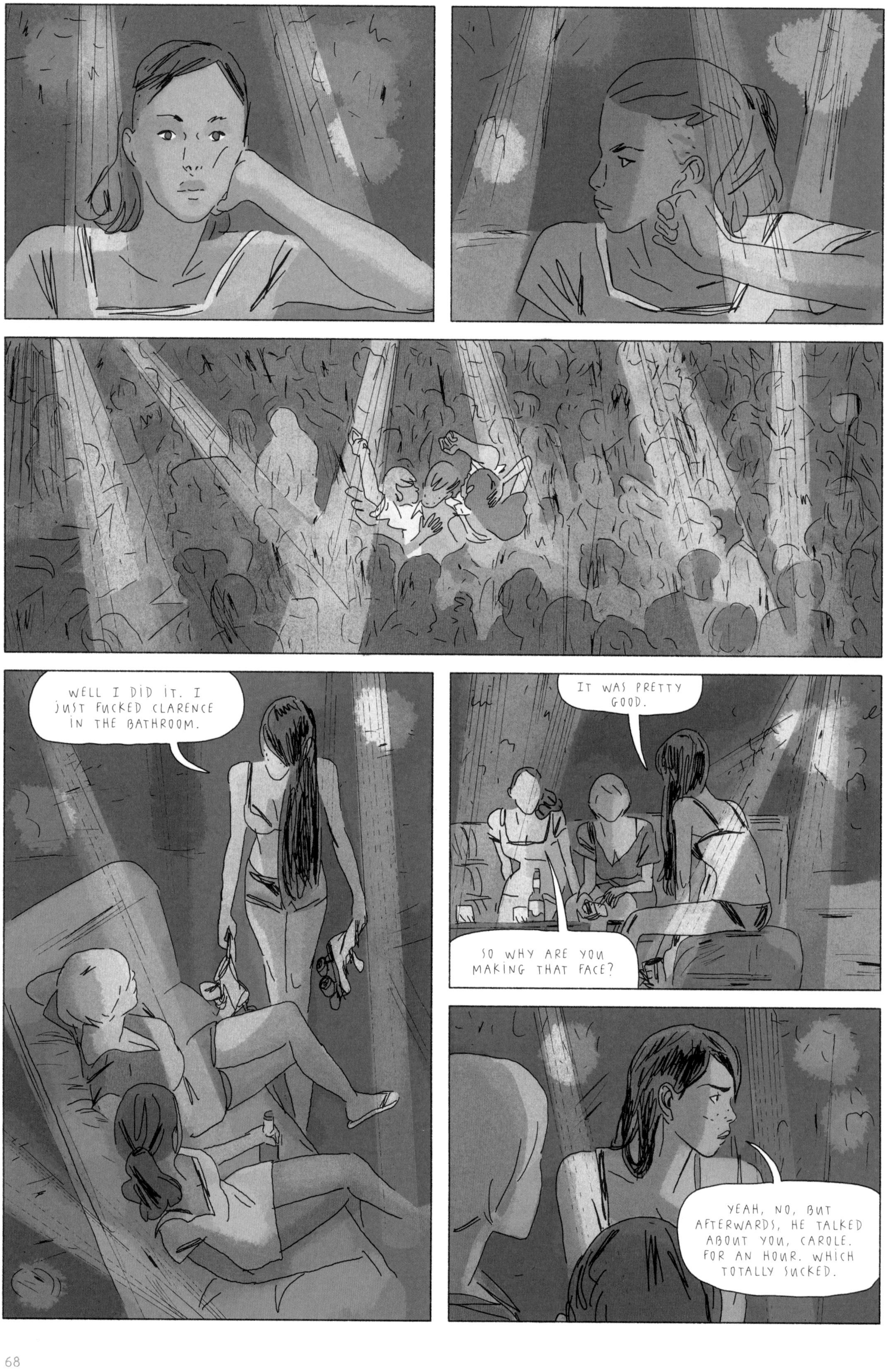

WELL I DID IT. I JUST FUCKED CLARENCE IN THE BATHROOM.
IT WAS PRETTY GOOD.
SO WHY ARE YOU MAKING THAT FACE?
YEAH, NO, BUT AFTERWARDS, HE TALKED ABOUT YOU, CAROLE. FOR AN HOUR. WHICH TOTALLY SUCKED.

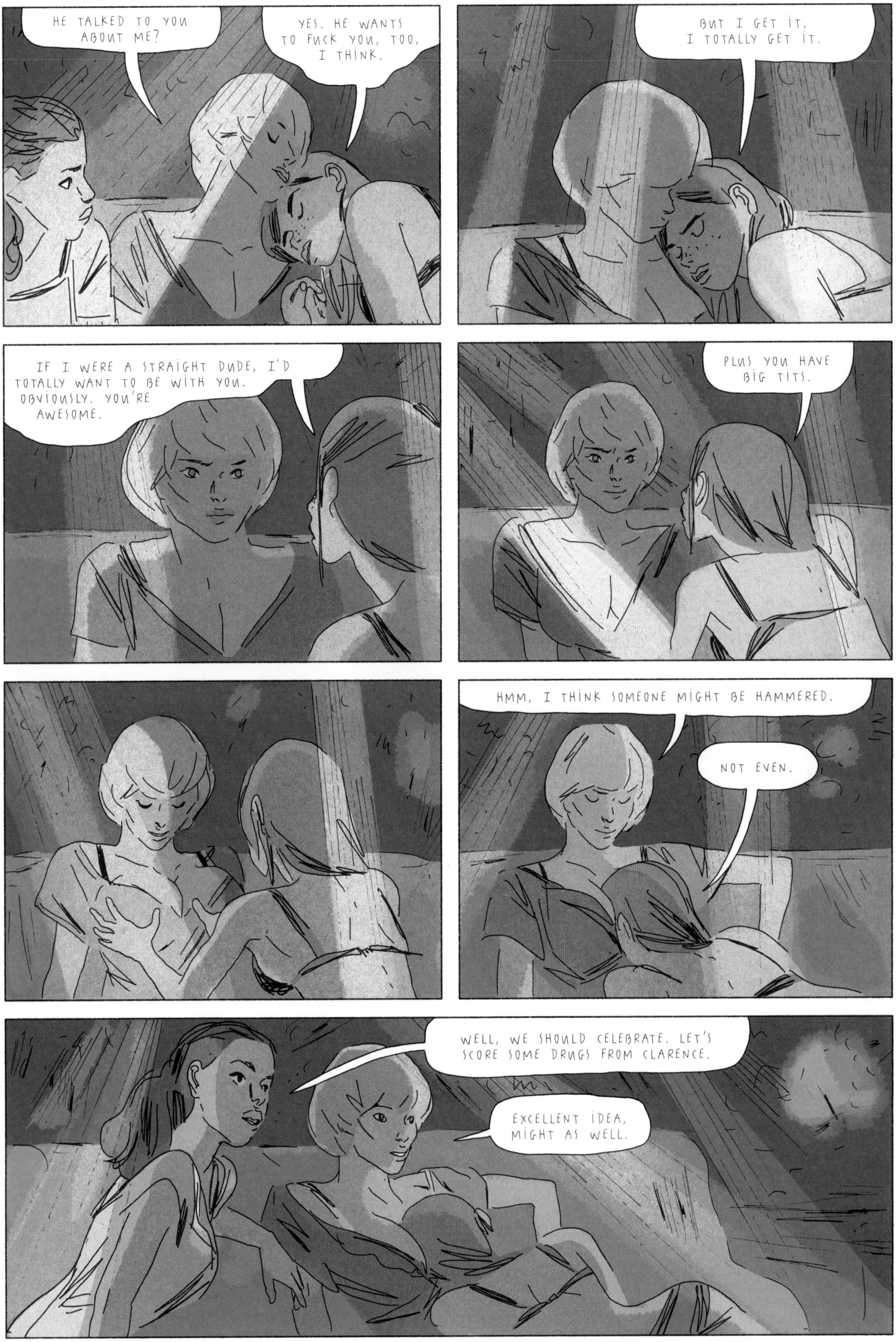
HE TALKED TO YOU ABOUT ME?
YES. HE WANTS TO FUCK YOU, TOO, I THINK.
BUT I GET IT, I TOTALLY GET IT.
IF I WERE A STRAIGHT DUDE, I'D TOTALLY WANT TO BE WITH YOU. OBVIOUSLY. YOU'RE AWESOME.
PLUS YOU HAVE BIG TITS.
HMM, I THINK SOMEONE MIGHT BE HAMMERED.
NOT EVEN.
WELL, WE SHOULD CELEBRATE. LET'S SCORE SOME DRUGS FROM CLARENCE.
EXCELLENT IDEA, MIGHT AS WELL.

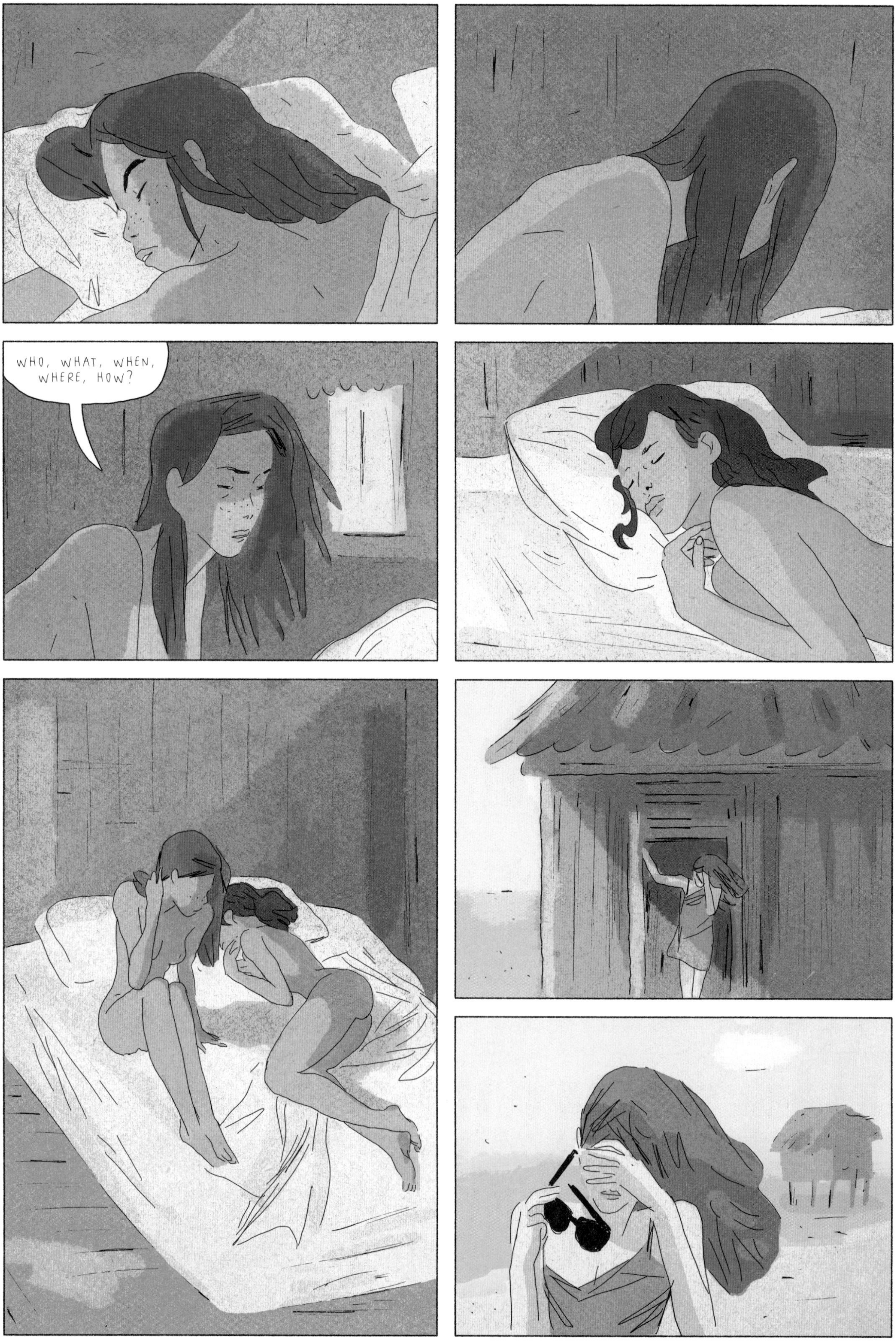
WHO, WHAT, WHEN, WHERE, HOW?

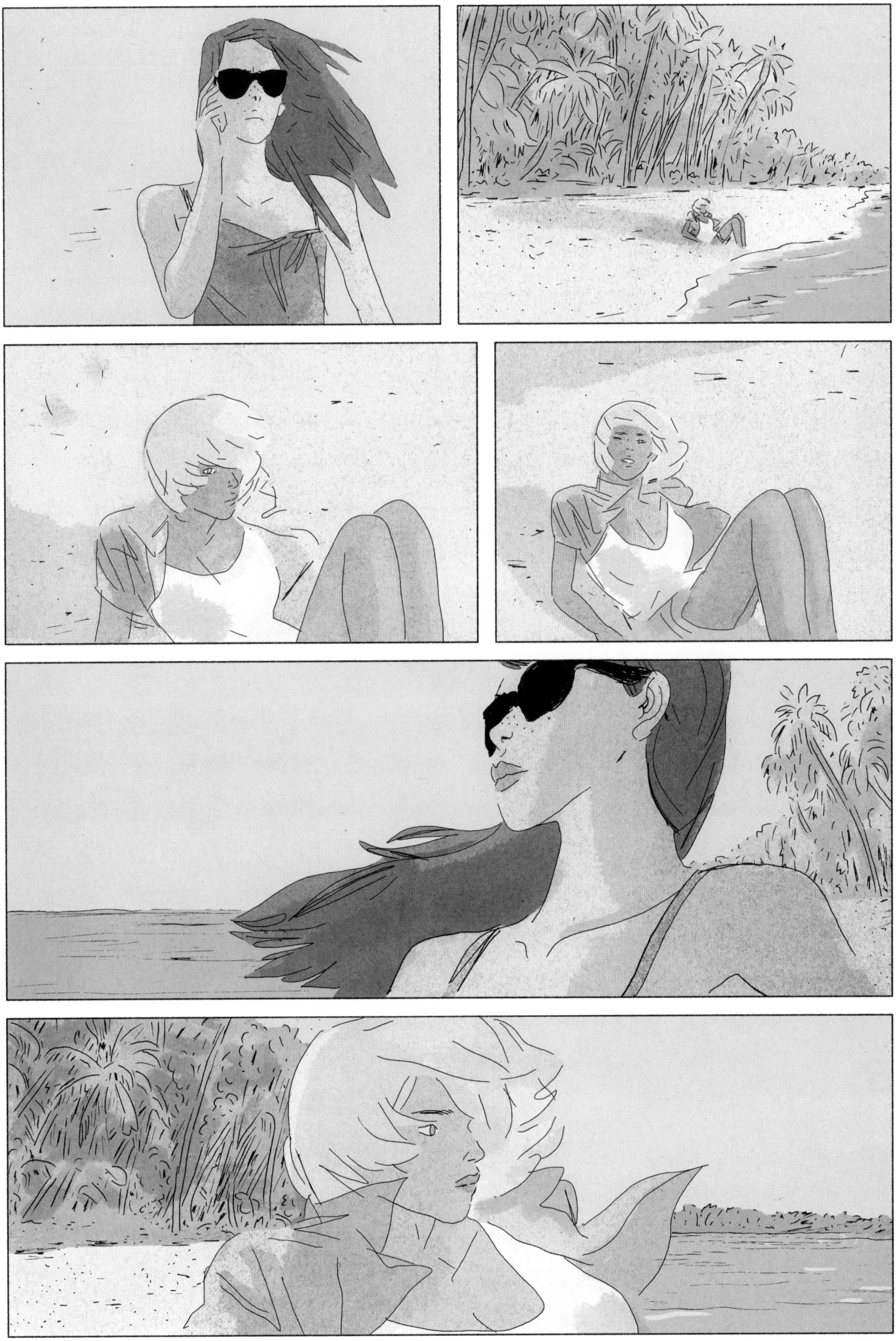

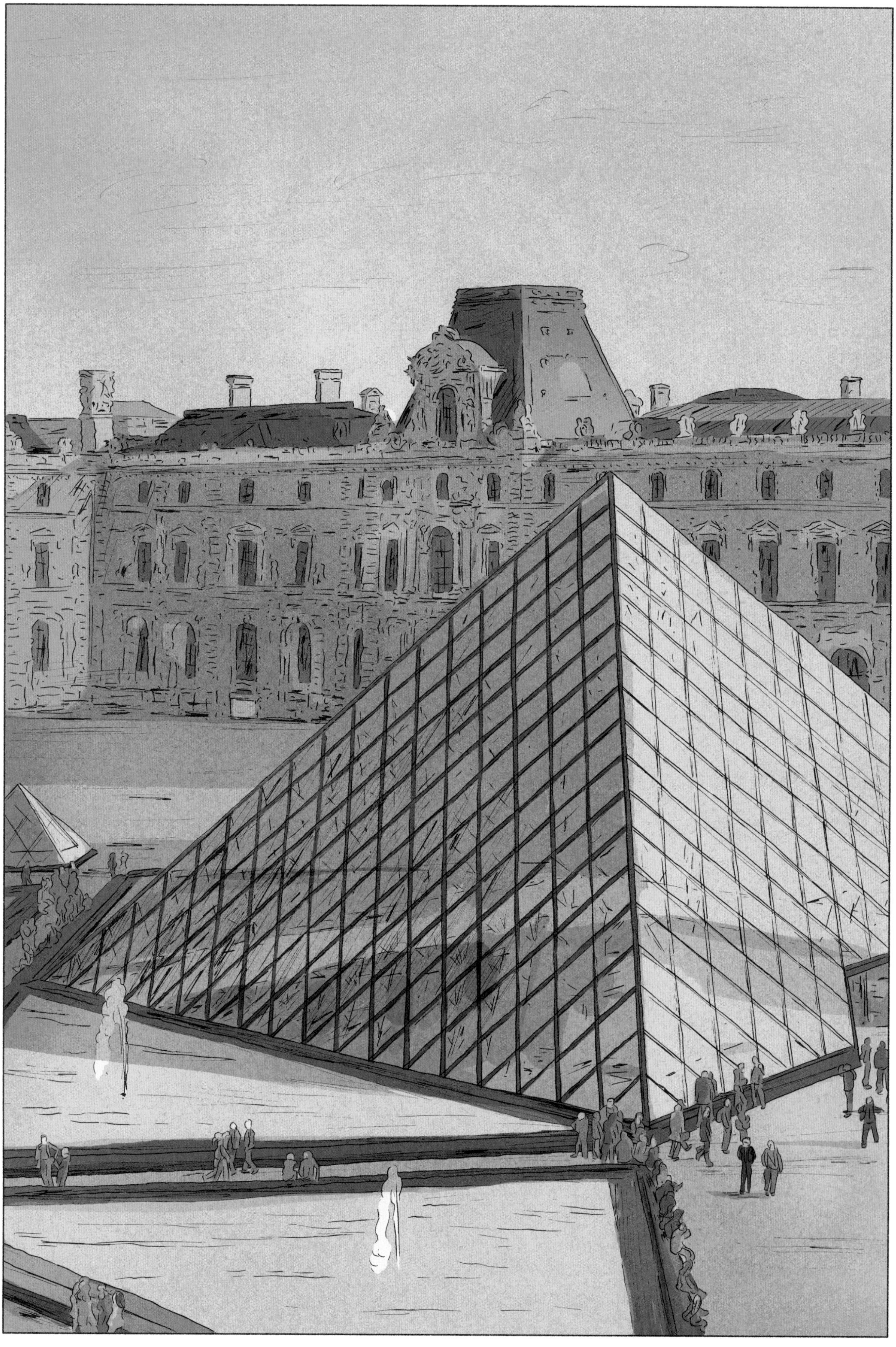

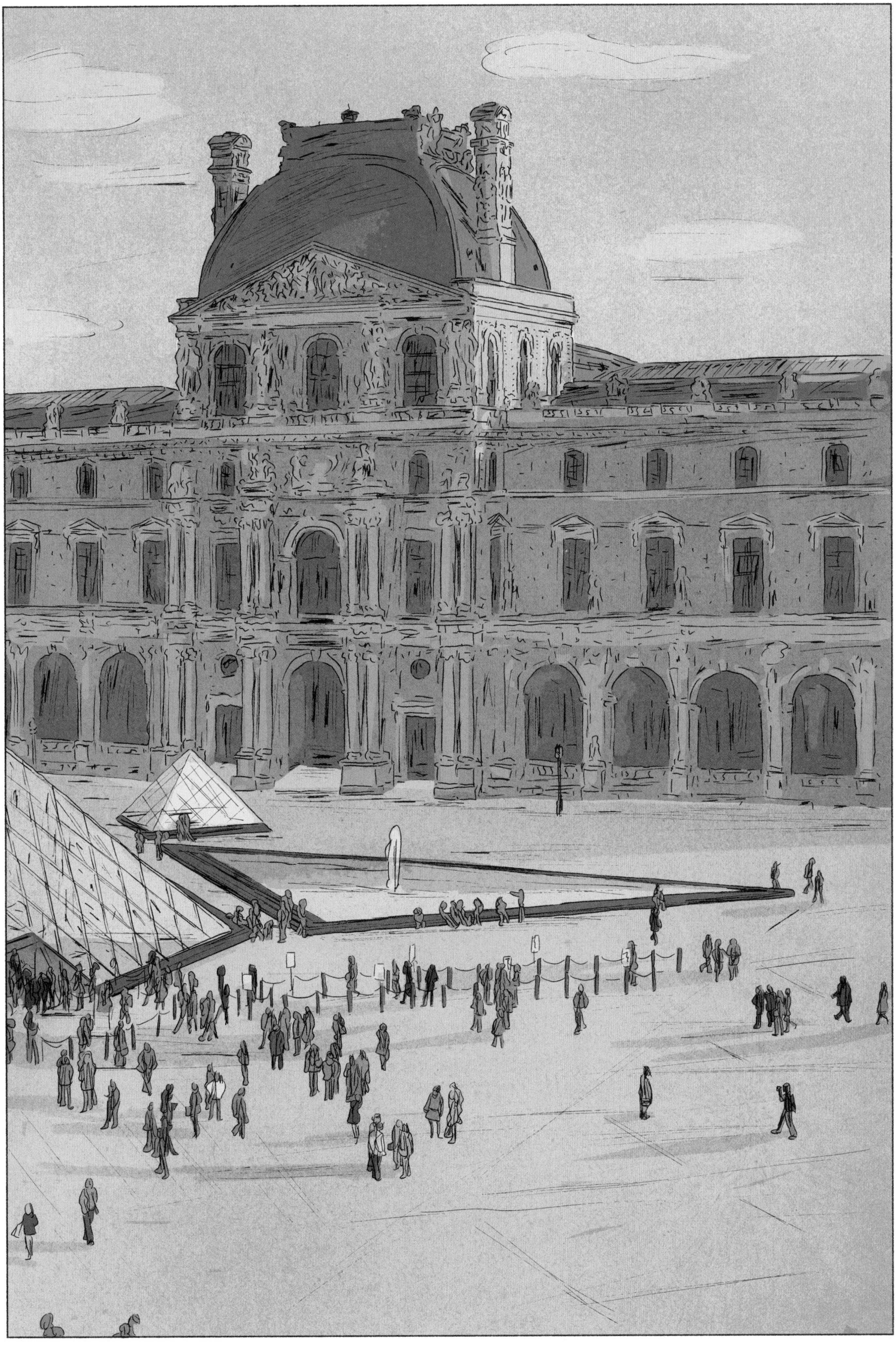

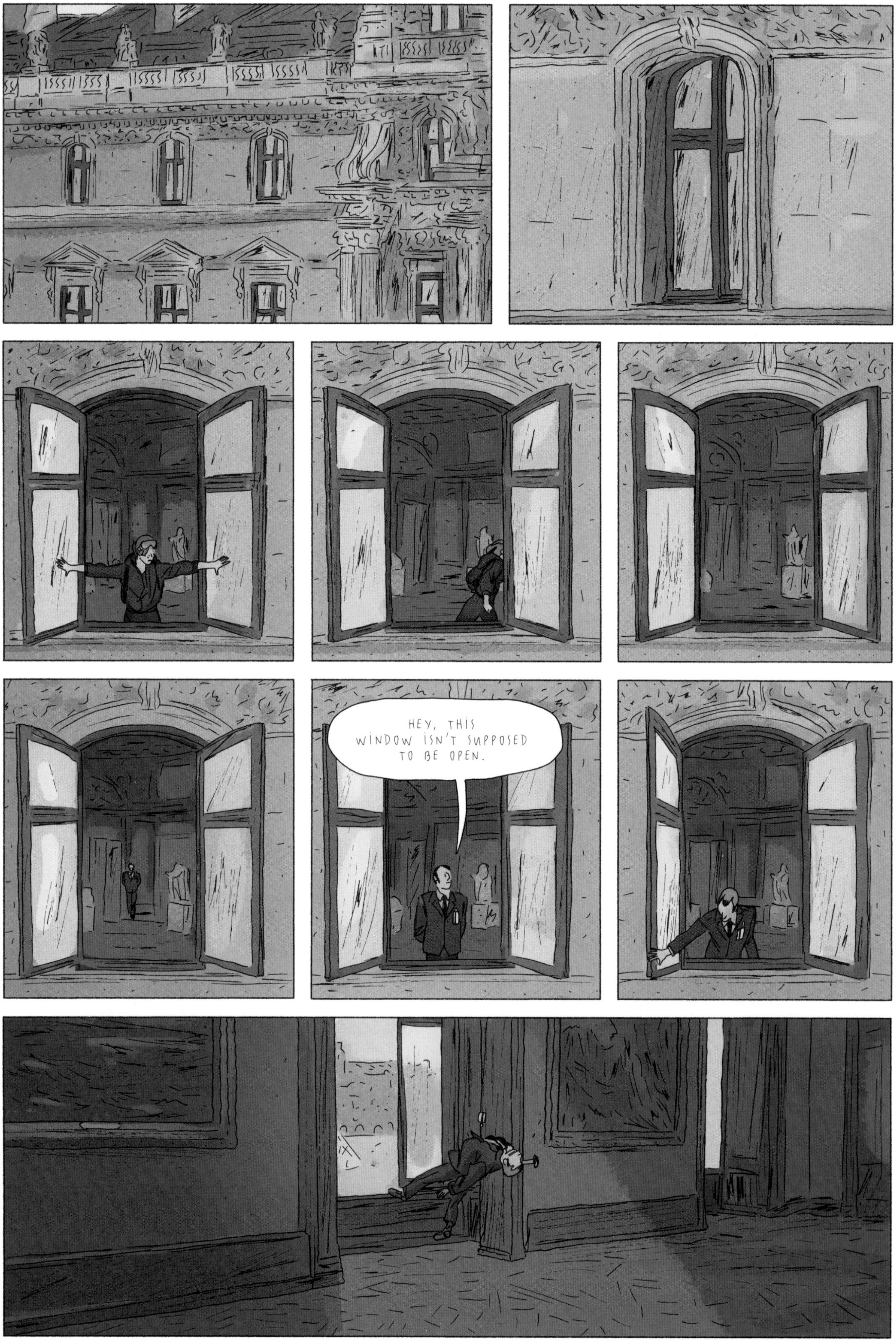
HEY, THIS WINDOW ISN'T SUPPOSED TO BE OPEN.

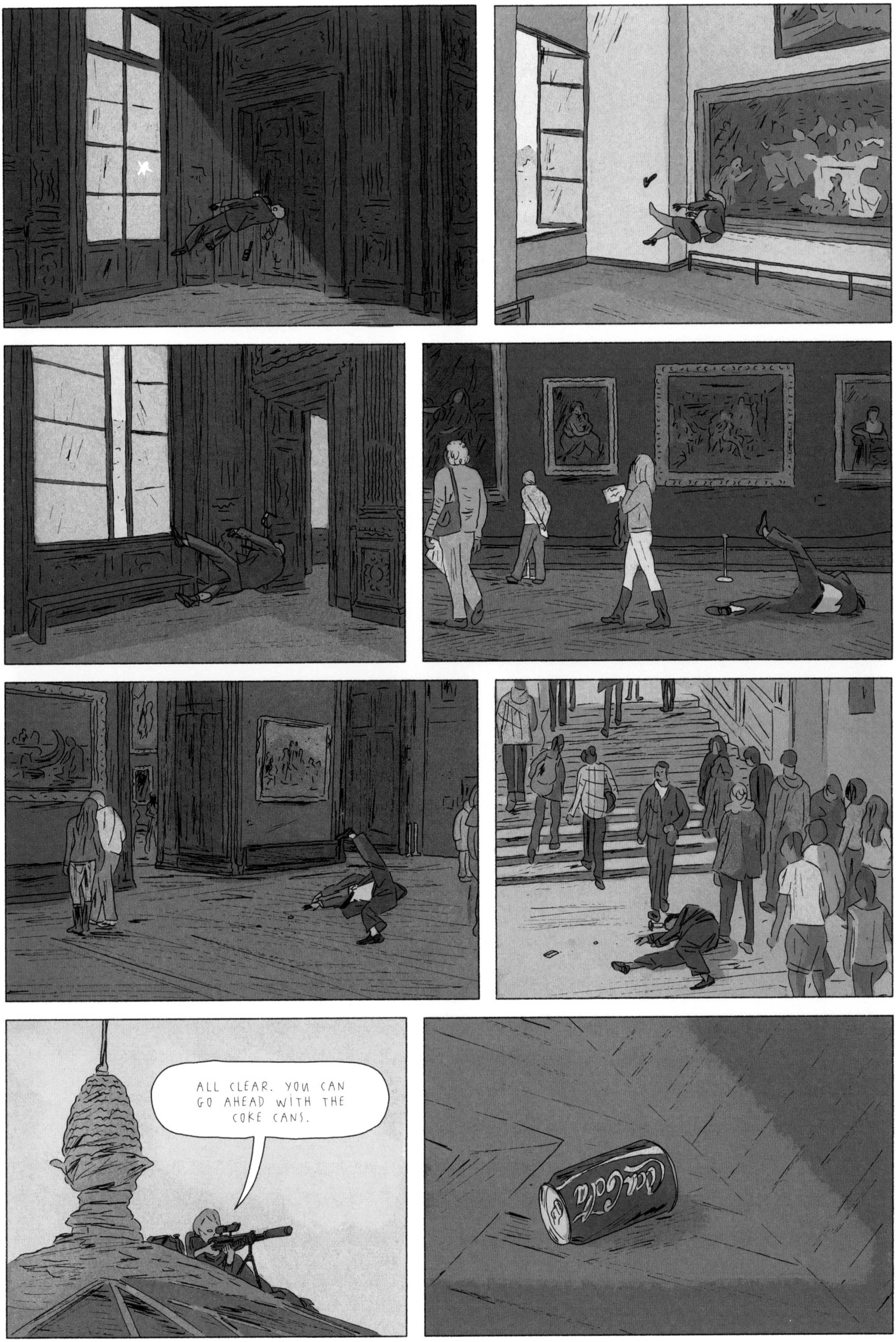
ALL CLEAR. YOU CAN GO AHEAD WITH THE COKE CANS.

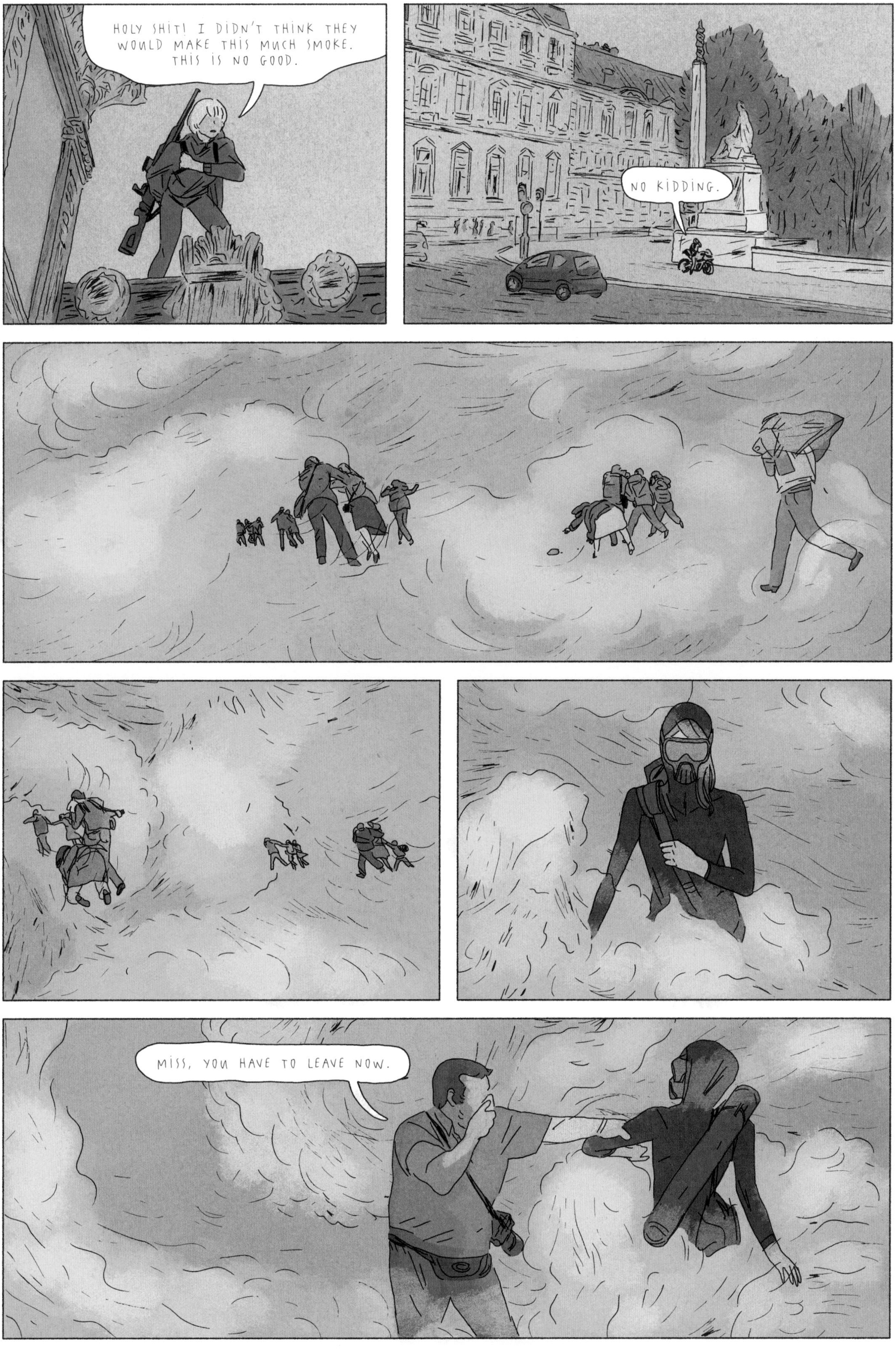
HOLY SHIT! I DIDN'T THINK THEY WOULD MAKE THIS MUCH SMOKE. THIS IS NO GOOD.
NO KIDDING.
MISS, YOU HAVE TO LEAVE NOW.

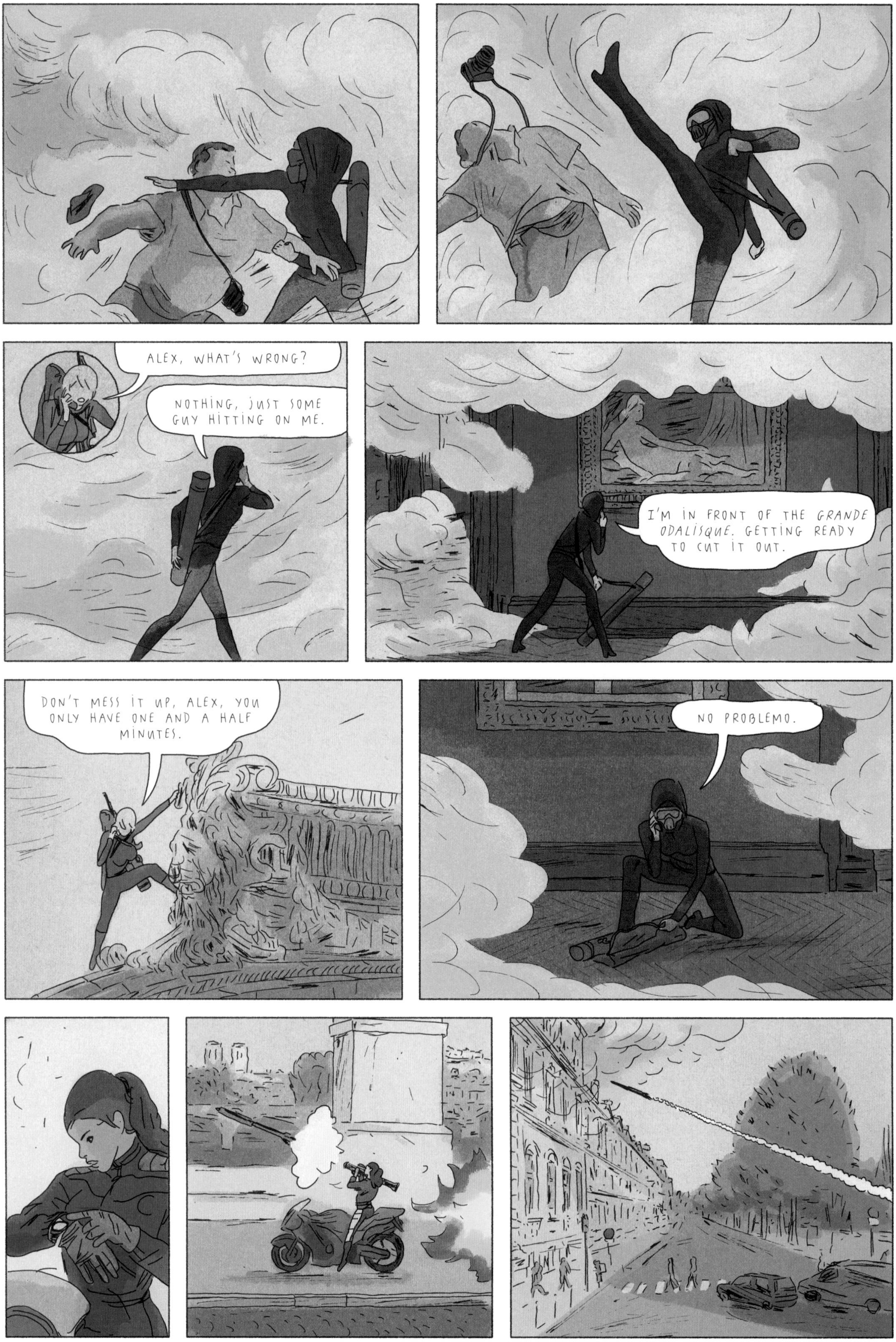
ALEX, WHAT'S WRONG?
NOTHING, JUST SOME GUY HITTING ON ME.
I'M IN FRONT OF THE GRANDE ODALISQUE. GETTING READY TO CUT IT OUT.
DON'T MESS IT UP, ALEX, YOU ONLY HAVE ONE AND A HALF MINUTES.
NO PROBLEMO.

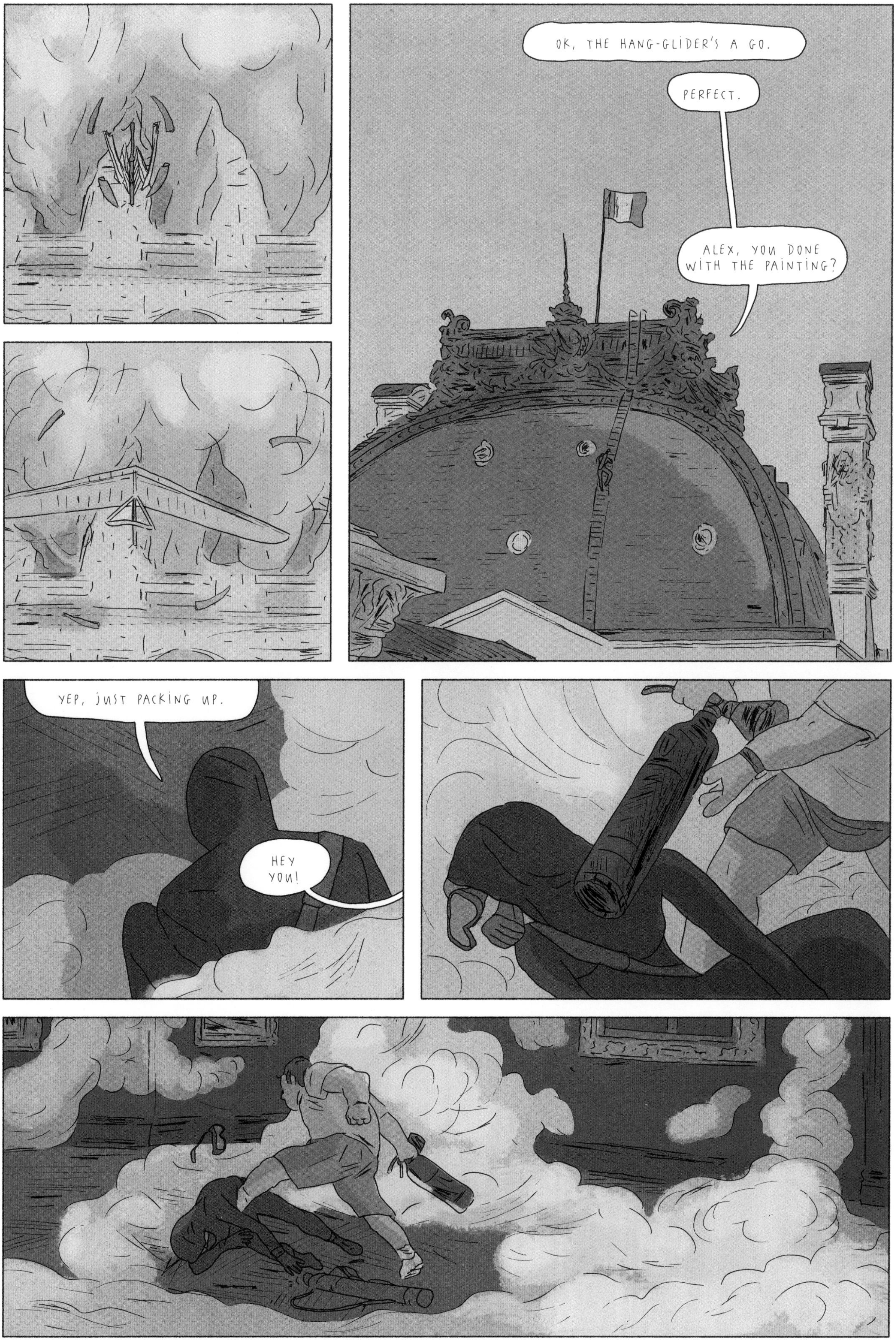
OK, THE HANG-GLIDER'S A GO.
PERFECT.
ALEX, YOU DONE WITH THE PAINTING?
YEP, JUST PACKING UP.
HEY YOU!

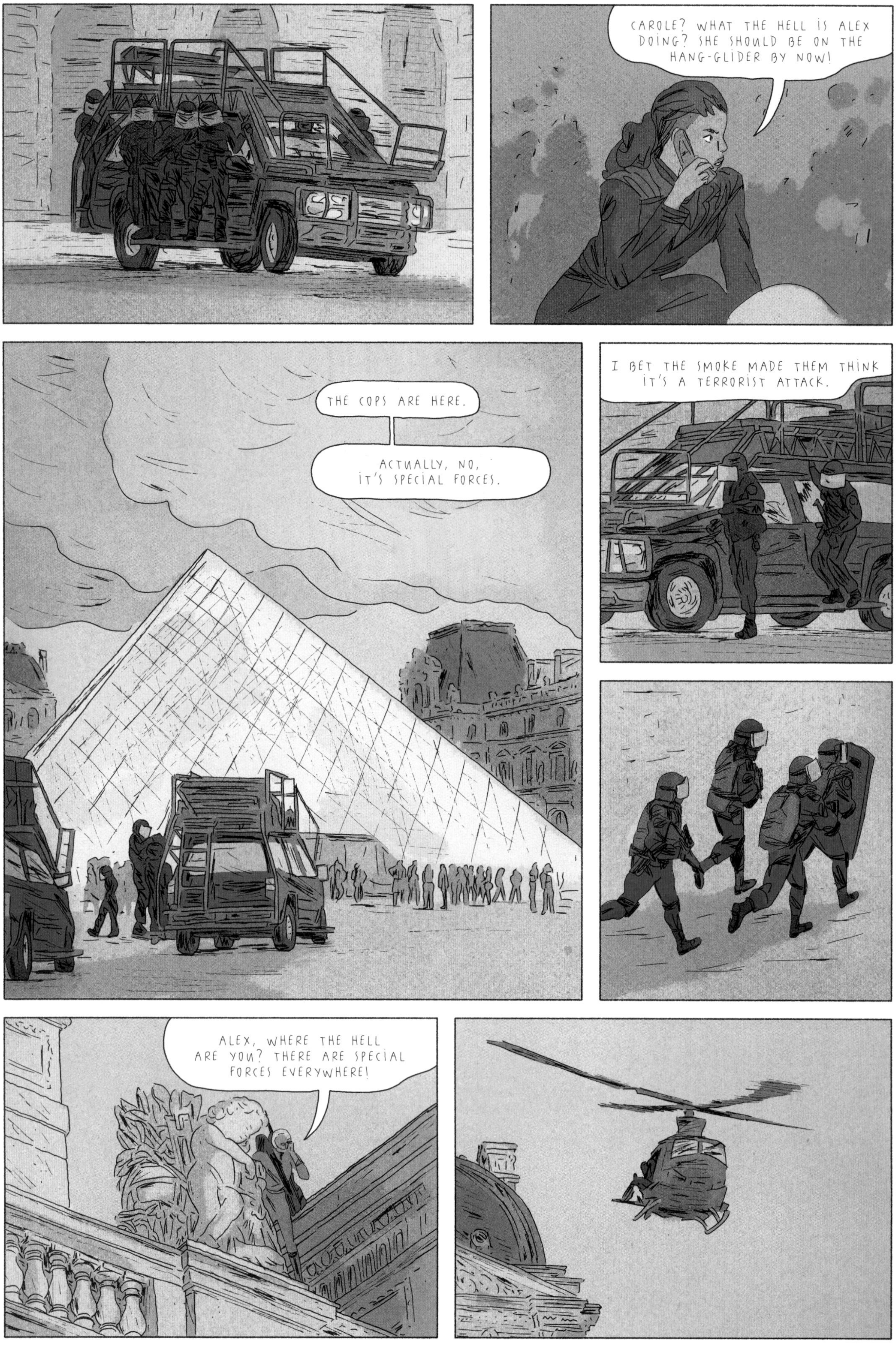
CAROLE? WHAT THE HELL IS ALEX DOING? SHE SHOULD BE ON THE HANG-GLIDER BY NOW!
THE COPS ARE HERE.
ACTUALLY, NO, IT'S SPECIAL FORCES.
I BET THE SMOKE MADE THEM THINK IT'S A TERRORIST ATTACK.
ALEX, WHERE THE HELL ARE YOU? THERE ARE SPECIAL FORCES EVERYWHERE!

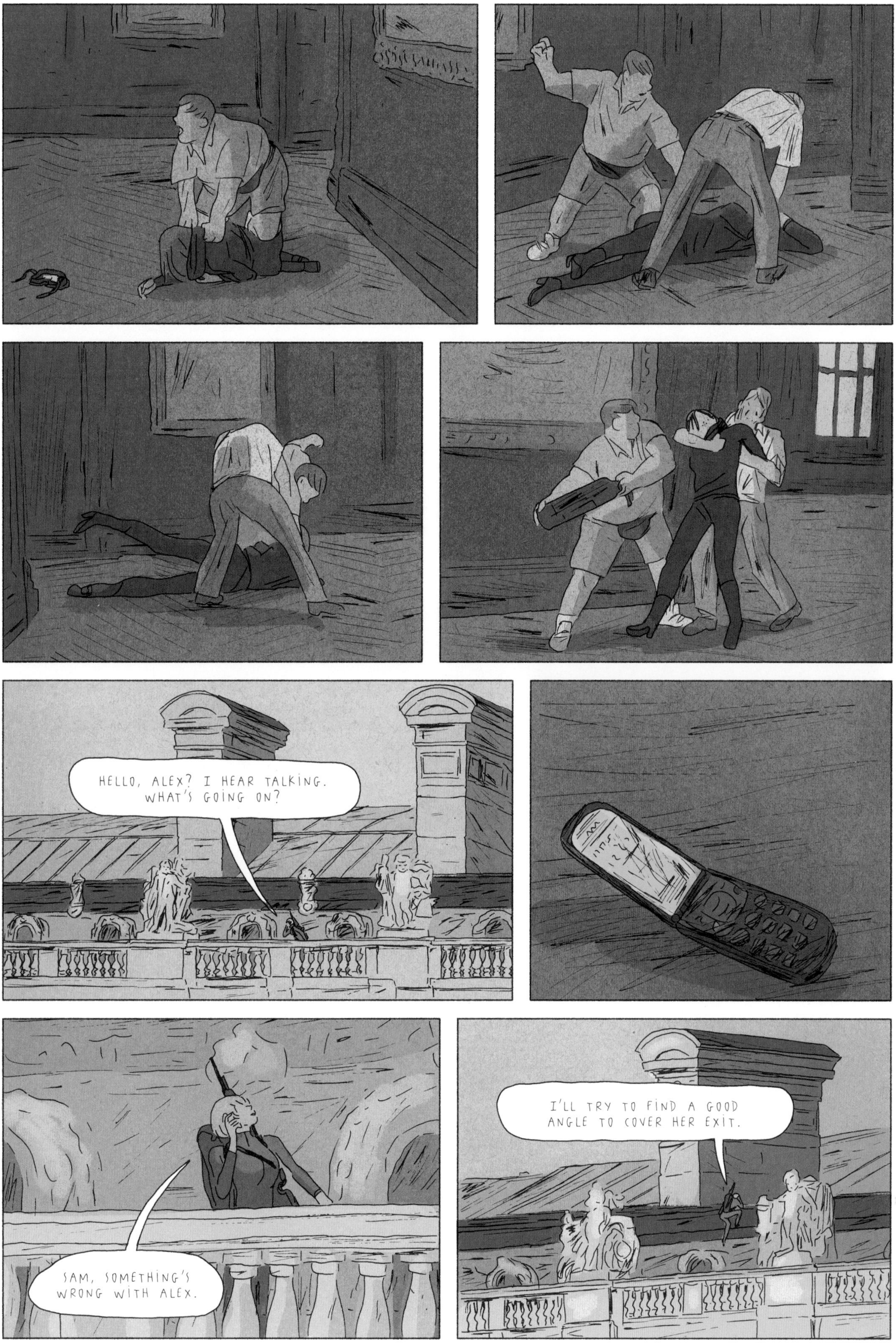
HELLO, ALEX? I HEAR TALKING. WHAT'S GOING ON?
SAM, SOMETHING'S WRONG WITH ALEX.
I'LL TRY TO FIND A GOOD ANGLE TO COVER HER EXIT.

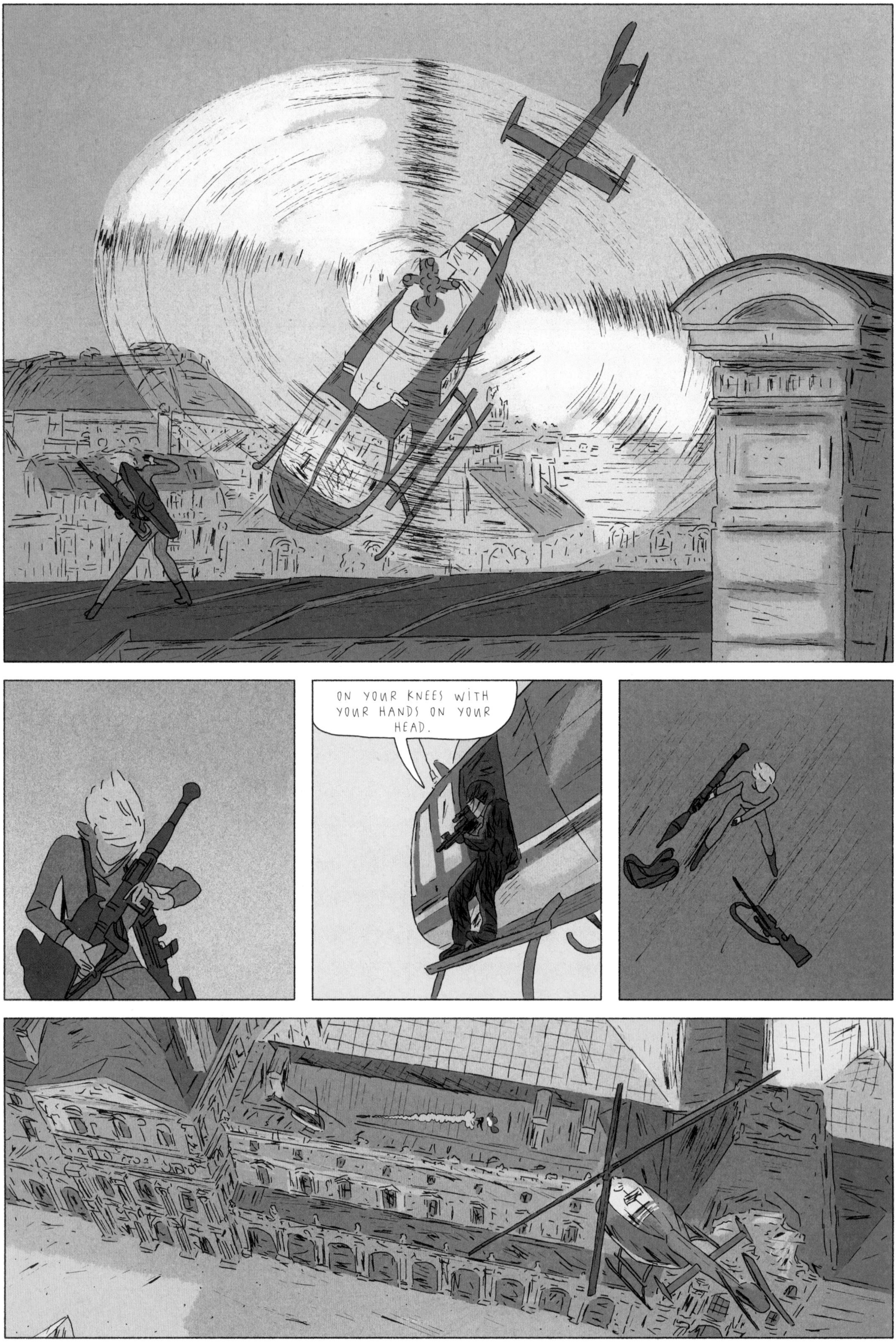
ON YOUR KNEES WITH YOUR HANDS ON YOUR HEAD.

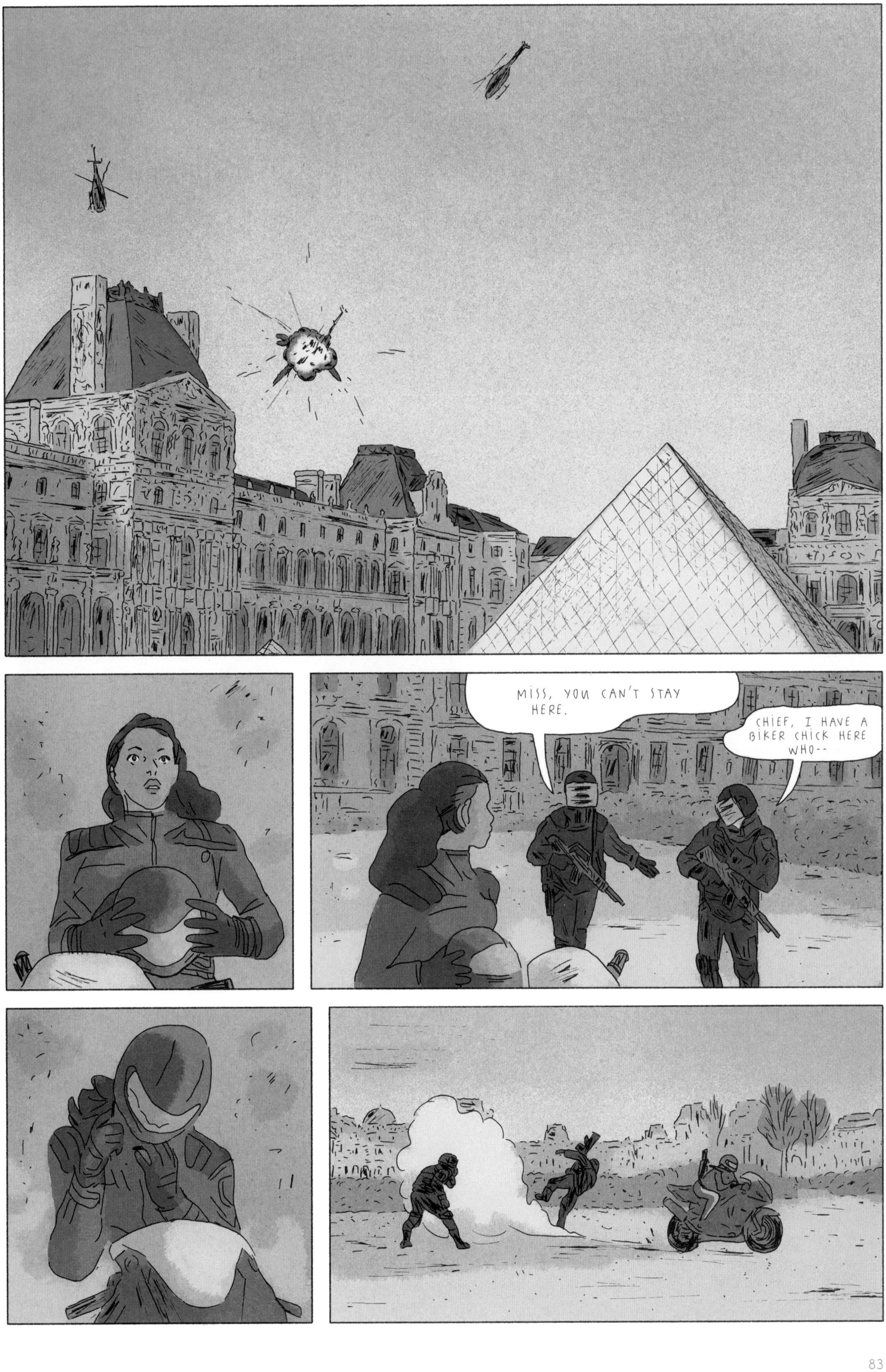
MISS, YOU CAN'T STAY HERE.
CHIEF, I HAVE A BIKER CHICK HERE WHO--

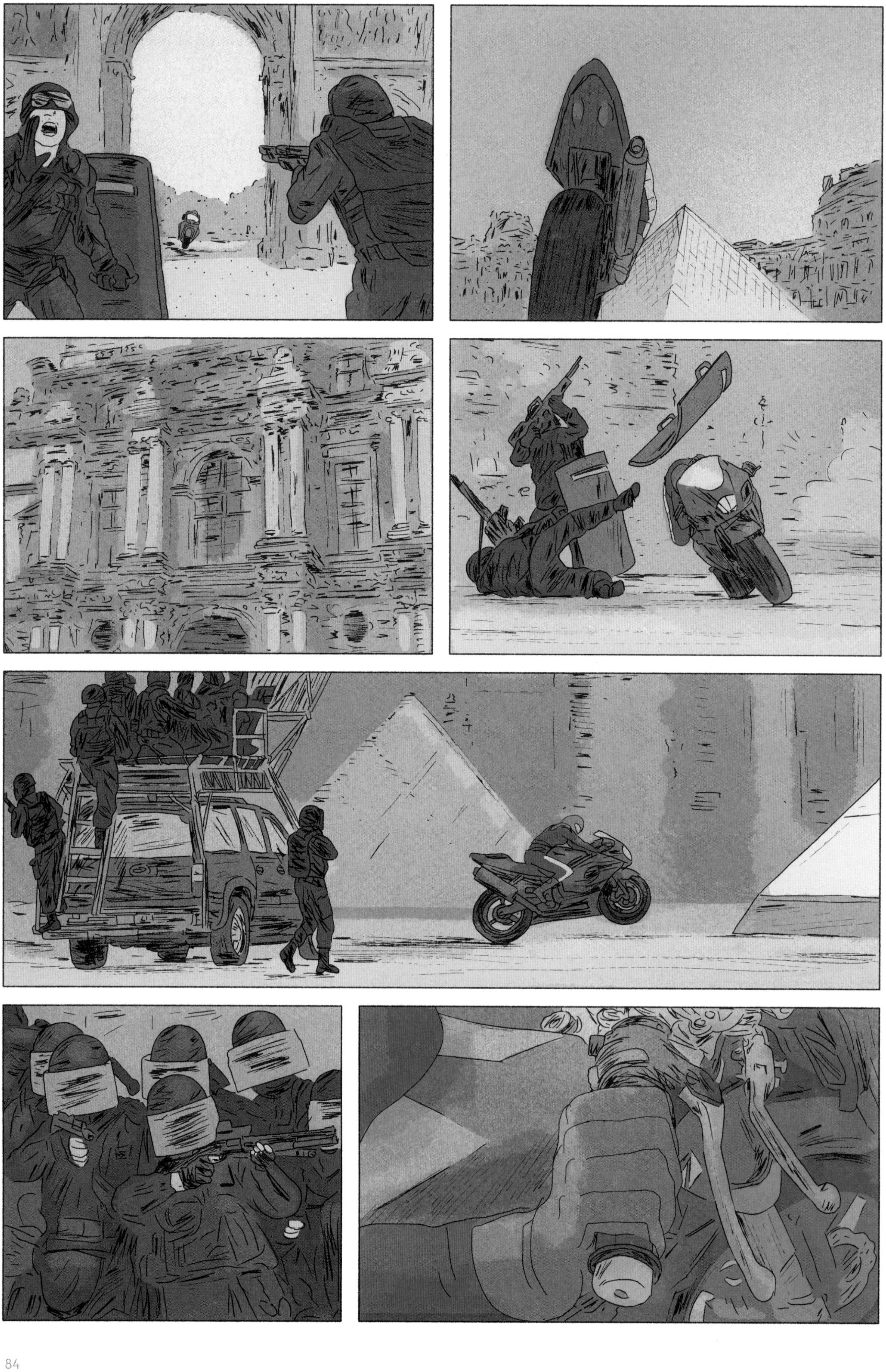

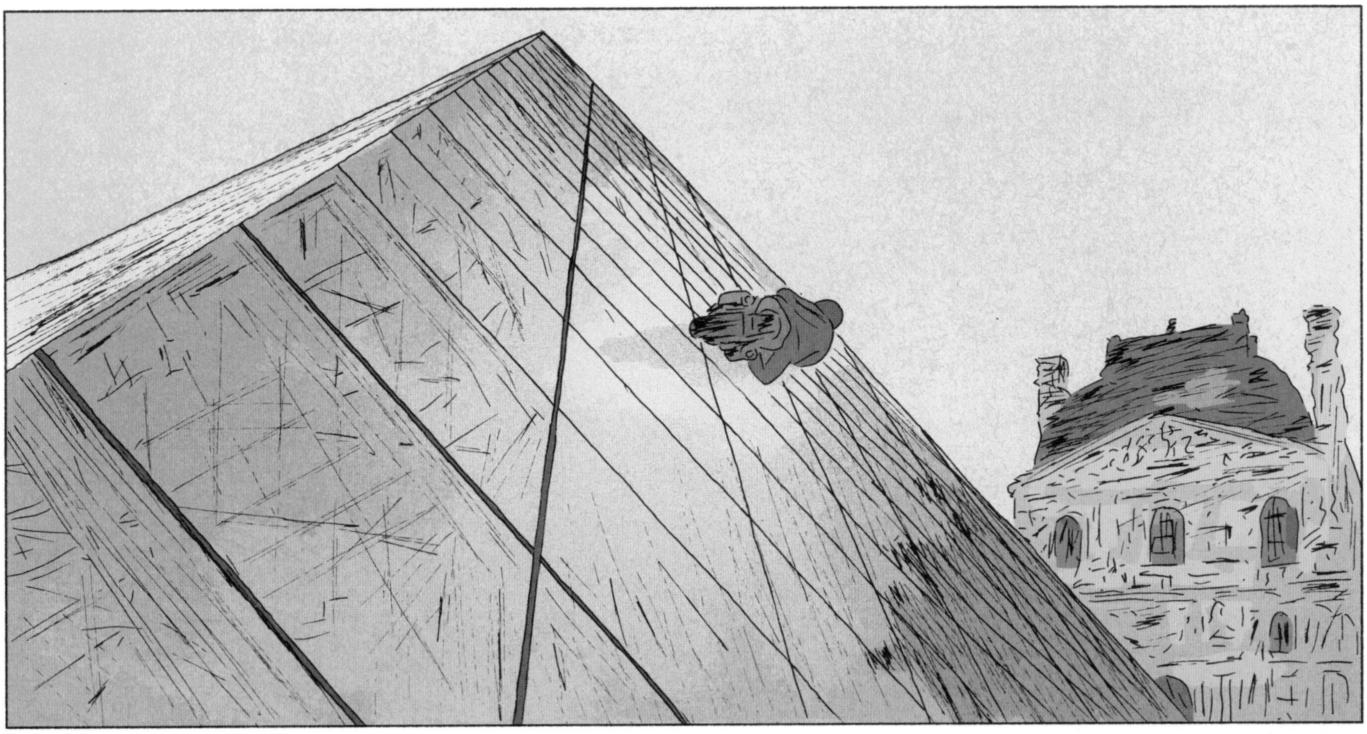

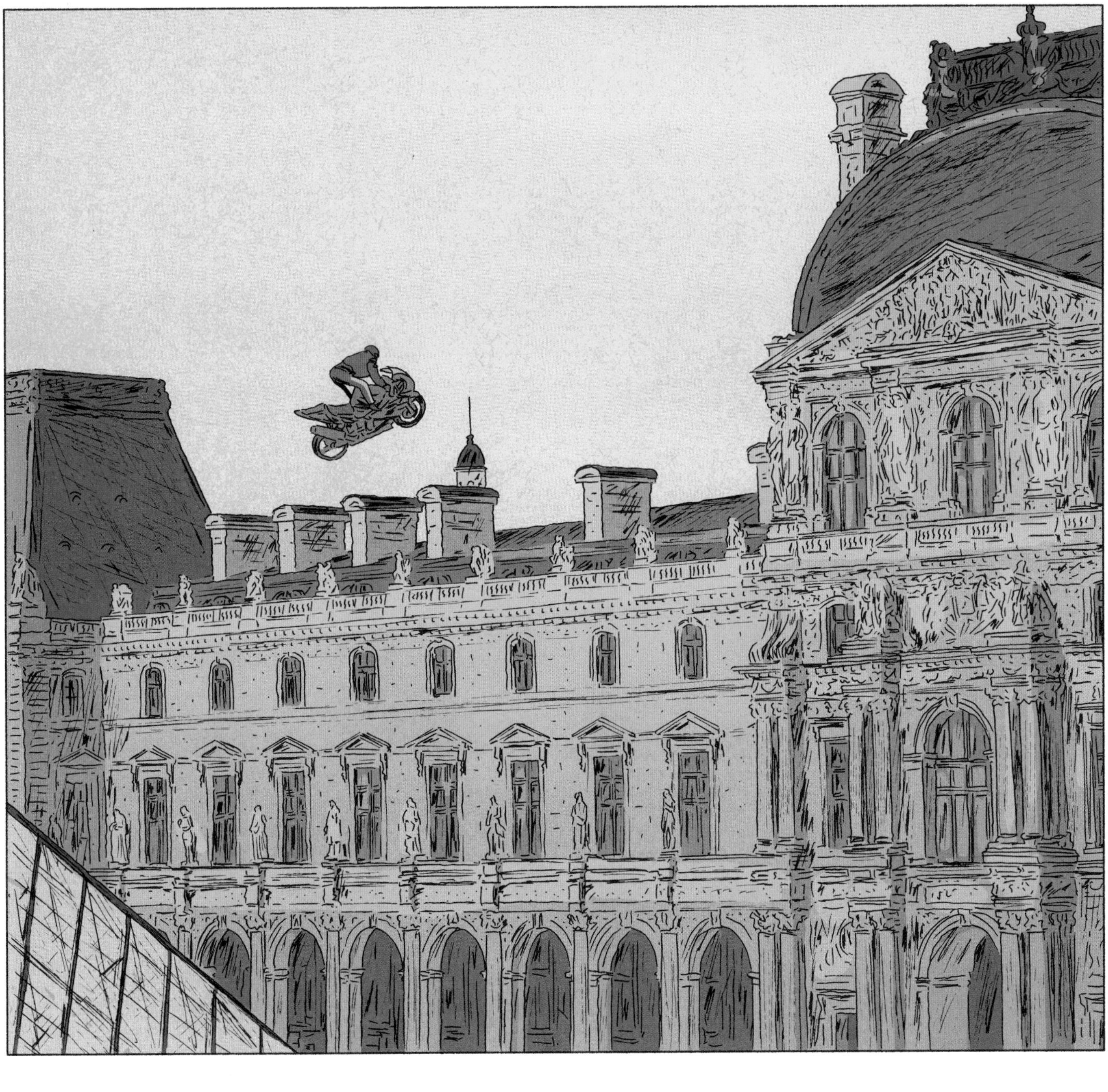

VERY WELL, SIR.
IT'S ALRIGHT. THE POLICE ARE COMING.

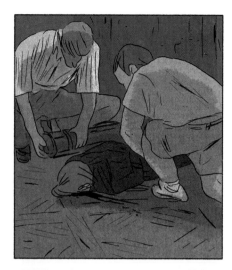

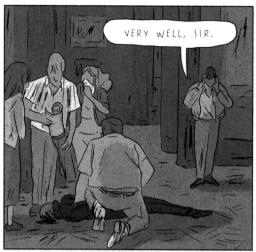

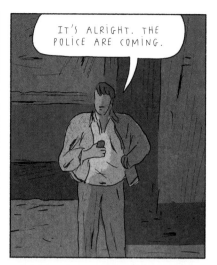

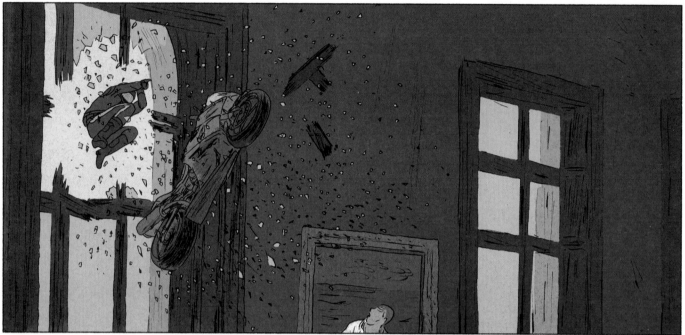

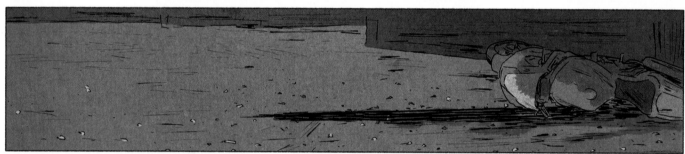

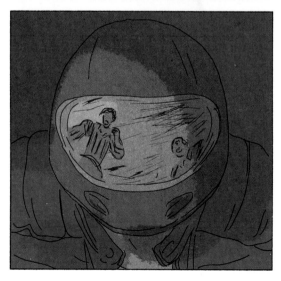

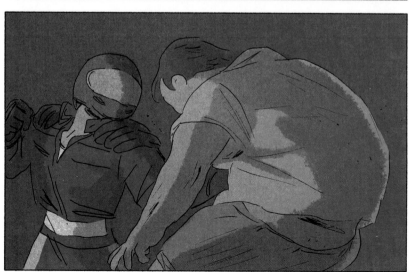

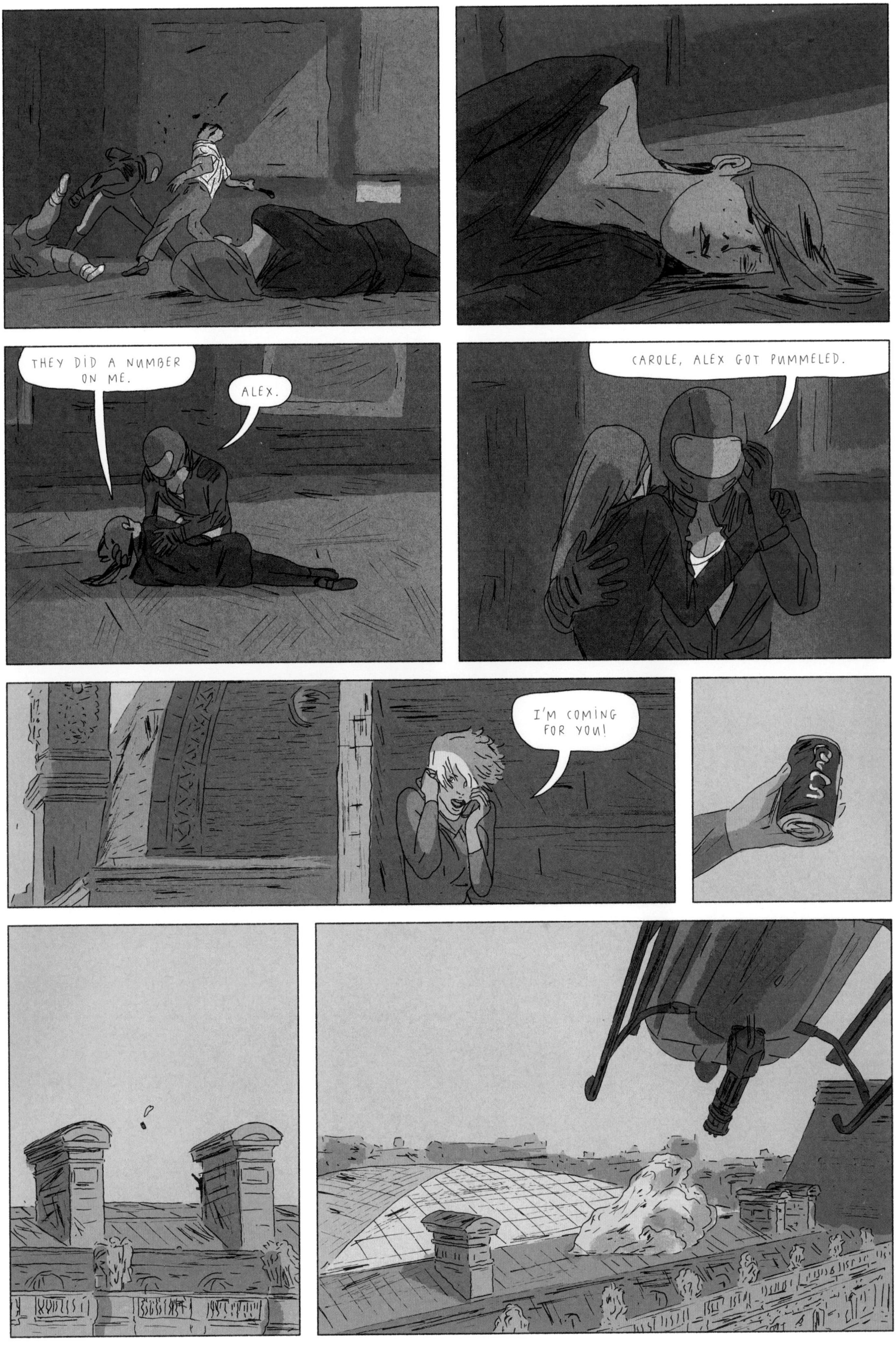
THEY DID A NUMBER ON ME.
ALEX.
CAROLE, ALEX GOT PUMMELED.
I'M COMING FOR YOU!

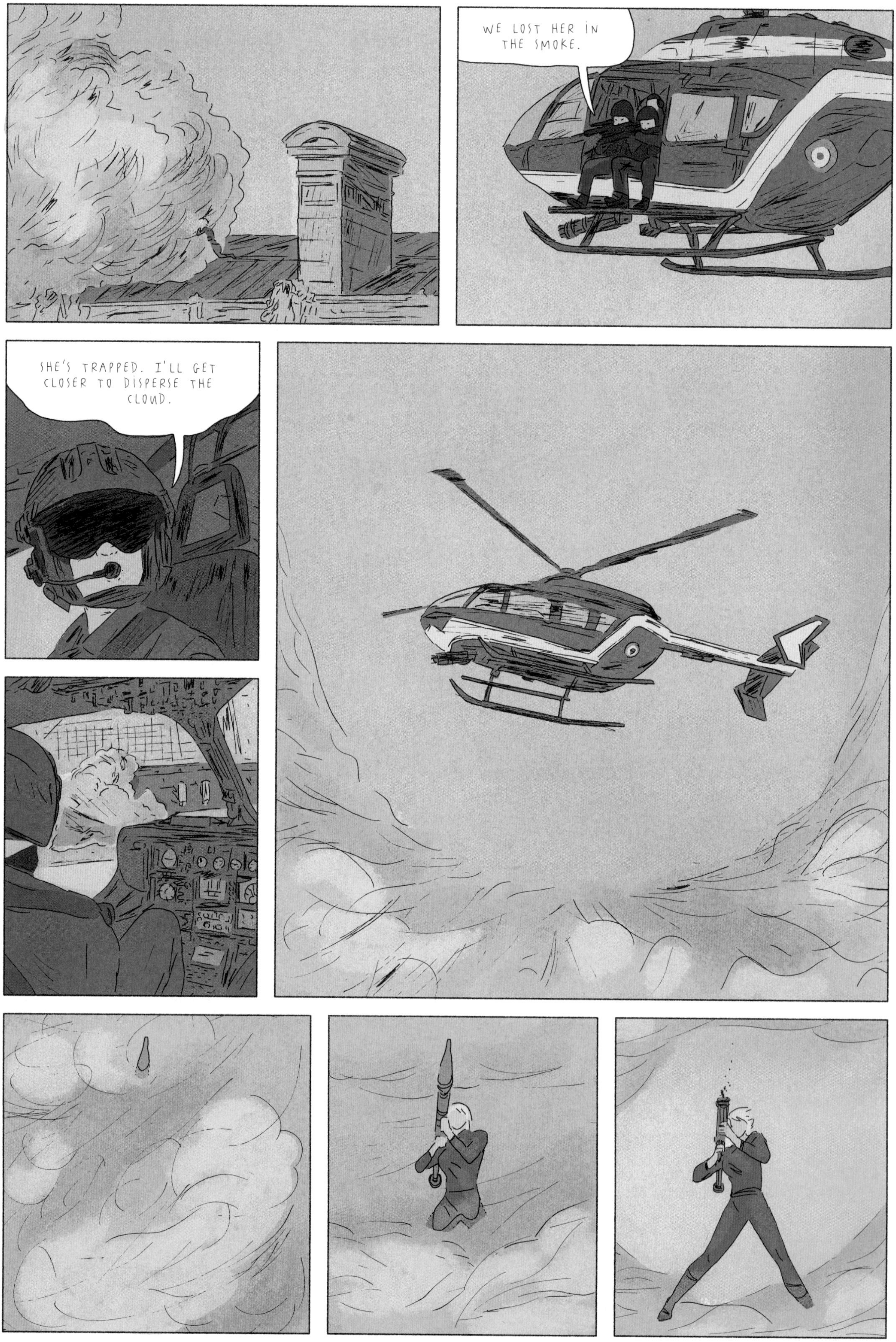
WE LOST HER IN THE SMOKE.
SHE'S TRAPPED. I'LL GET CLOSER TO DISPERSE THE CLOUD.

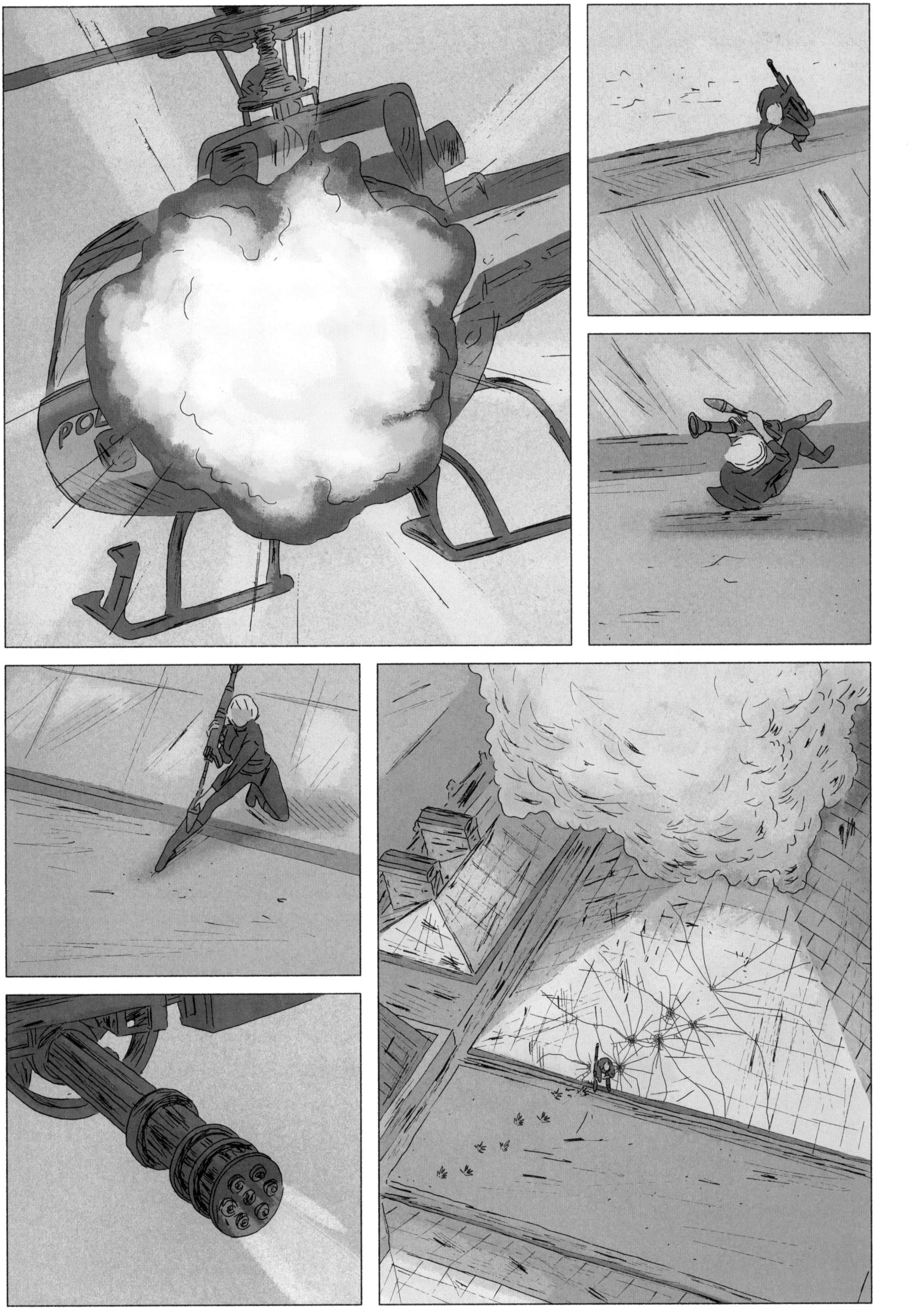

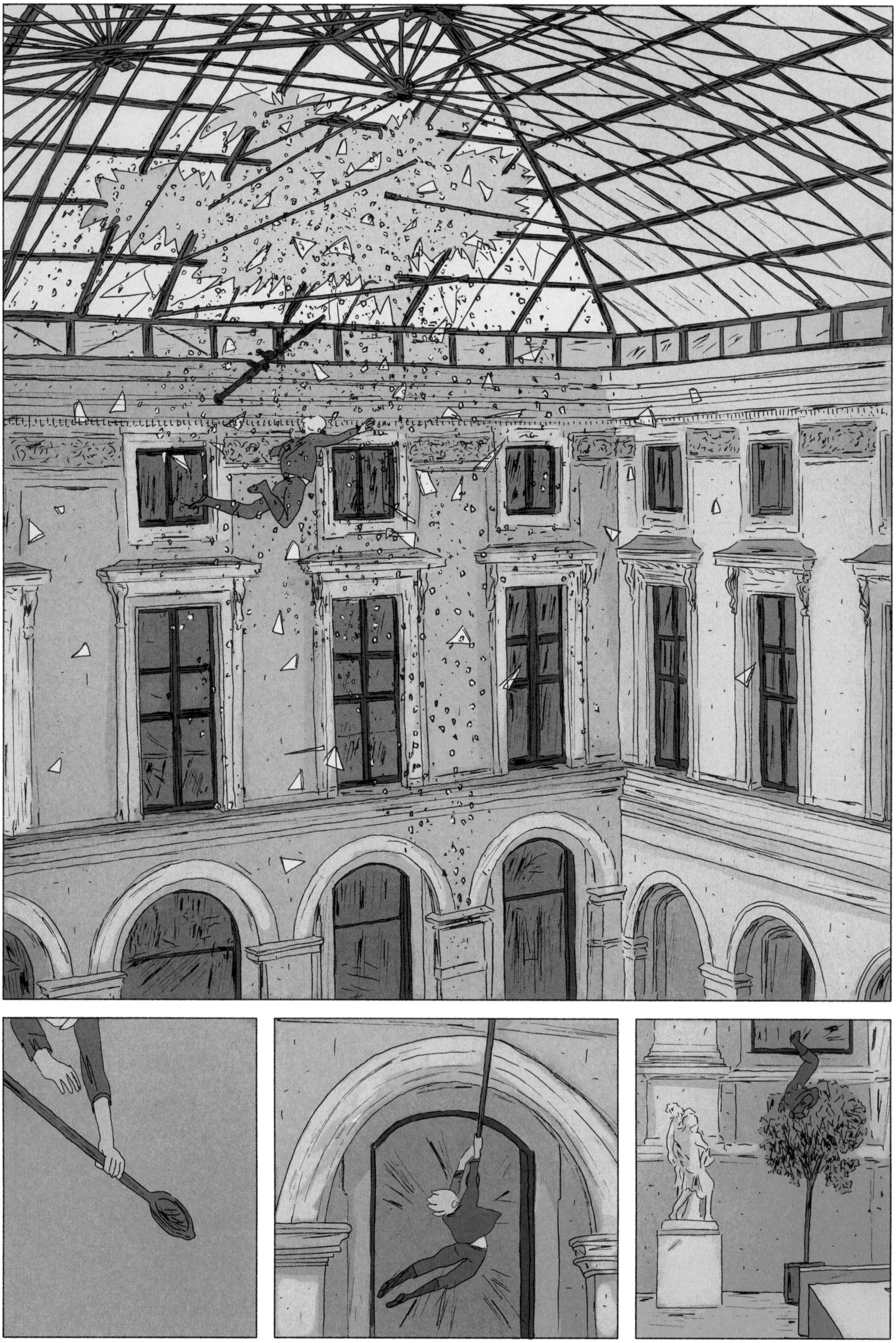

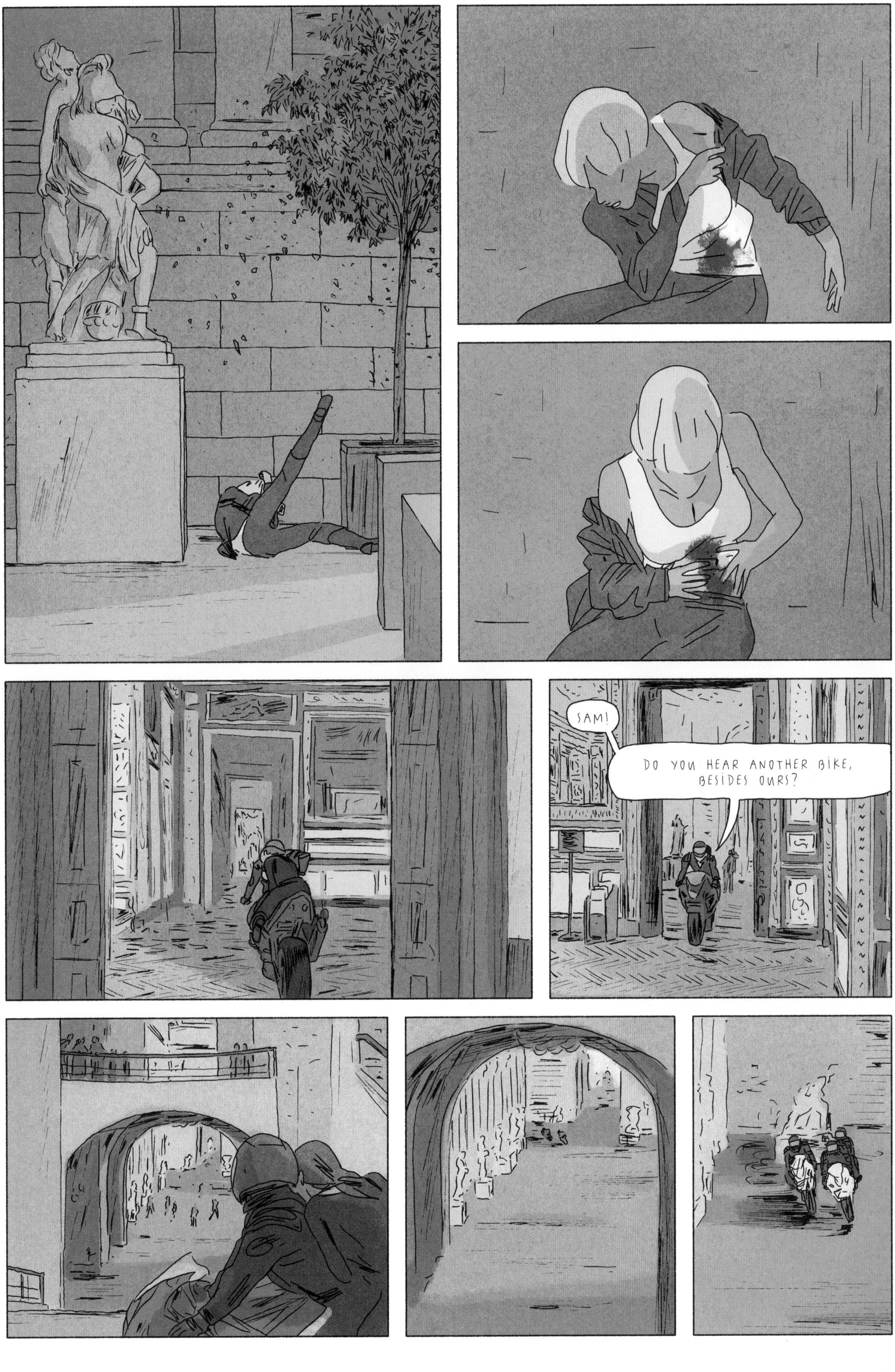
SAM!
DO YOU HEAR ANOTHER BIKE, BESIDES OURS?

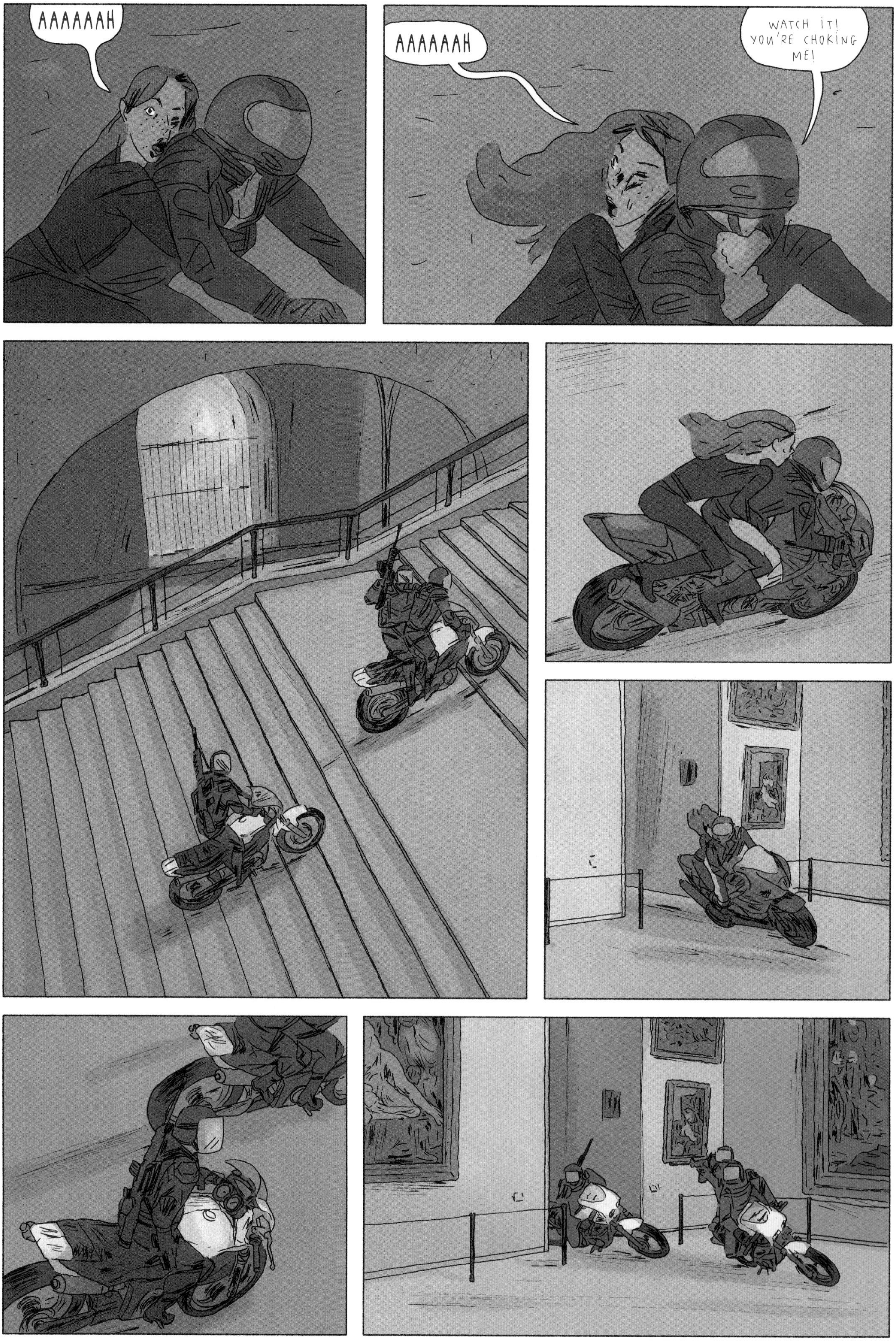
AAAAAAH
AAAAAAH
WATCH IT! YOU'RE CHOKING ME!

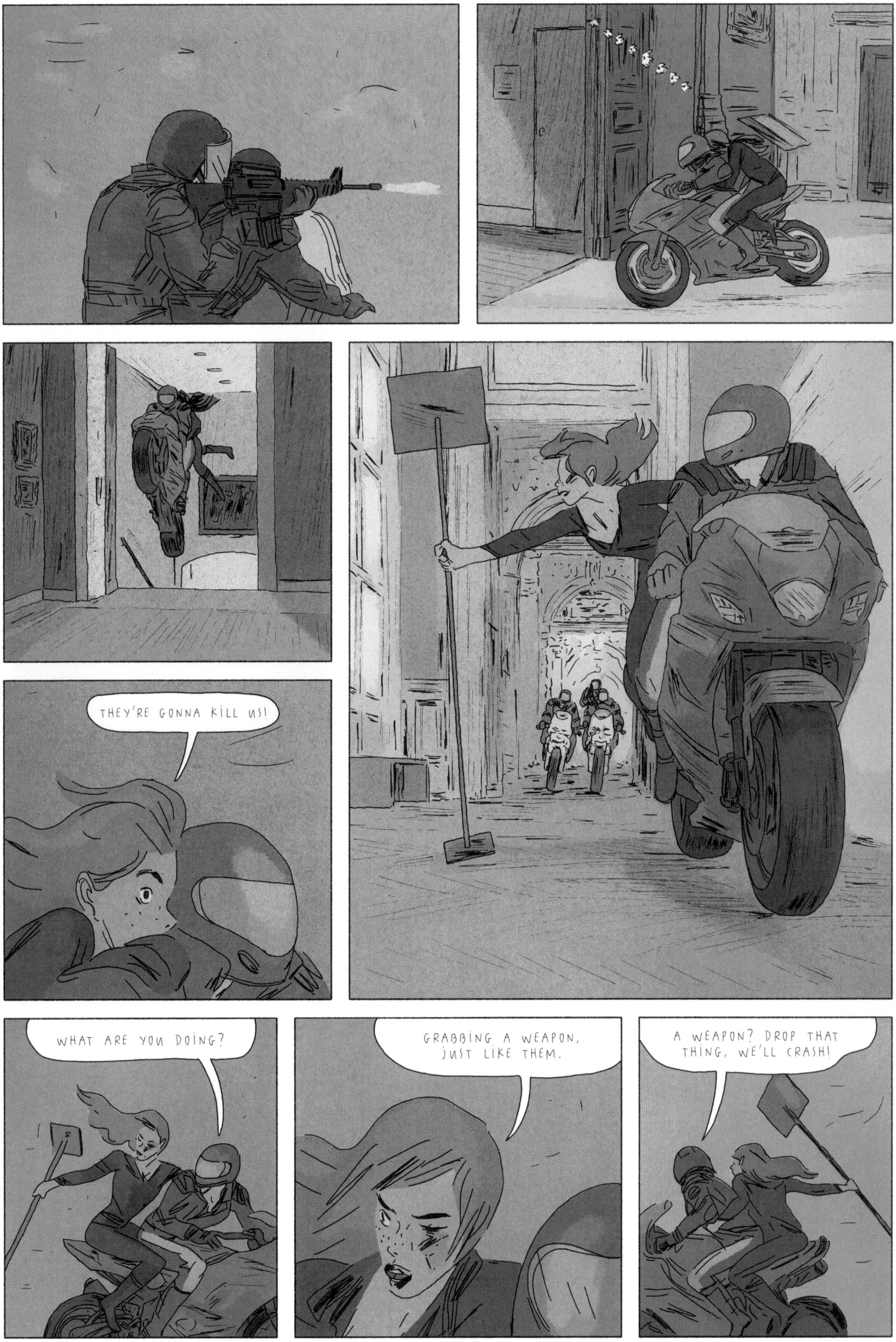
THEY'RE GONNA KILL US!
WHAT ARE YOU DOING?
GRABBING A WEAPON, JUST LIKE THEM.
A WEAPON? DROP THAT THING, WE'LL CRASH!

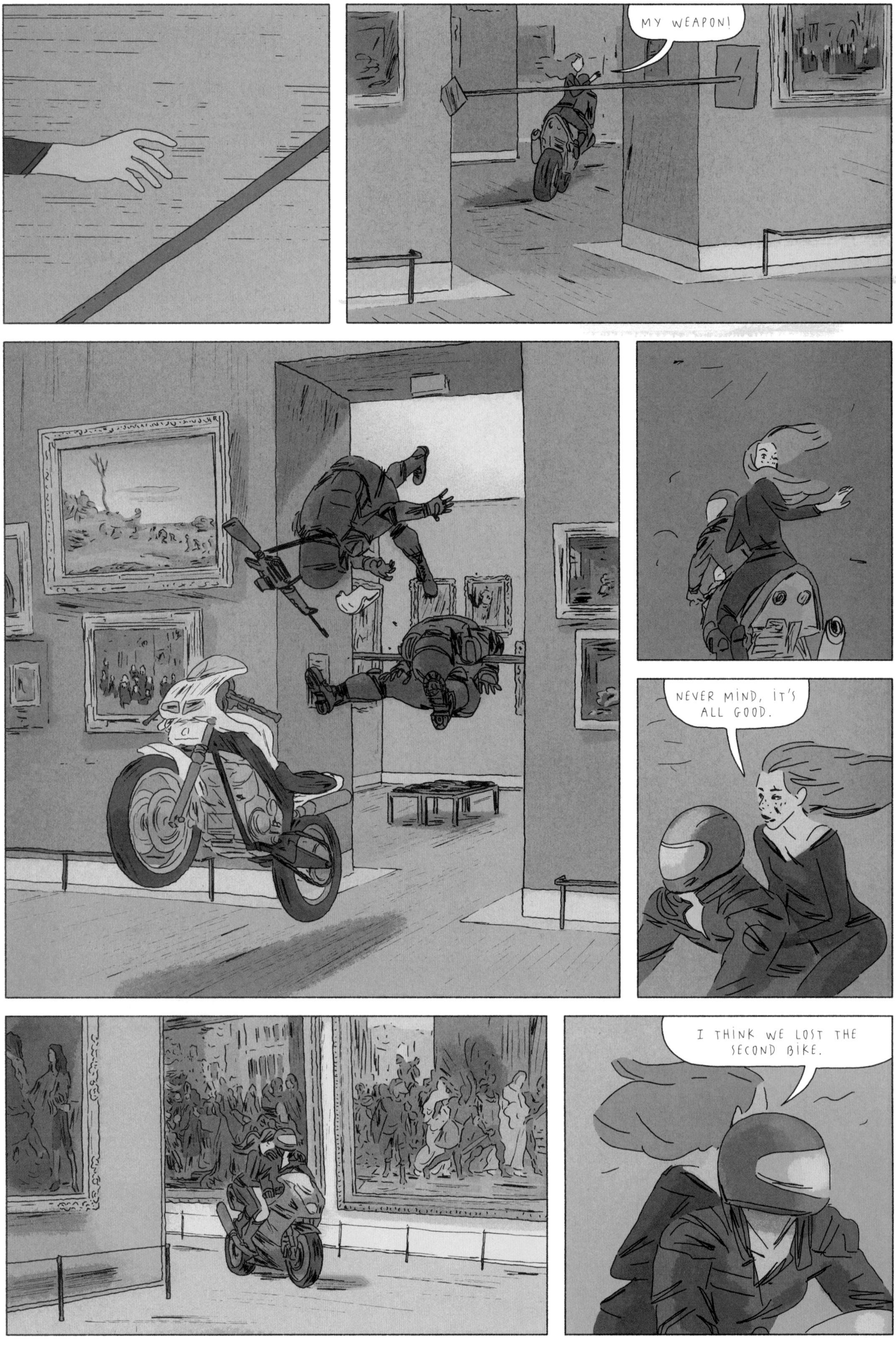
MY WEAPON!
NEVER MIND, IT'S ALL GOOD.
I THINK WE LOST THE SECOND BIKE.

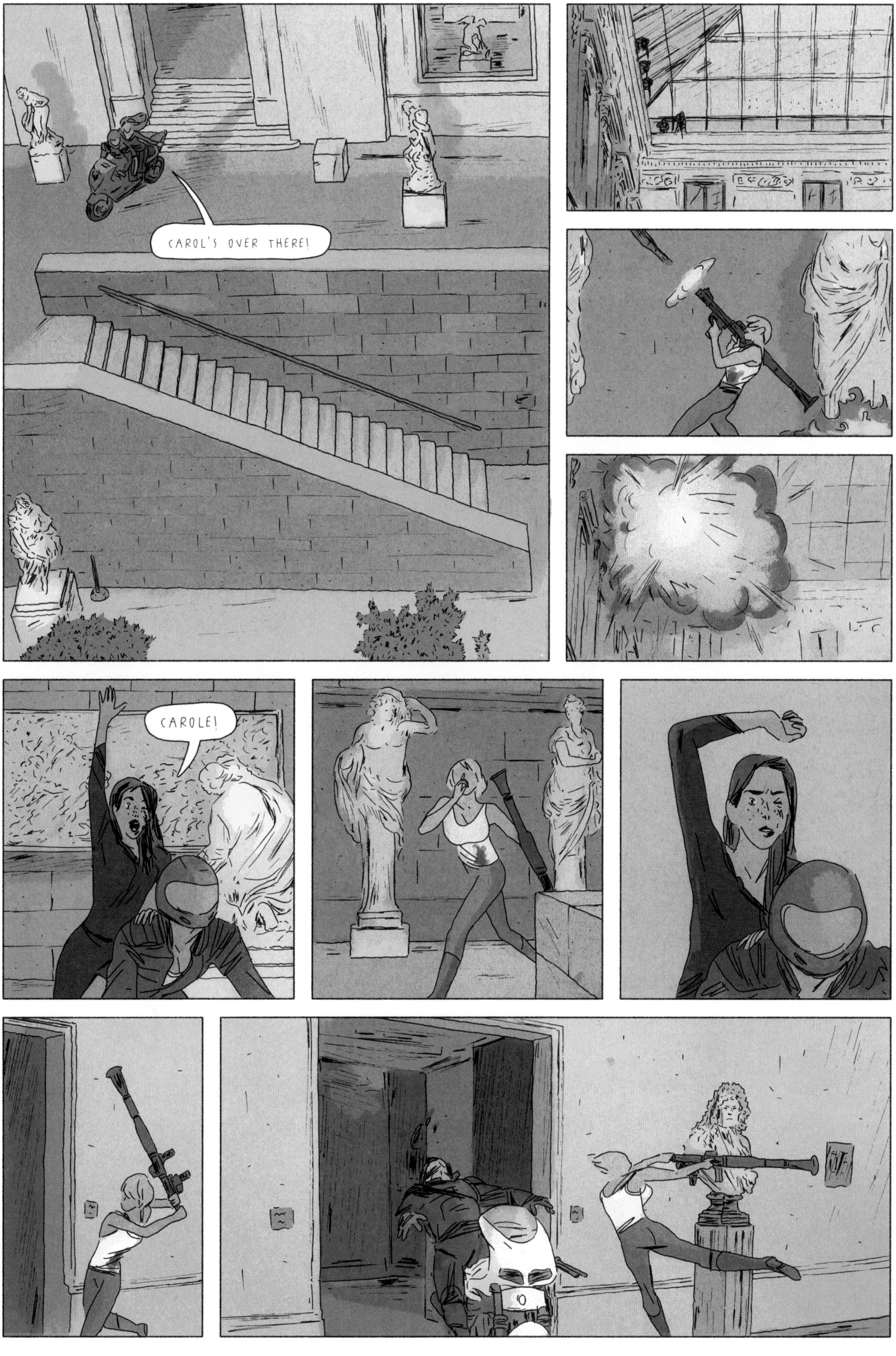
CAROL'S OVER THERE!
CAROLE!

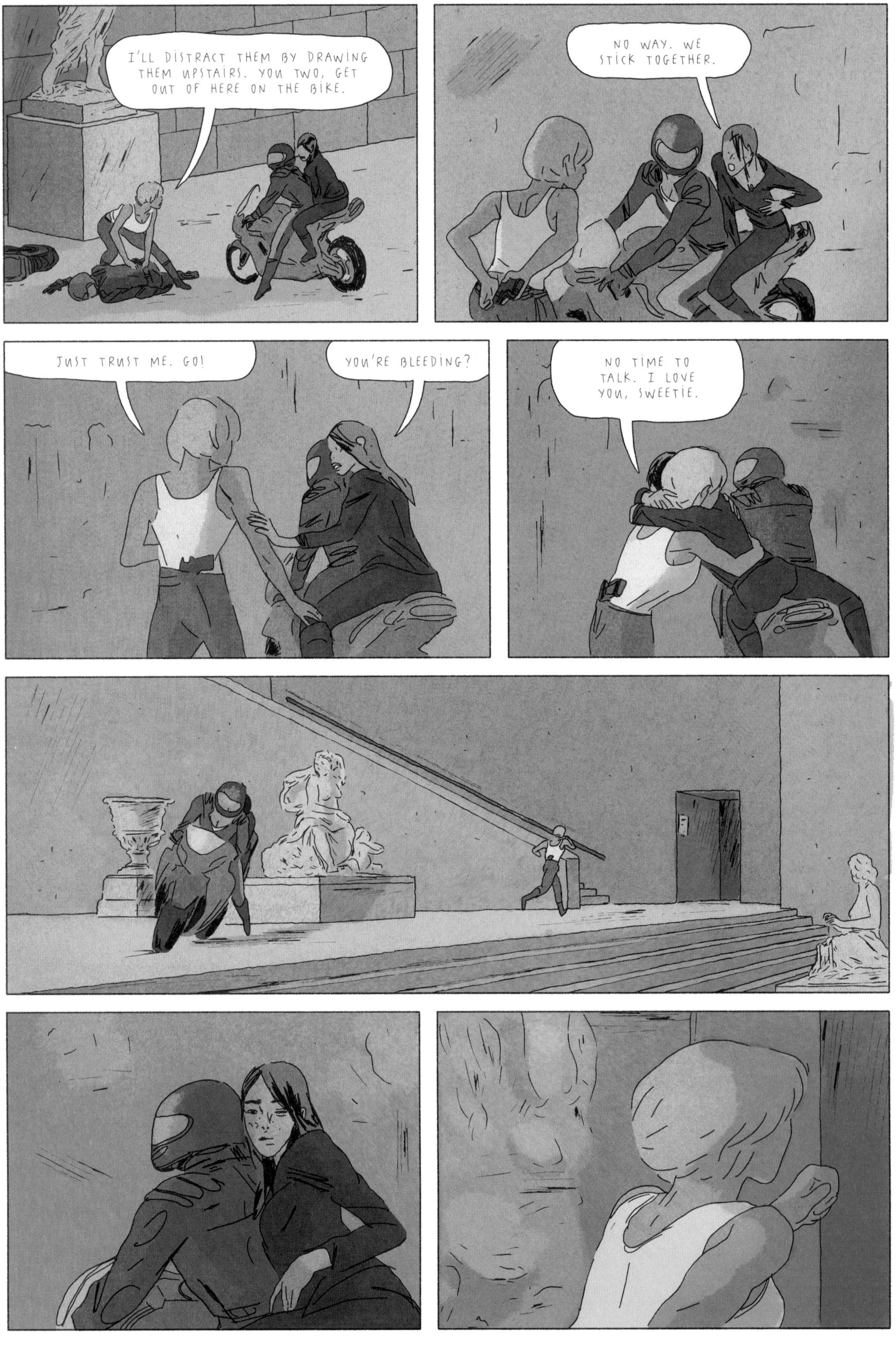
I'LL DISTRACT THEM BY DRAWING THEM UPSTAIRS. YOU TWO, GET OUT OF HERE ON THE BIKE.
NO WAY. WE STICK TOGETHER.
JUST TRUST ME. GO!
YOU'RE BLEEDING?
NO TIME TO TALK. I LOVE YOU, SWEETIE.

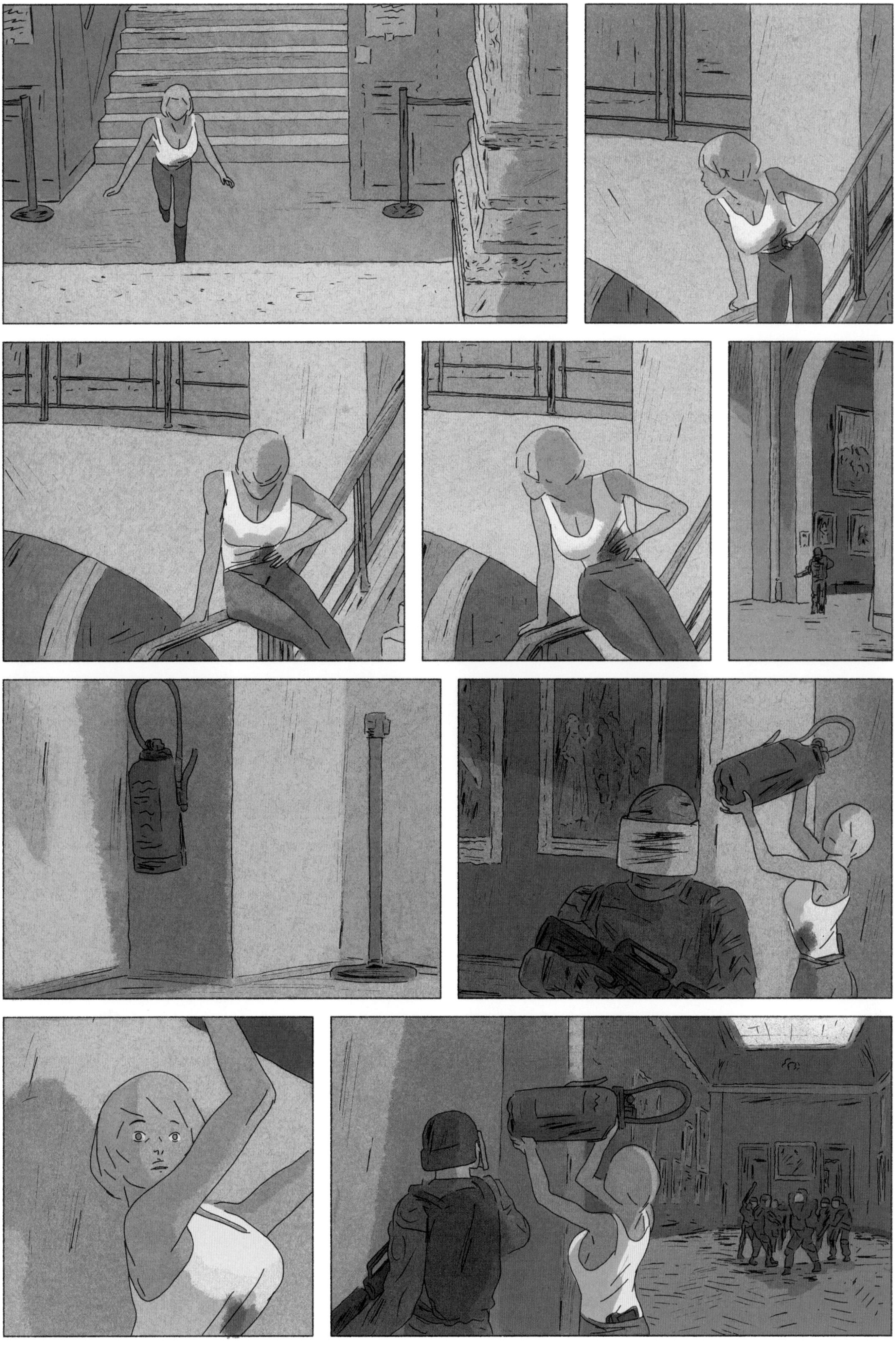

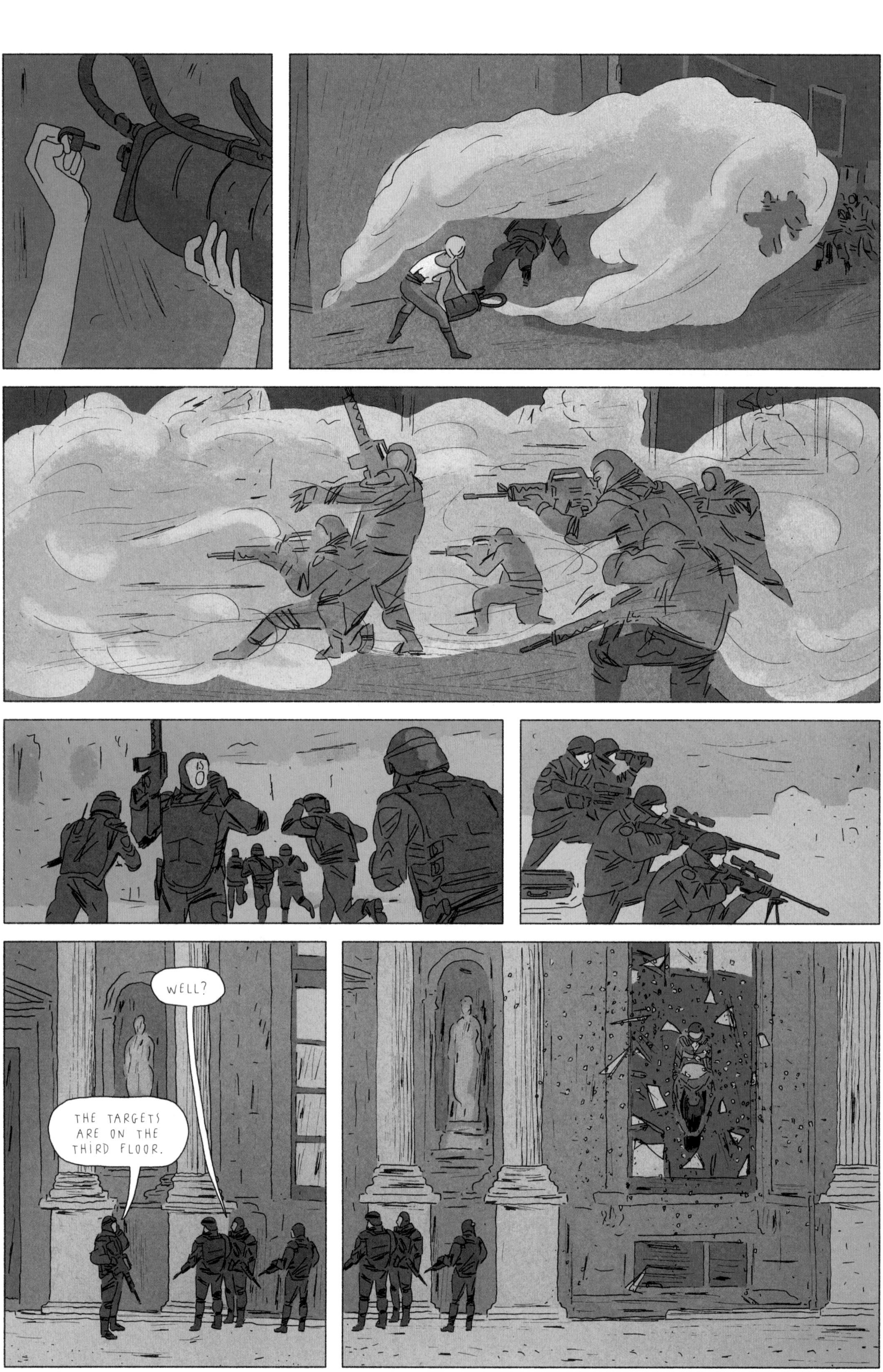
WELL?
THE TARGETS ARE ON THE THIRD FLOOR.

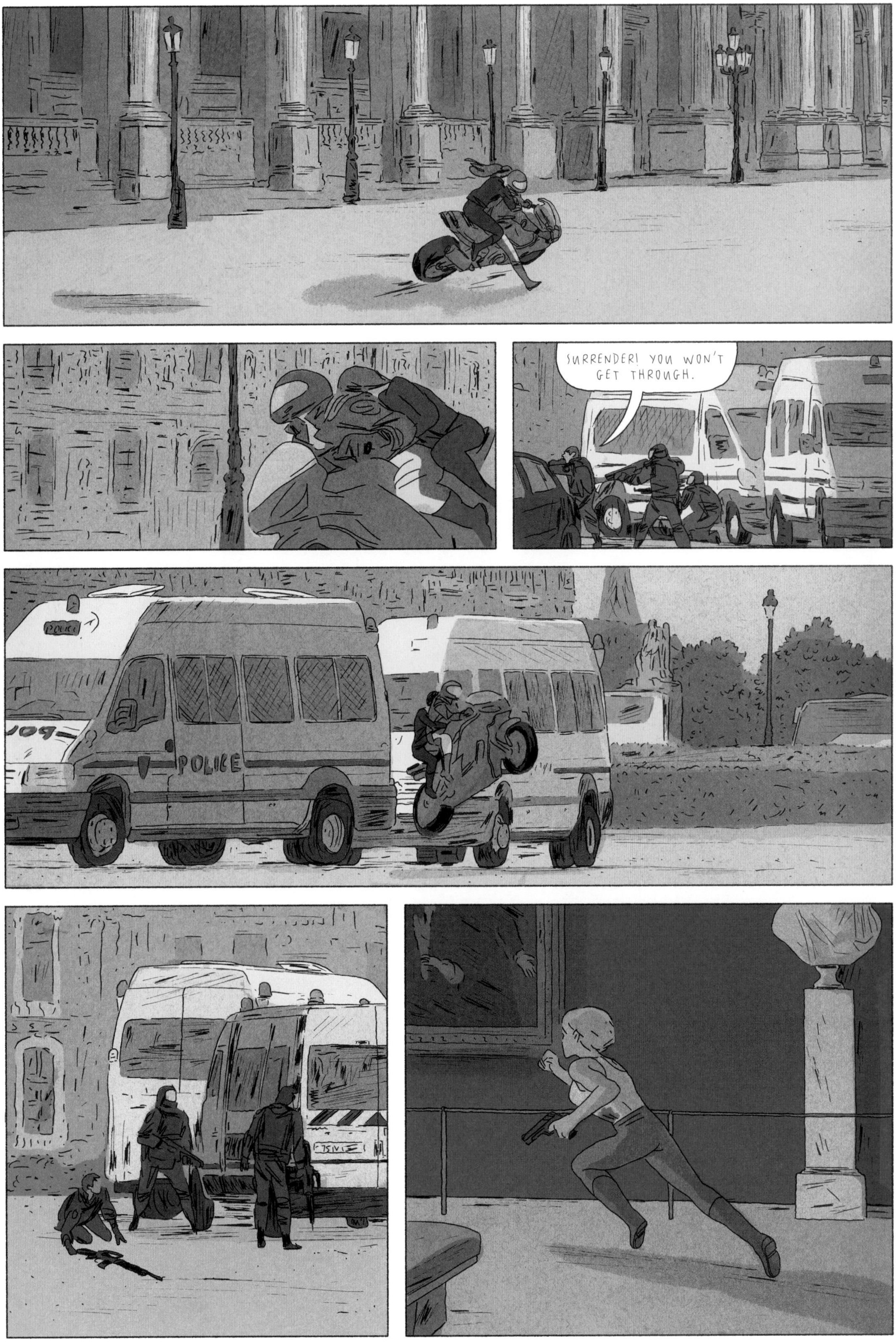
SURRENDER! YOU WON'T GET THROUGH.
POLICE
POLICE

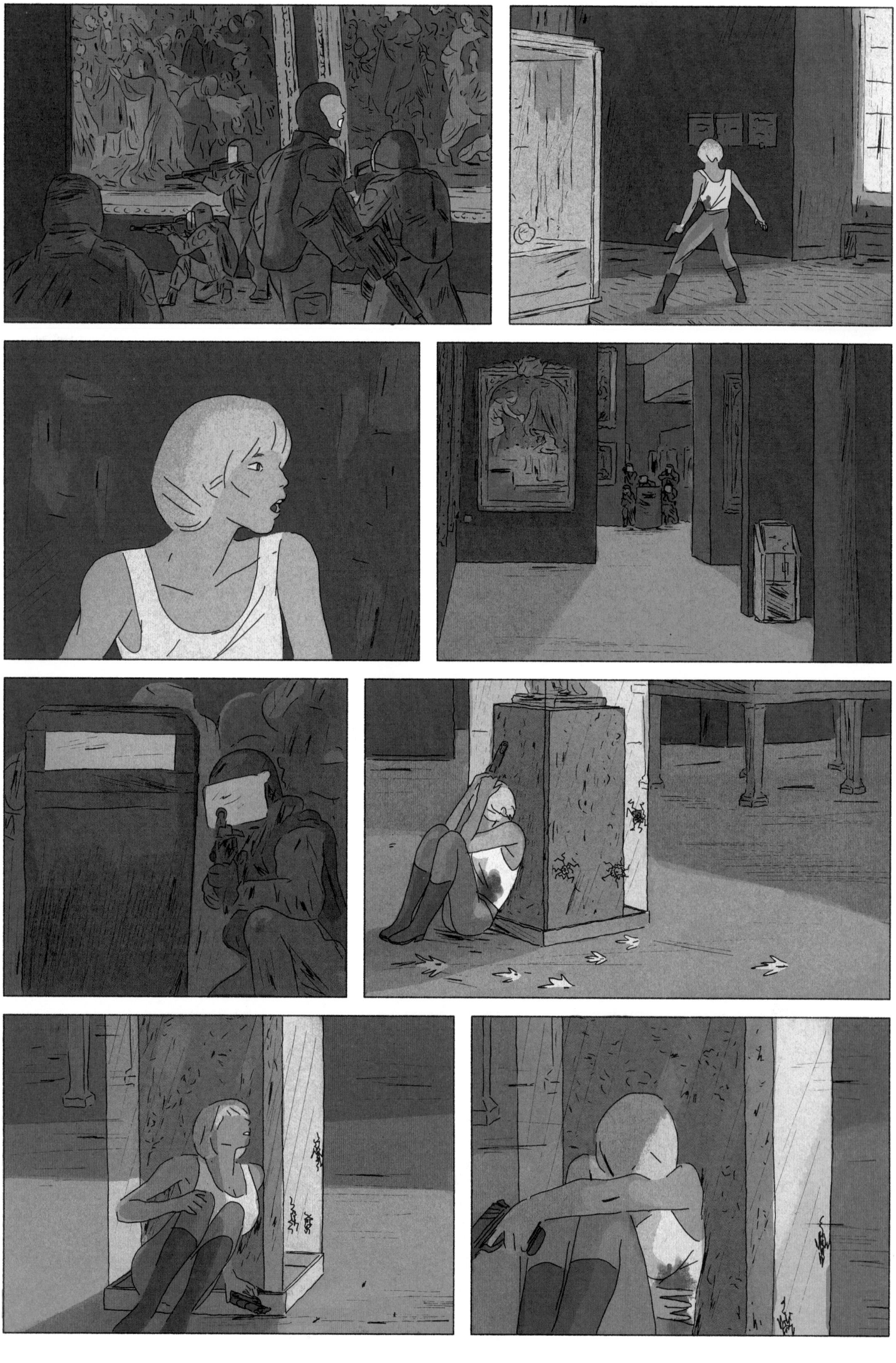

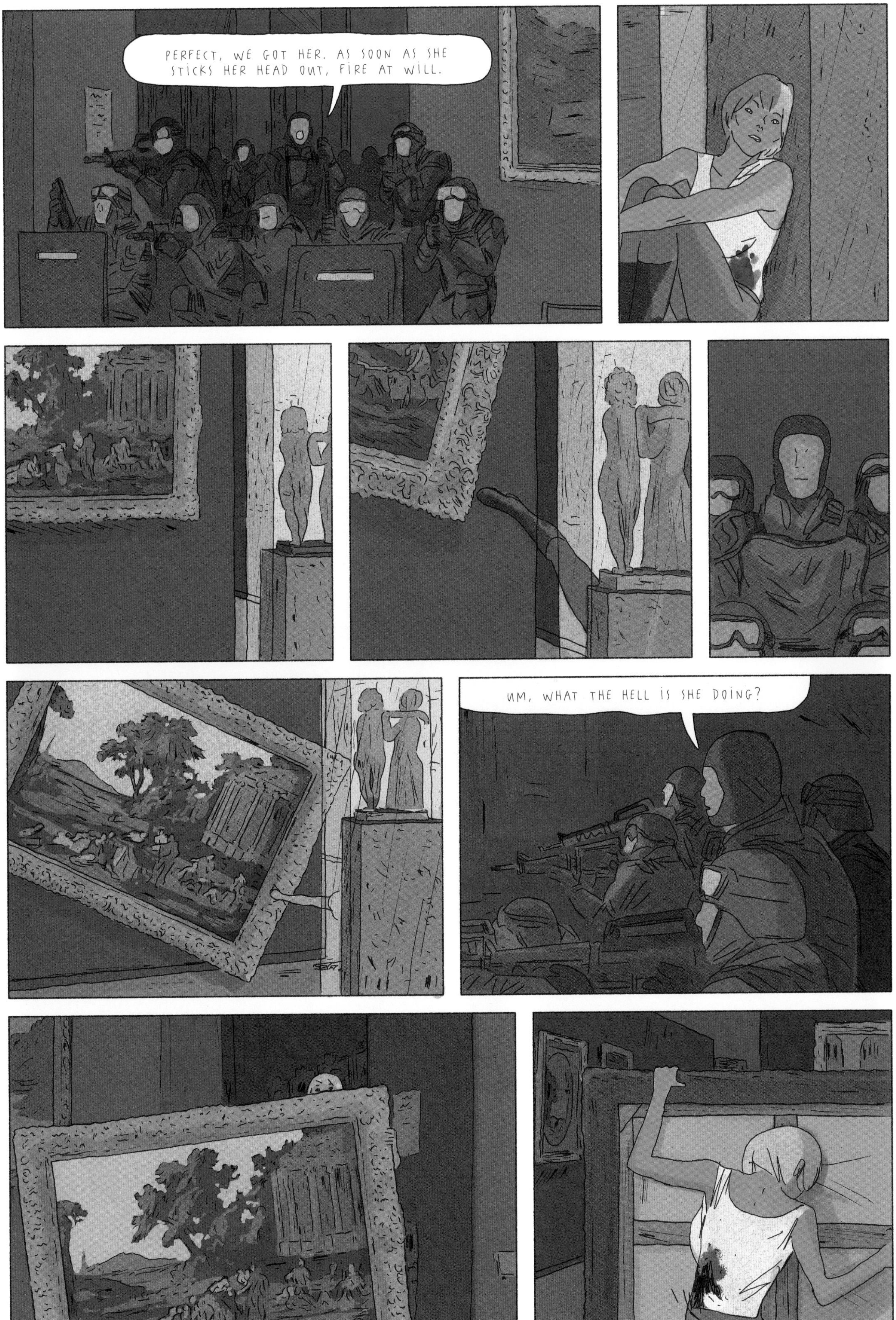
PERFECT, WE GOT HER. AS SOON AS SHE STICKS HER HEAD OUT, FIRE AT WILL.
UM, WHAT THE HELL IS SHE DOING?

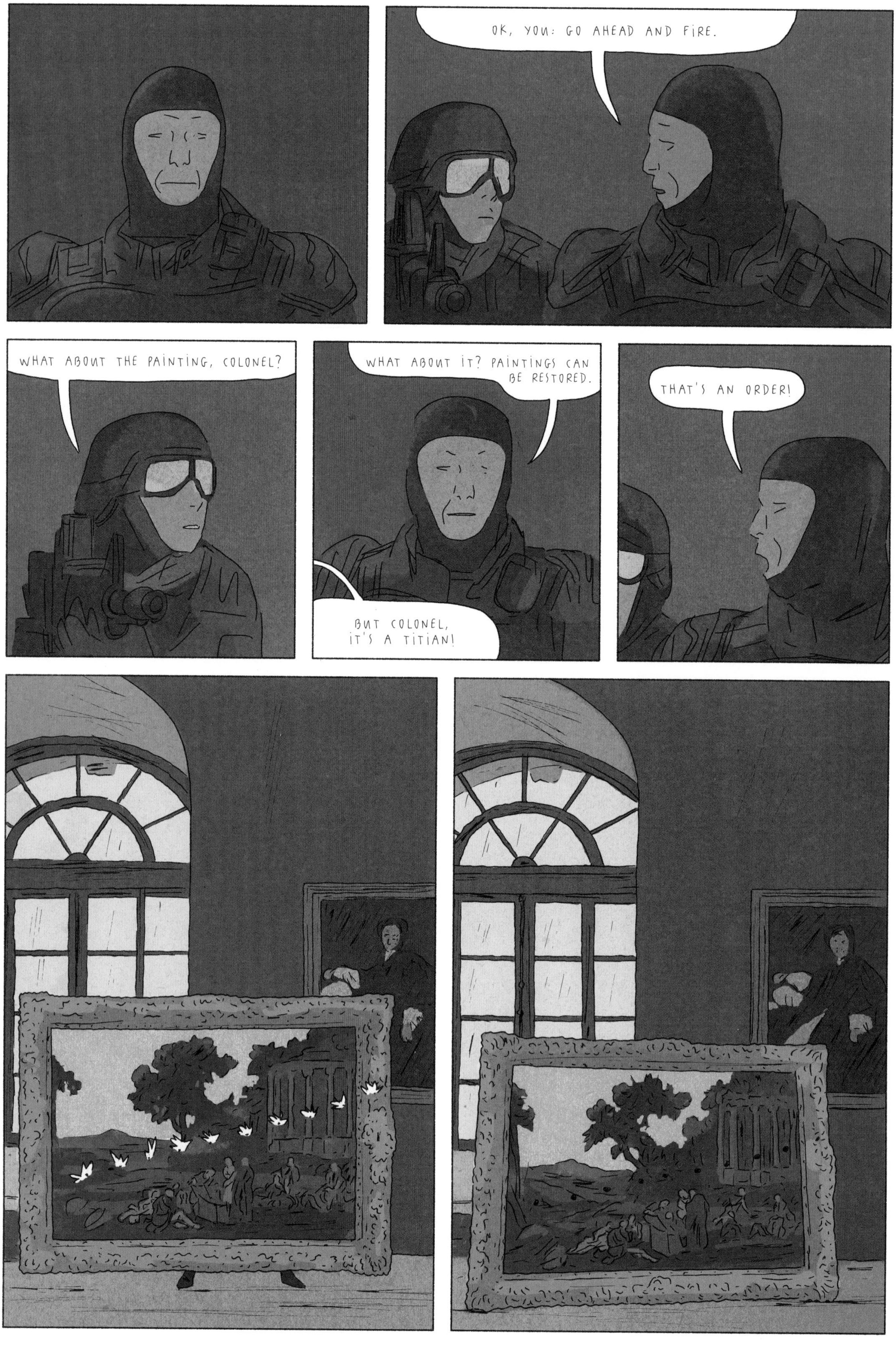
OK, YOU: GO AHEAD AND FIRE.
WHAT ABOUT THE PAINTING, COLONEL?
WHAT ABOUT IT? PAINTINGS CAN BE RESTORED.
BUT COLONEL, IT'S A TITIAN!
THAT'S AN ORDER!

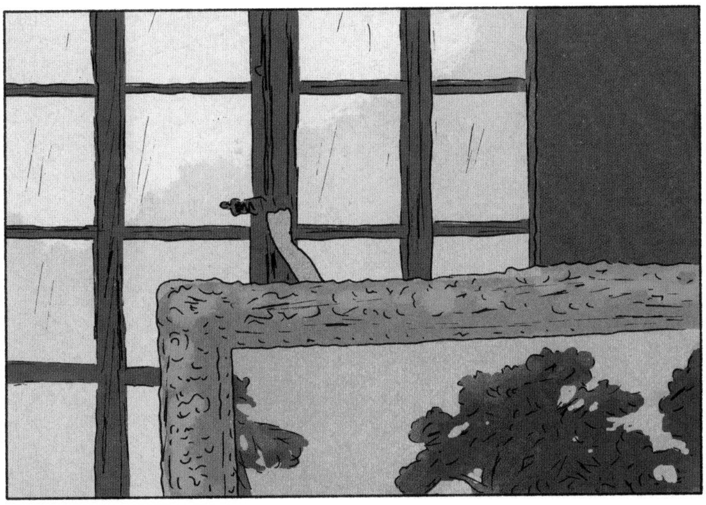

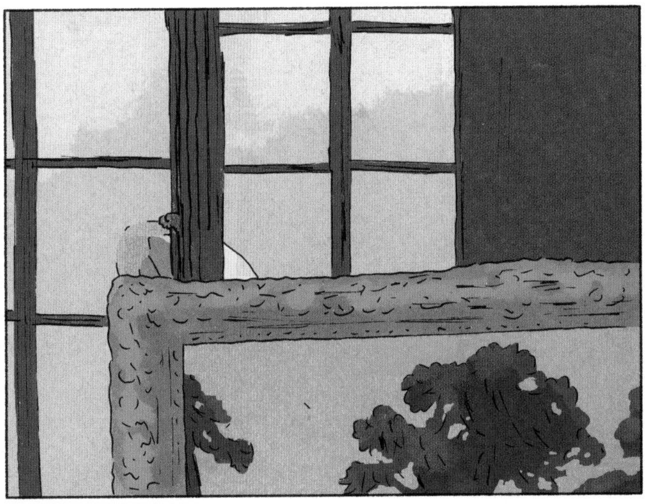

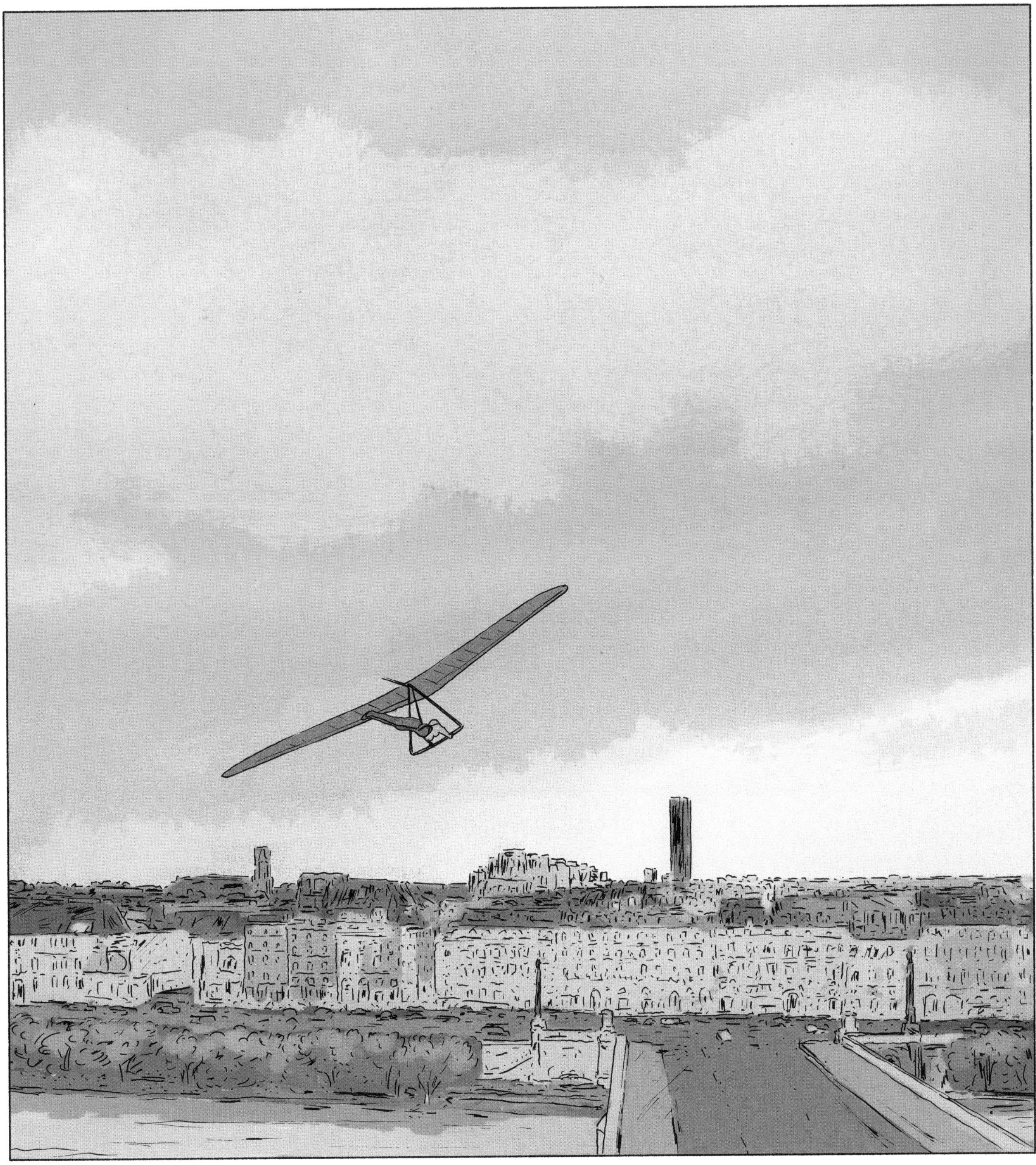

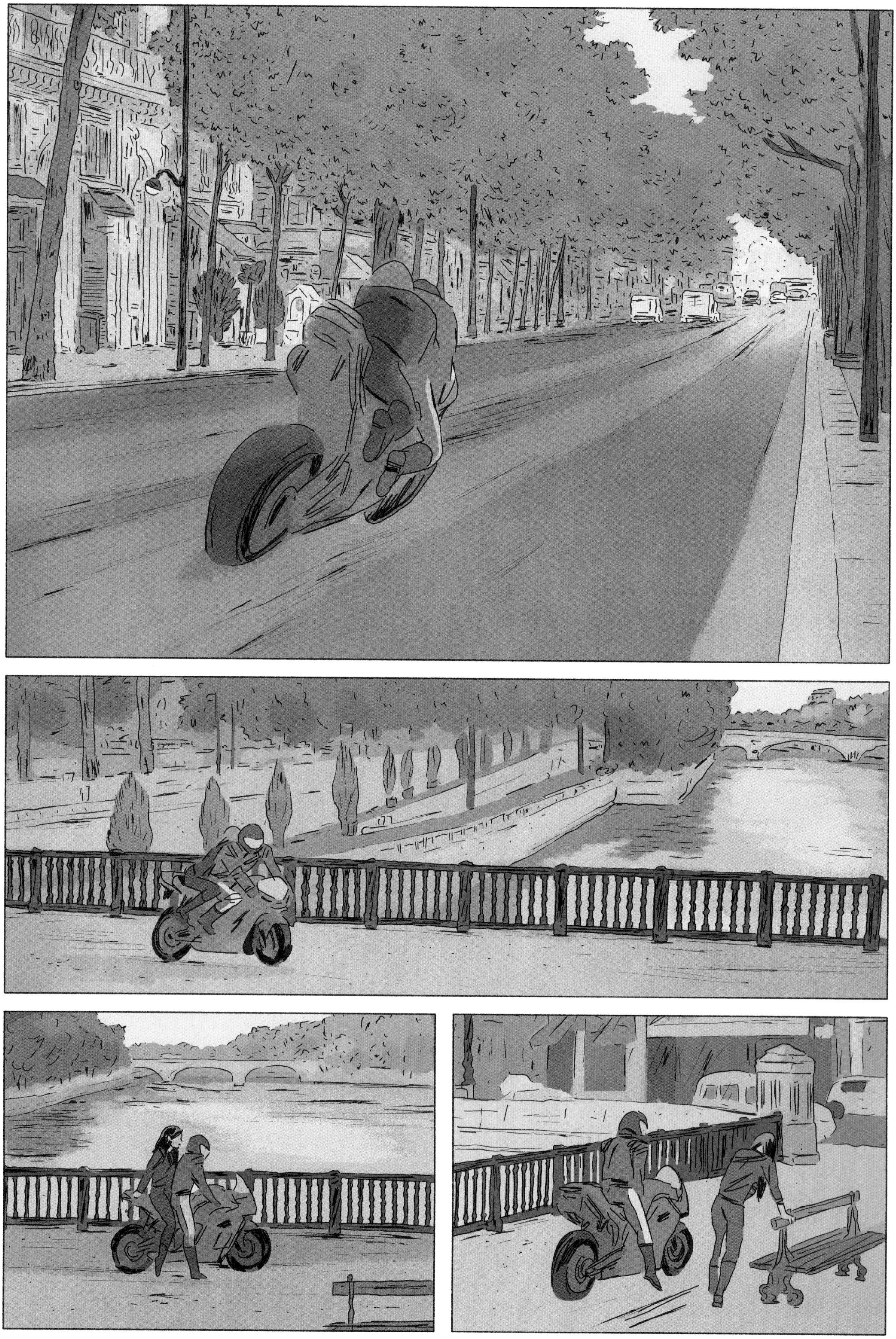

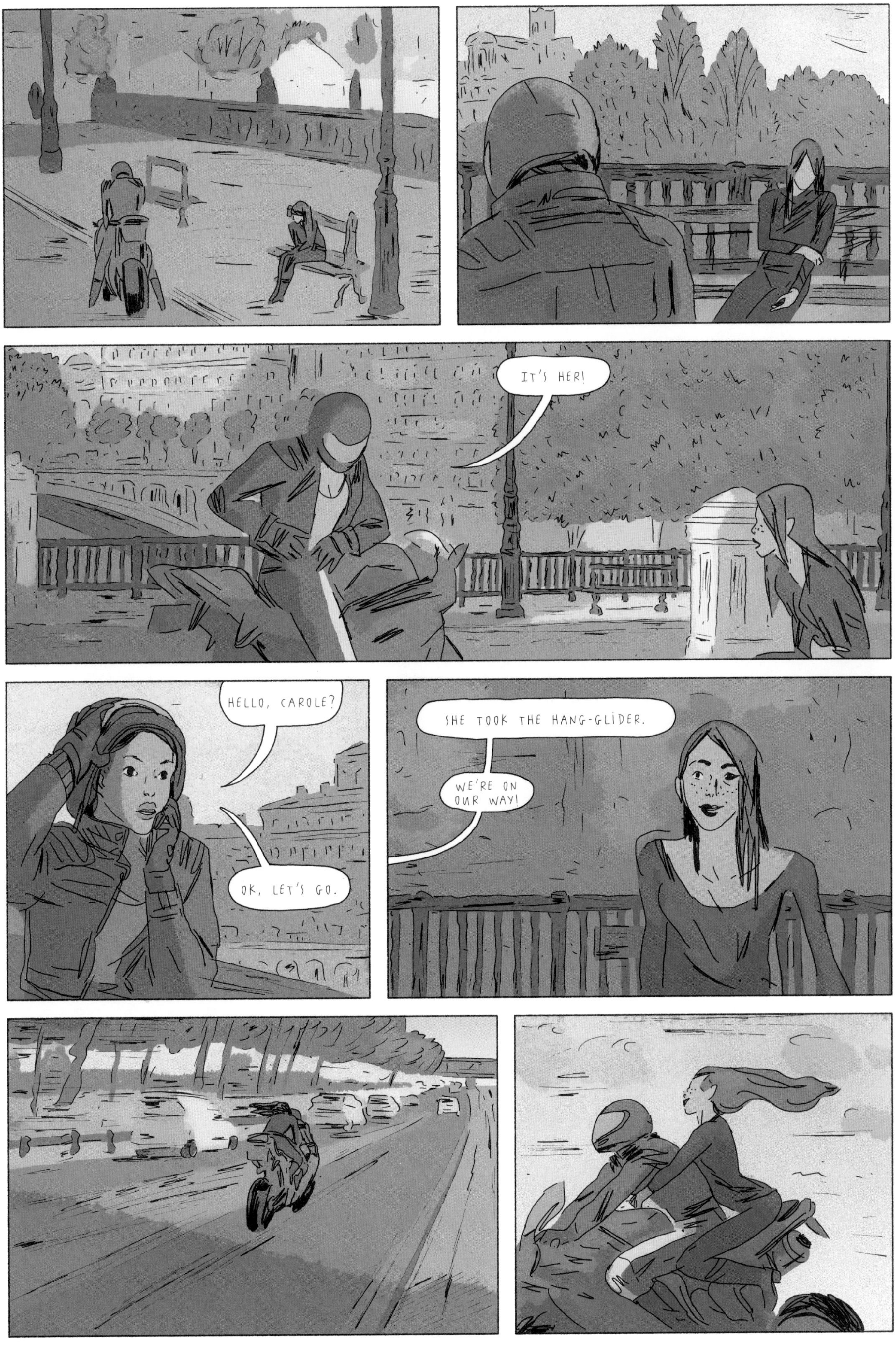
IT'S HER!
HELLO, CAROLE?
OK, LET'S GO.
SHE TOOK THE HANG-GLIDER.
WE'RE ON OUR WAY!

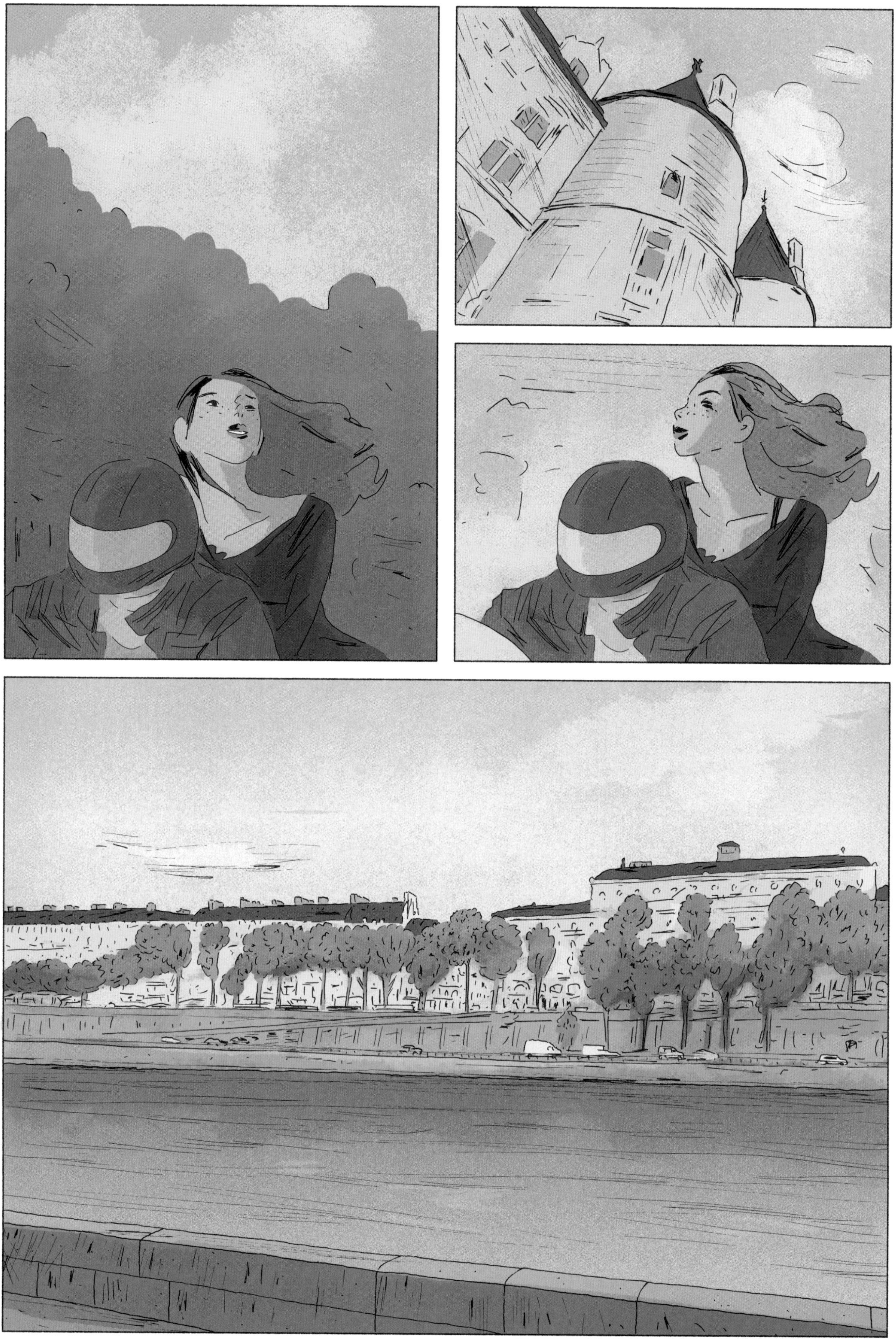

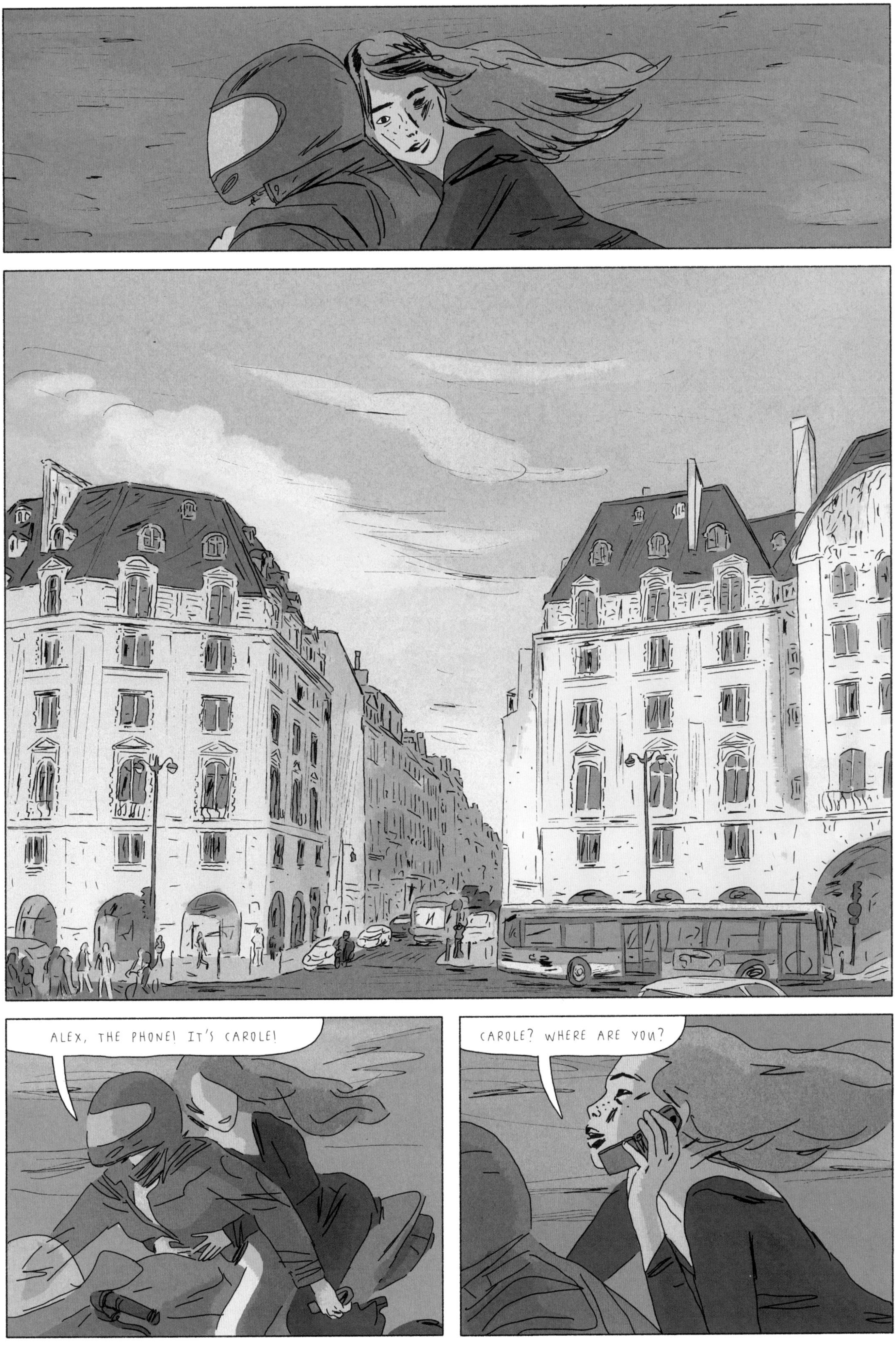
ALEX, THE PHONE! IT'S CAROLE!
CAROLE? WHERE ARE YOU?

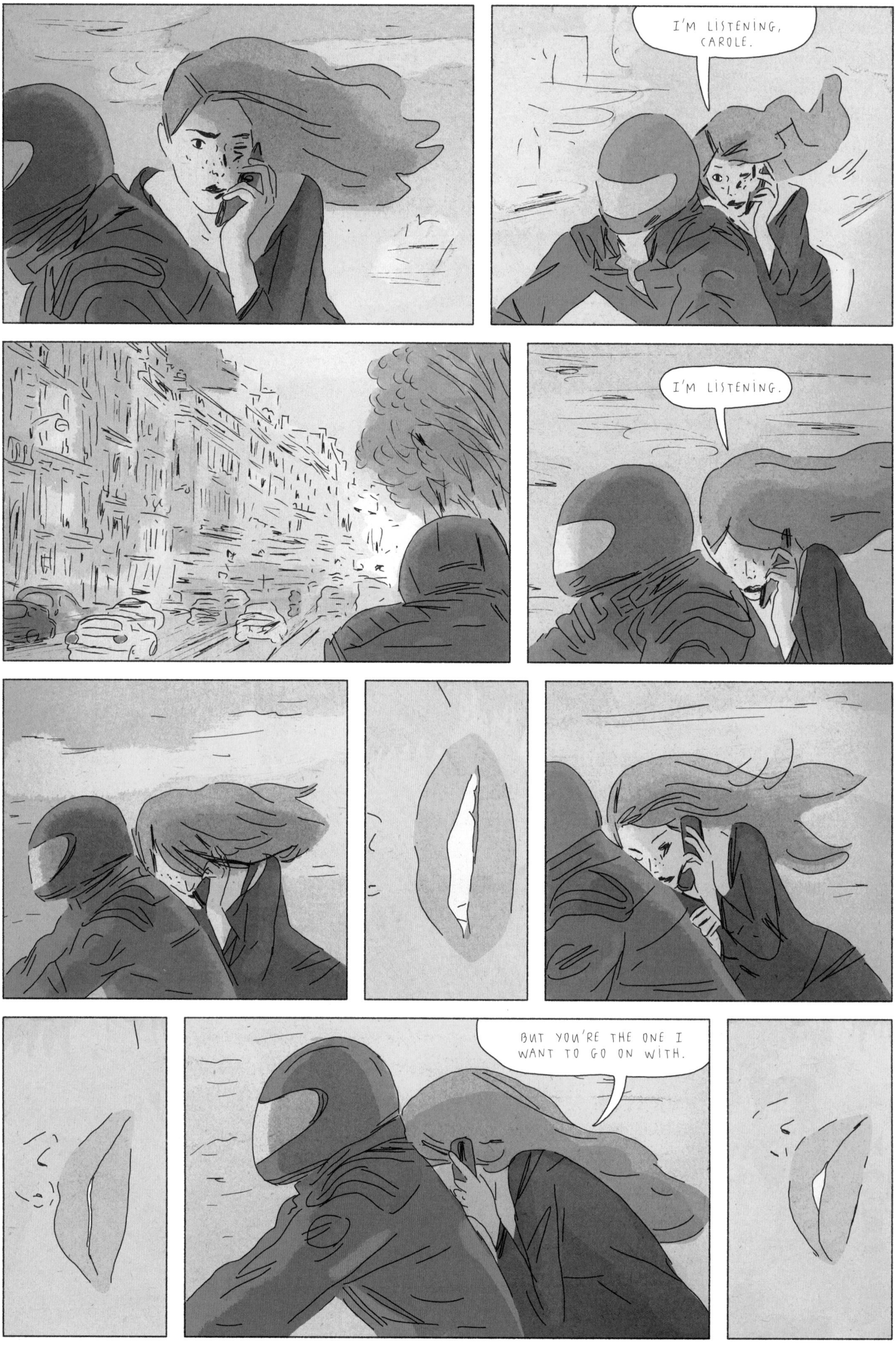
I'M LISTENING, CAROLE.
I'M LISTENING.
BUT YOU'RE THE ONE I WANT TO GO ON WITH.

DON'T LEAVE ME ALL ALONE, CAROLE... PLEASE.

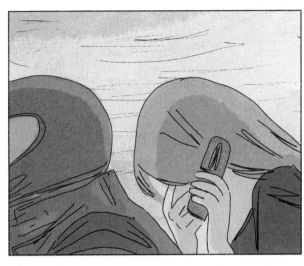

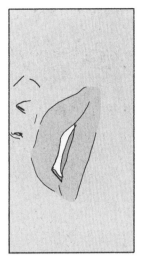

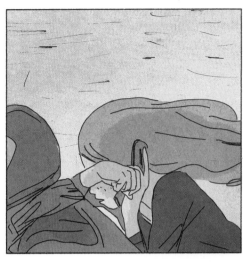

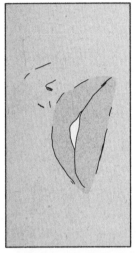

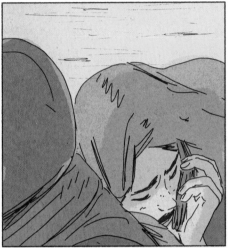

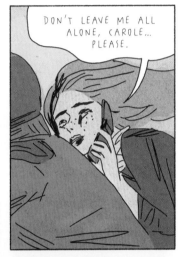

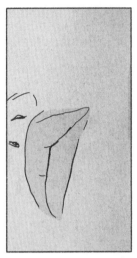

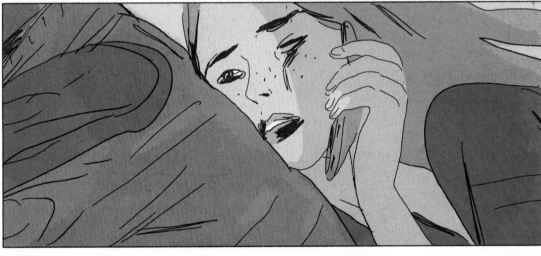

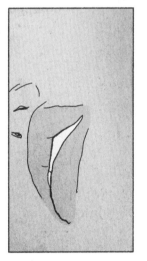

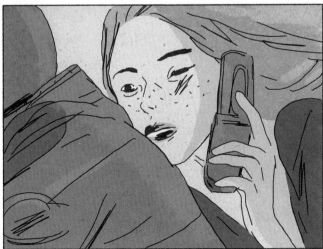

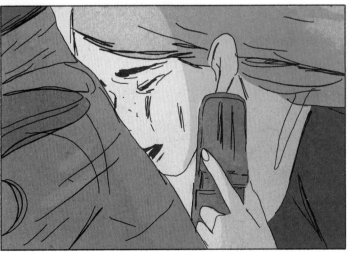

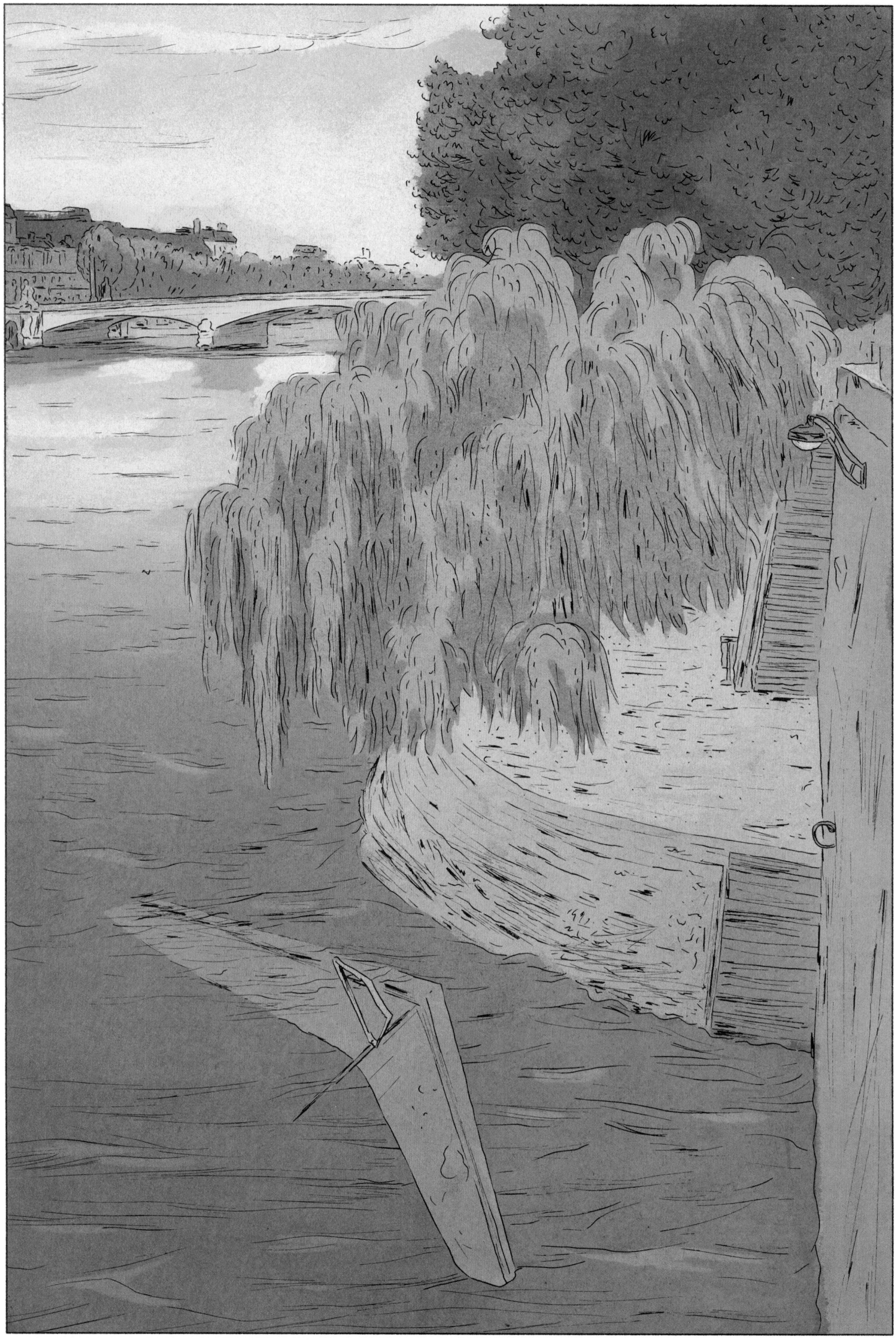

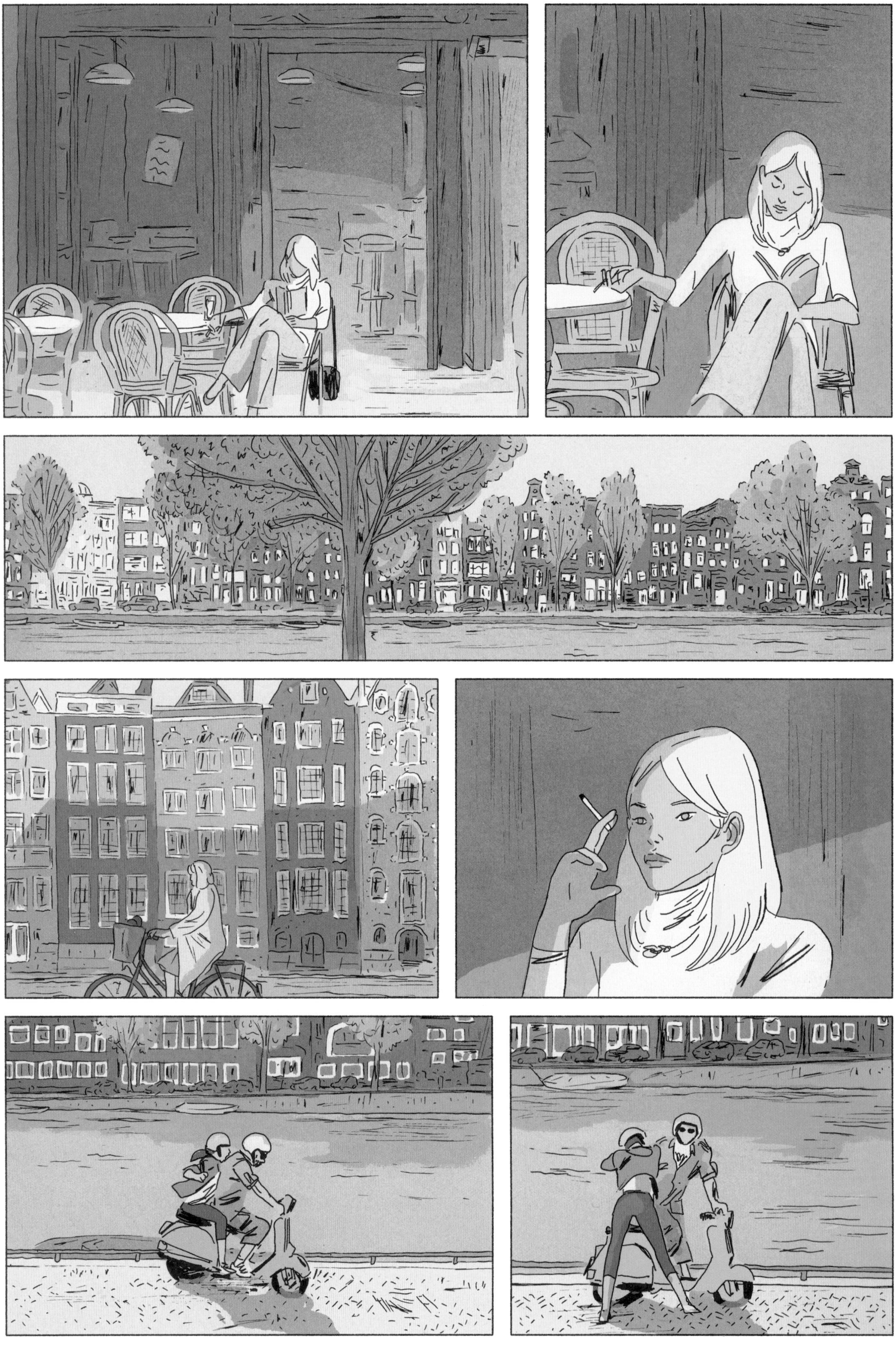

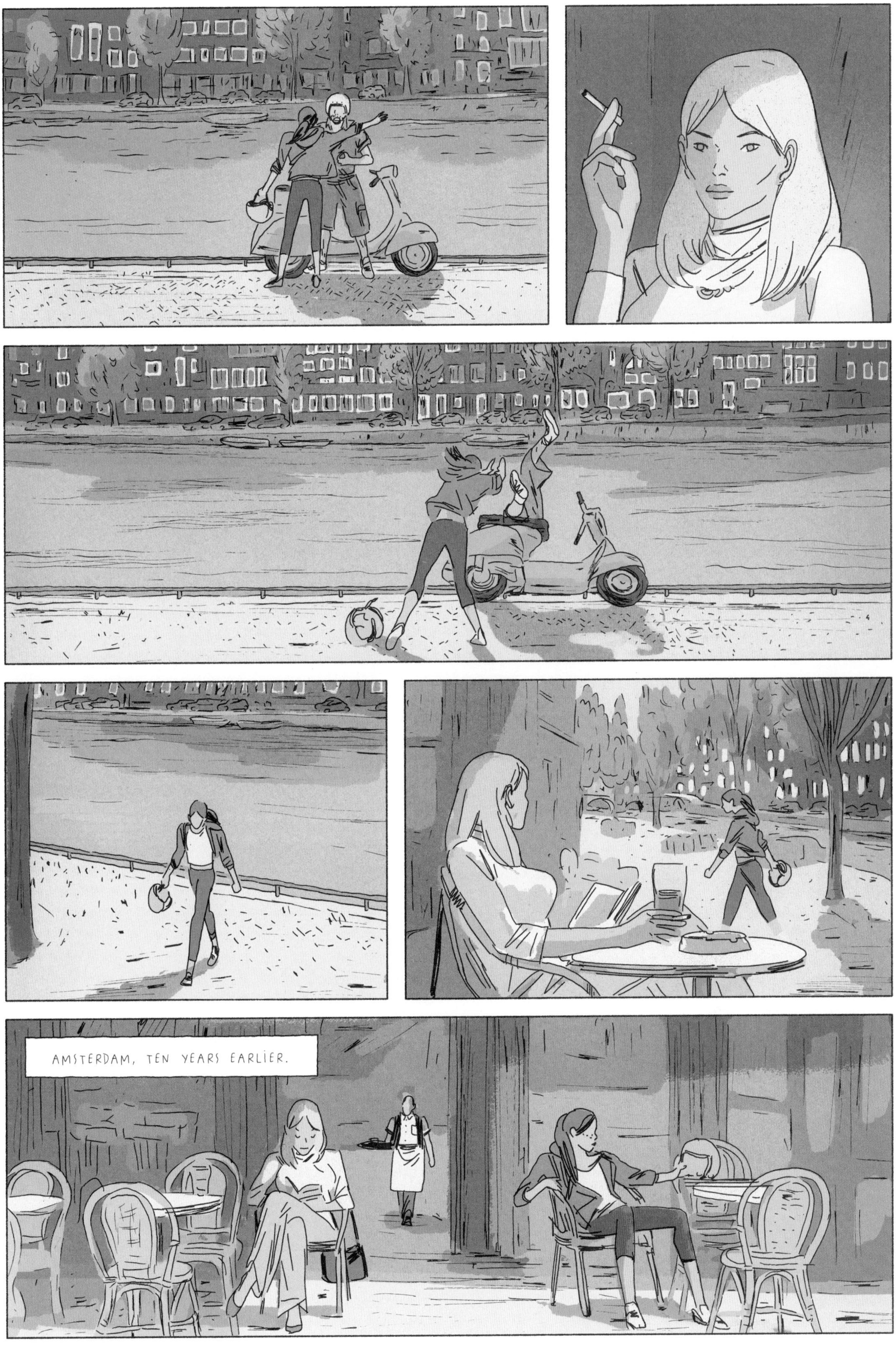
AMSTERDAM, TEN YEARS EARLIER.

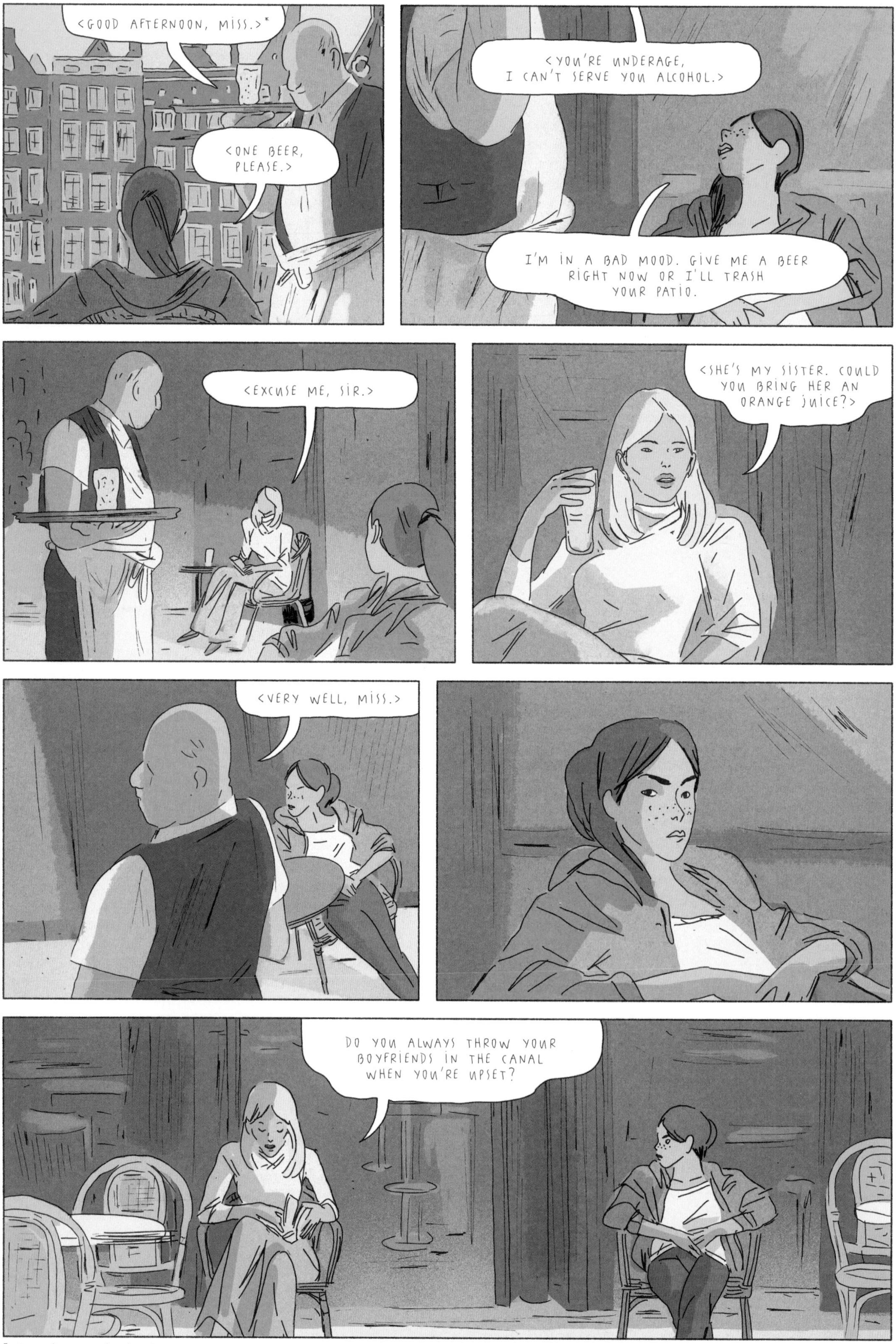
<GOOD AFTERNOON, MISS.>*
<ONE BEER, PLEASE.>
<YOU'RE UNDERAGE, I CAN'T SERVE YOU ALCOHOL.>
I'M IN A BAD MOOD. GIVE ME A BEER RIGHT NOW OR I'LL TRASH YOUR PATIO.
<EXCUSE ME, SIR.>
<SHE'S MY SISTER. COULD YOU BRING HER AN ORANGE JUICE?>
<VERY WELL, MISS.>
DO YOU ALWAYS THROW YOUR BOYFRIENDS IN THE CANAL WHEN YOU'RE UPSET?

*TEXT IN <> IS IN DUTCH, MAN

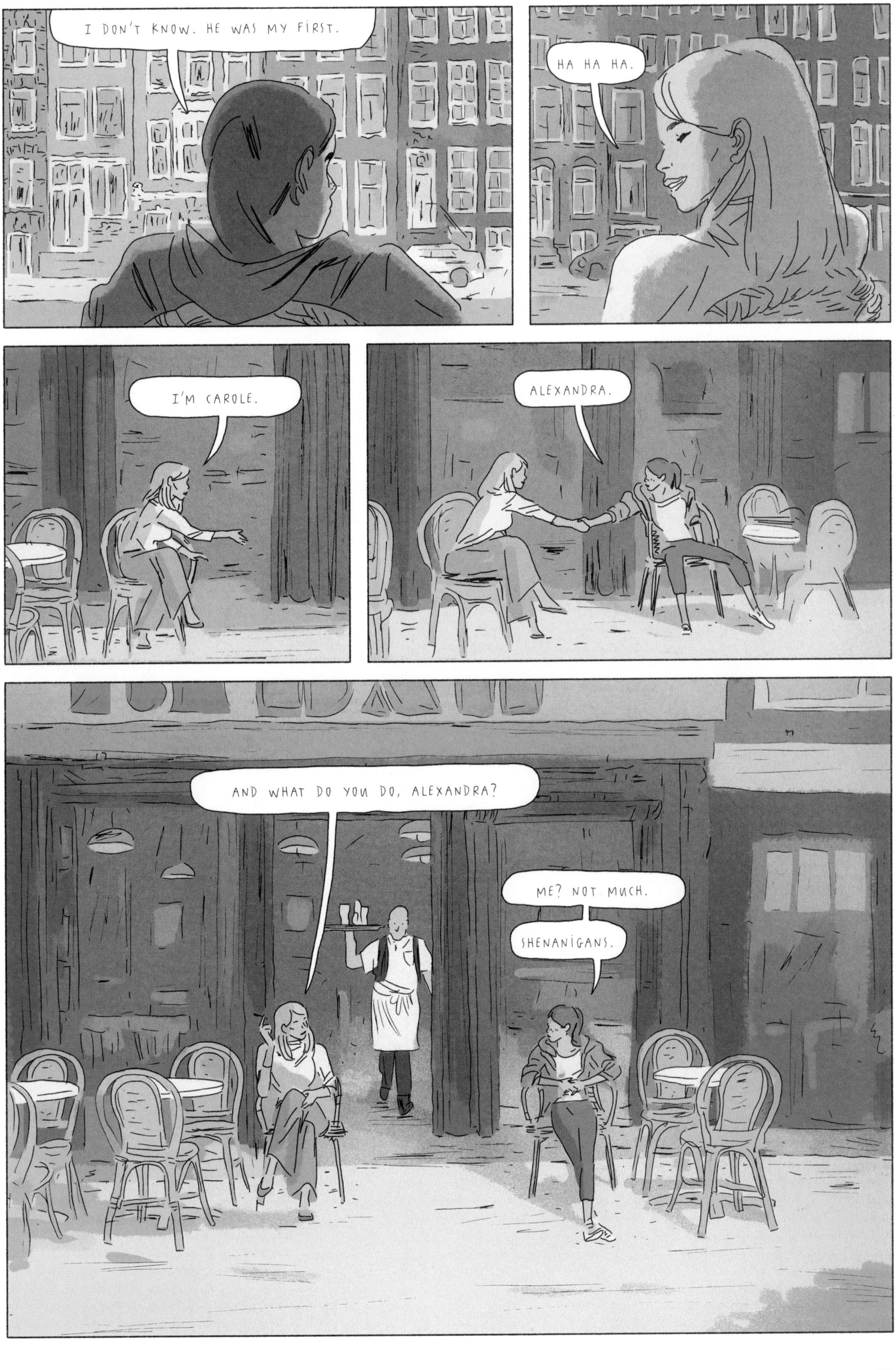
I DON'T KNOW. HE WAS MY FIRST.
HA HA HA.
I'M CAROLE.
ALEXANDRA.
AND WHAT DO YOU DO, ALEXANDRA?
ME? NOT MUCH.
SHENANIGANS.

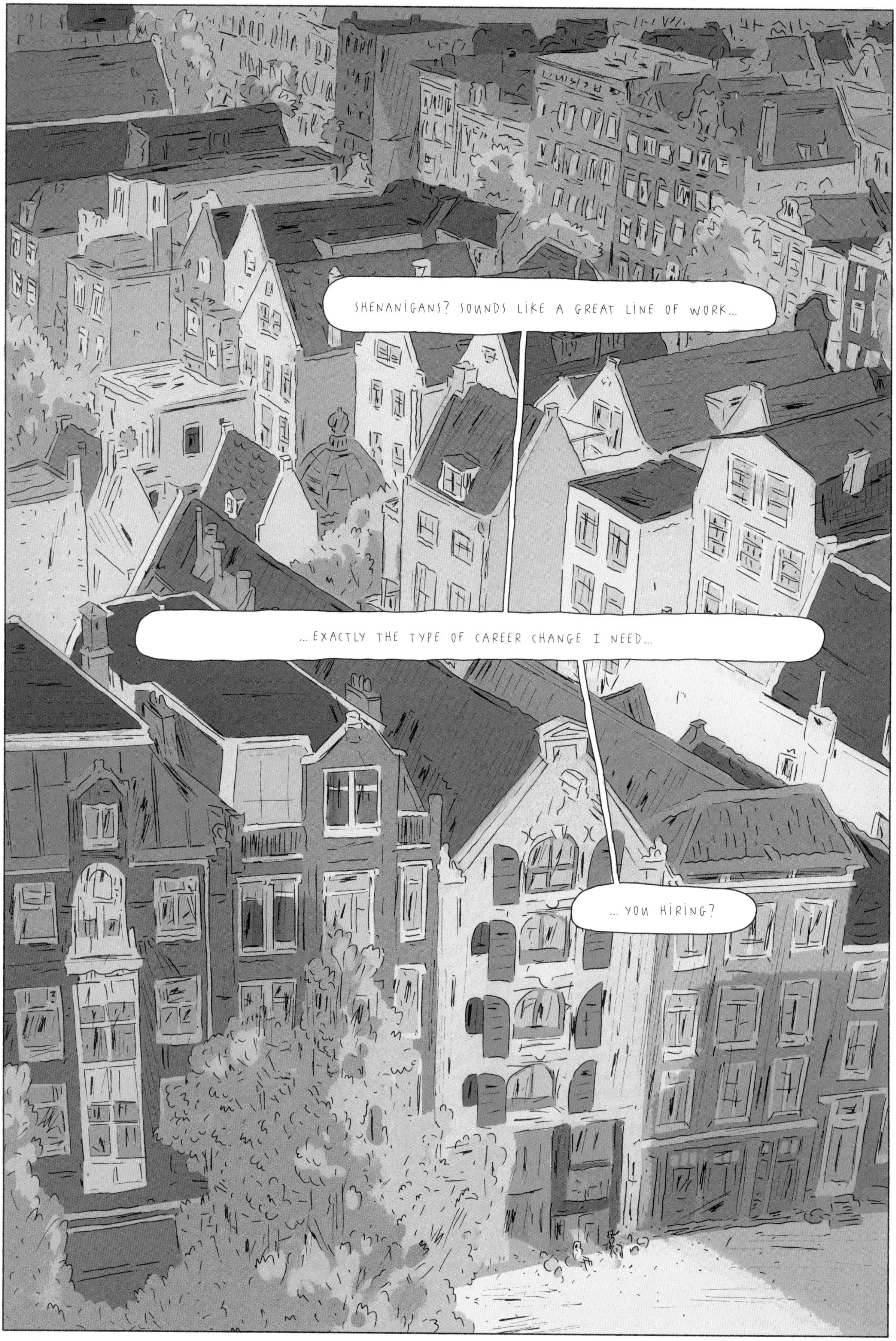
SHENANIGANS? SOUNDS LIKE A GREAT LINE OF WORK...
...EXACTLY THE TYPE OF CAREER CHANGE I NEED...
...YOU HIRING?

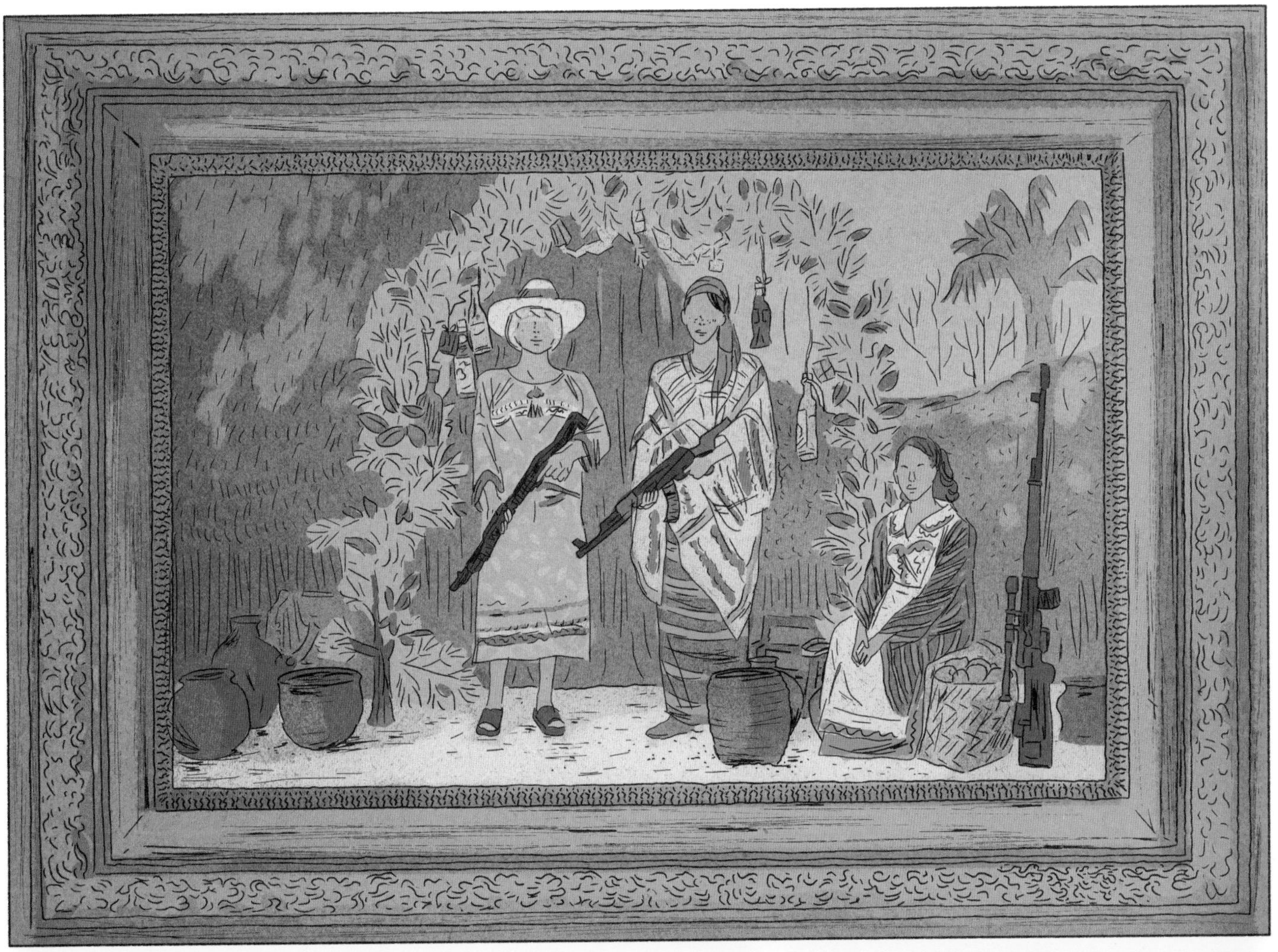
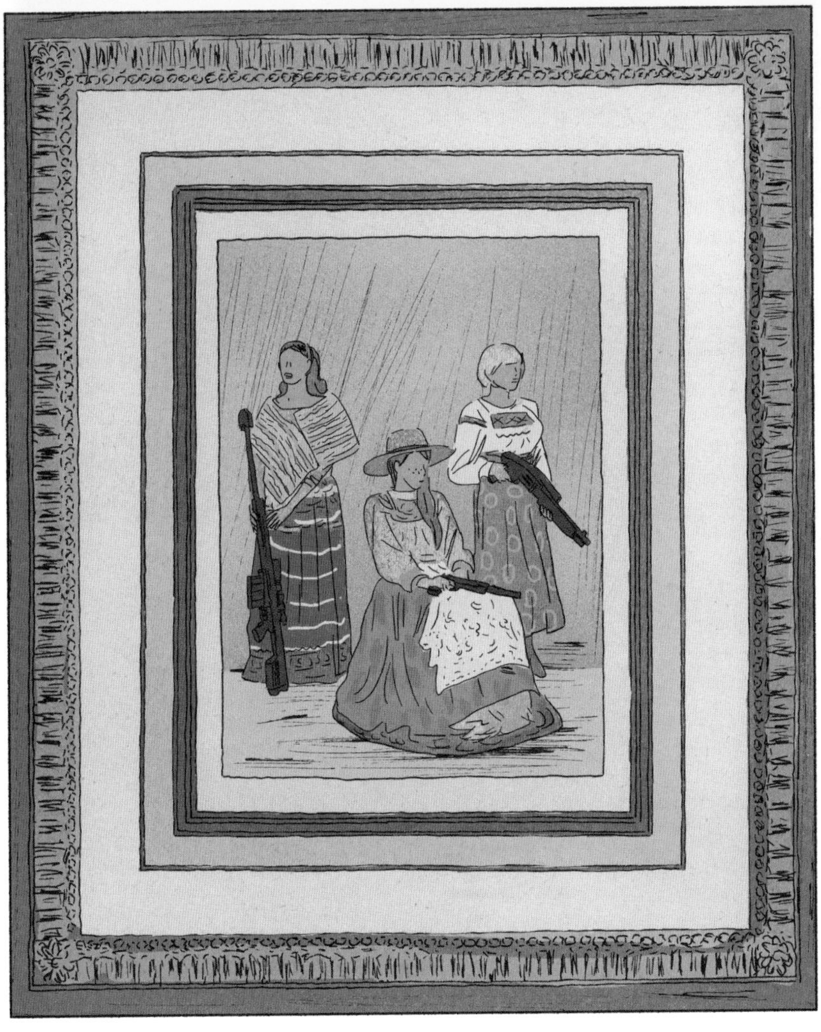
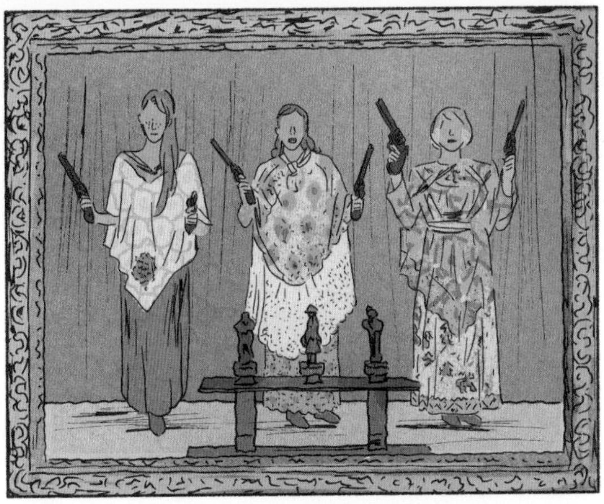
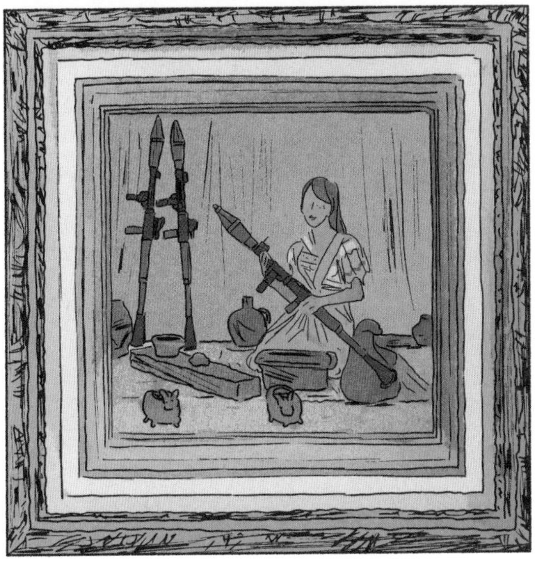

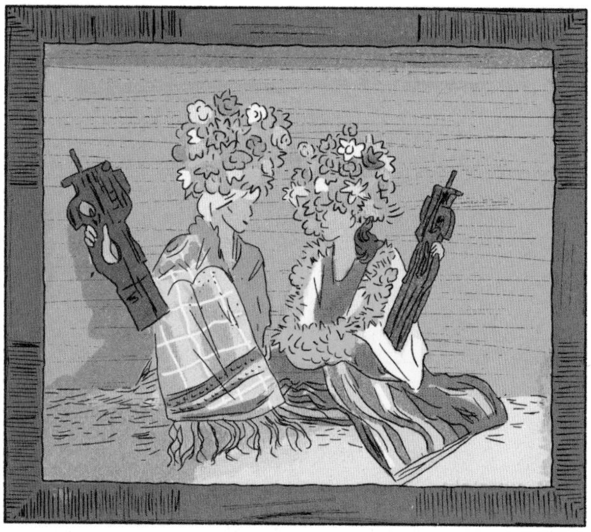

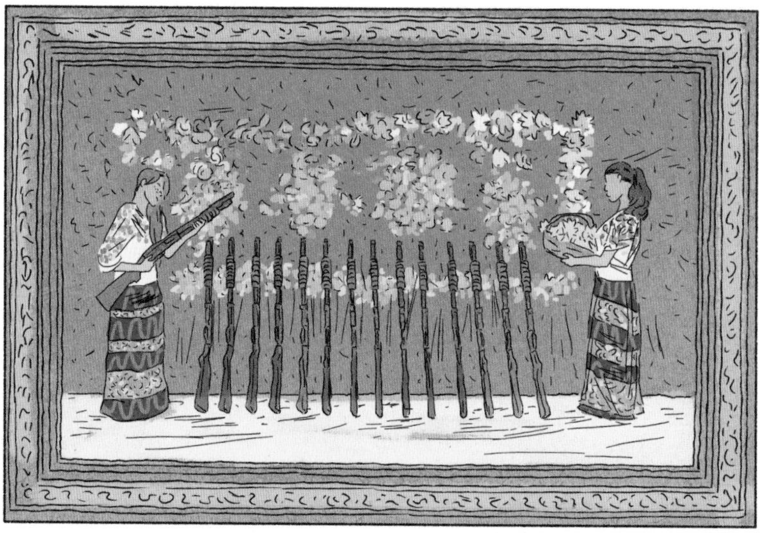

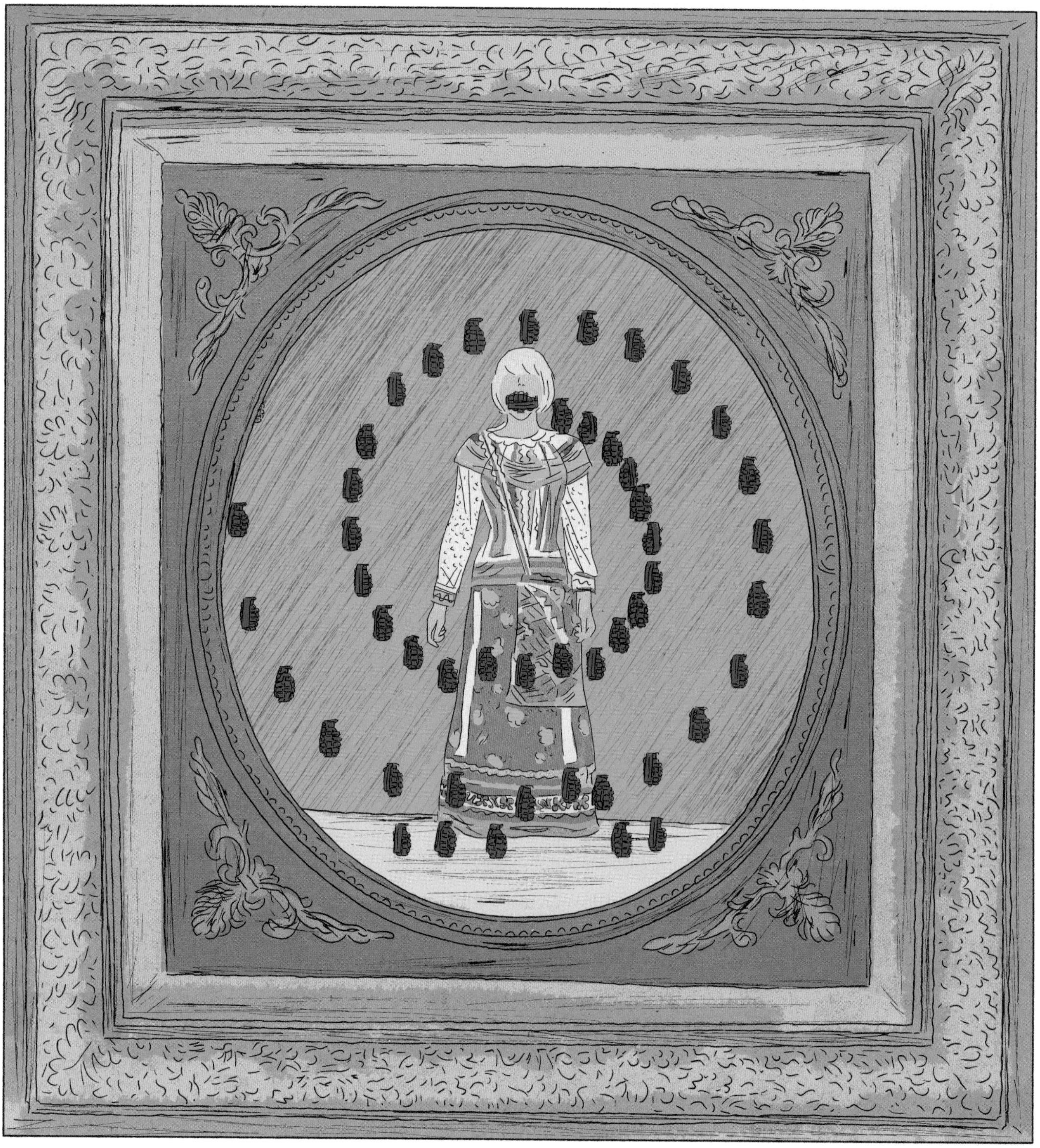

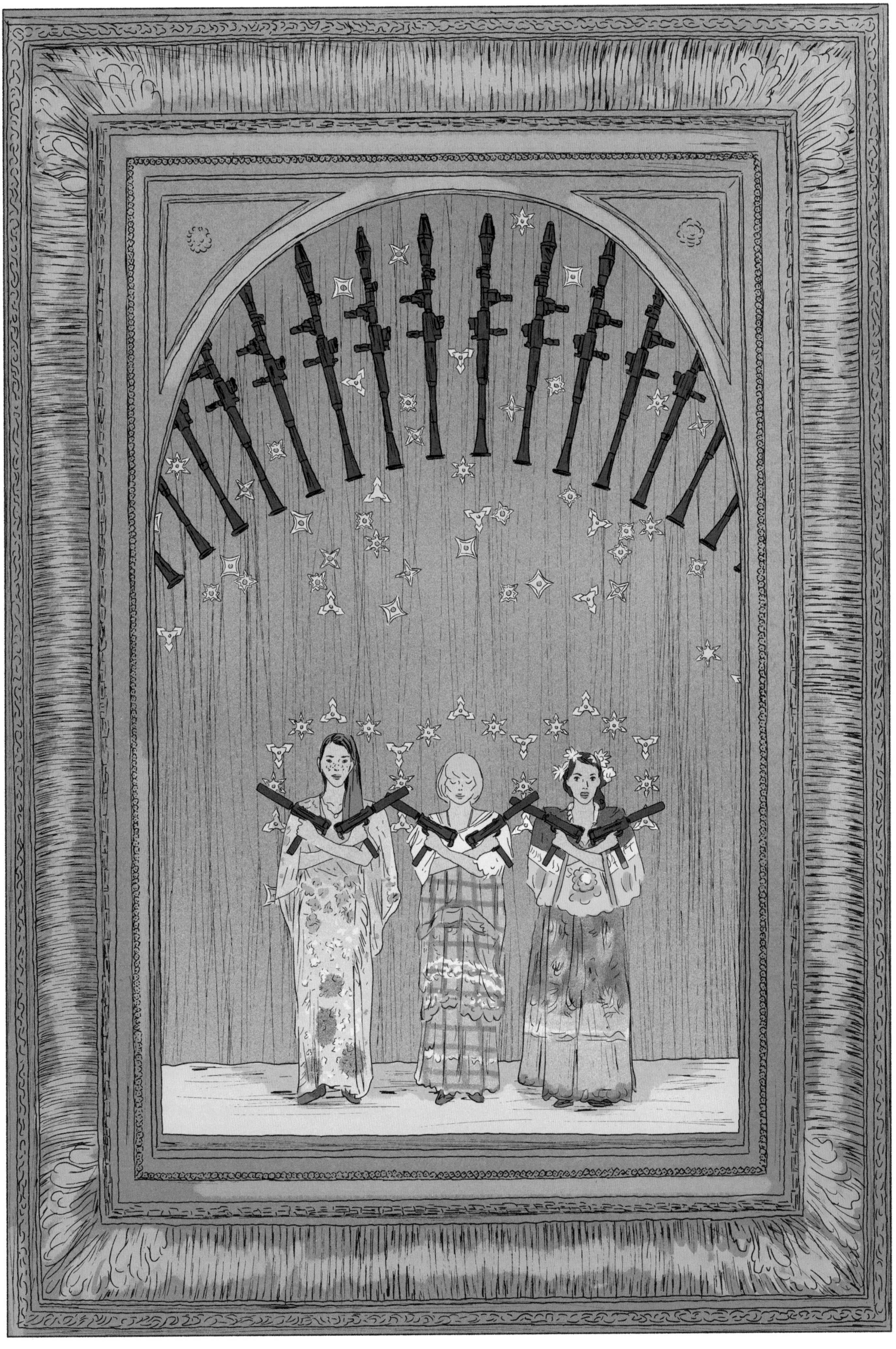

Carole, Alex, & Sam will return
in *Olympia*.

Thanks to Martin, for believing in the project.

—VIVÈS, RUPPERT & MULOT

RUPPERT & MULOT are best known for their seamless comics collaborations together; each French artist both writes and draws. The two met at the National School of Art in Dijon and began publishing their creations in their fanzine *Del Adventure*. Together they won the Revelation Prize from the Angouleme International Comics Festival for *Barrel of Monkeys* (*Panier de Singe*). In 2019, Fantagraphics published their graphic novel, *The Perineum Technique*.

BASTIEN VIVÉS is a Parisian who has drawn or collaborated on more than a dozen graphic novels since his published debut in 2006. The Angouleme Comics Festival granted Vives the Revelation Prize in 2009 and the prize for best series in 2015.

FANTAGRAPHICS BOOKS INC.
7563 Lake City Way NE • Seattle, Washington, 98115
W W W . F A N T A G R A P H I C S . C O M

Editor & Associate Publisher: Eric Reynolds
Translator: Montana Kane
Designer: Chelsea Wirtz
Type Designer: Cromatik Ltd
Production: Paul Baresh
Publisher: Gary Groth

I S B N 978-1-68396-402-5
Library of Congress Control Number 2020941627

First printing: February 2021
Printed in China

W W W . D U P U I S . C O M